*Published in cooperation with the
National Association for
Foreign Student Affairs*

Educating Students from Other Nations

American Colleges
and Universities
in International
Educational Interchange

Hugh M. Jenkins
and Associates

Foreword by J. William Fulbright

Educating Students from Other Nations

Jossey-Bass Publishers

San Francisco • Washington • London • 1983

EDUCATING STUDENTS FROM OTHER NATIONS
*American Colleges and Universities
in International Educational Interchange*
by Hugh M. Jenkins and Associates

Copyright © 1983 by: Jossey-Bass Inc., Publishers
433 California Street
San Francisco, California 94104
&
Jossey-Bass Limited
28 Banner Street
London EC1Y 8QE

Library of Congress Cataloging in Publication Data

Jenkins, Hugh M.
        Educating students from other nations.

        Bibliography: p. 334
        Includes index.
        1. Educational exchanges—Addresses, essays, lectures.
2. Foreign study—Addresses, essays, lectures.
3. Students, Foreign—United States—Addresses, essays,
lectures. I. Title.
LB2283.J4   1983   370.19'6   82-49043
ISBN 0-87589-559-X

Manufactured in the United States of America

The paper in this book meets the guidelines for
permanence and durability of the Committee on
Production Guidelines for Book Longevity of the
Council on Library Resources.

JACKET DESIGN BY WILLI BAUM

FIRST EDITION

Code 8311

The Jossey-Bass
Higher Education Series

Foreword

In this troubled period of our history, it is appropriate and timely for the National Association for Foreign Student Affairs to sponsor the publication of this book on the significance of international educational exchange. This century has already witnessed two devastating world wars and several destructive regional wars in which our country has been involved. In the recent past, we have witnessed the invasions of Afghanistan and Chad, the Iraqi-Iranian war, the Iranian hostage tragedy, the continuing devastation of Lebanon, our own tragic involvement in Vietnam, and many other examples of unrestrained violence in and between nations. Surely it is appropriate that serious attention now be given to activities that may contribute to the reestablishment of some semblance of order and tranquility to the world.

The traditional response to such ominous conflicts has been to increase armaments and prepare for the worst. Such measures have in the past resulted in the succession of conflicts with which we are familiar. In this volume NAFSA is reminding us that force and violence, the traditional arbiters of differences among nations, are not necessarily the only arbiters. Between the Super Powers especially, the traditional response is not a rational response. In this century two major efforts have been made to find a way other than force and violence to arbitrate international conflicts: the League of Nations, which failed; and the United Nations, which lacks the full support of the major nations and therefore the *power* to be effective.

This book reminds us that human beings are endowed with the capacity for reason, even though they have made little use of it. It also reminds us to consider seriously the proposition stated by Aristotle some two thousand years ago: "It is absurd to hold that a man ought to be ashamed of being unable to defend himself with his limbs, but not of being unable to defend himself with speech and reason, when the use of rational speech is more distinctive of a human being than the use of his limbs."

The interchange of students and scholars across national borders, which NAFSA facilitates so efficiently, is the most effective way to enable humankind to apply reason rather than arms to the arbitration of international problems. It is indeed an absurdity that modern man can go to the moon or project a nuclear missile around the world but is reluctant to apply an equal effort and resources to the solution of cultural and political differences that lead to conflict. Hydrogen bombs, vast quantities of which Super Powers possess, will not prove the validity of either system; they lead only to mutual destruction. Competition within the restraints of mutually accepted rules would provide a valid criterion of the relative merits of the respective polities. Cooperation between them would be the ultimate demonstration of the human capacity for rational conduct.

The idea that the superiority of a particular race, religion, or ideology may be proven by force and violence in this nuclear age is an anachronism, more irrelevant than the bow and arrow. Educational exchange between nations of different cultures is relevant to the reasonable solution of their differences and allows people to demonstrate their capacity for humane conduct.

February 1983   J. William Fulbright

Preface

The reason for this book may be found in the presence of over 300,000 foreign students in the universities and colleges across the United States. They form the largest part, but are only a part, of some one million students who are presently studying outside of their homelands. This massive acceleration in the transnational movement of students and scholars was one of the many new patterns that emerged following the war years of 1939–1945. Although now accepted as a fact of international life, foreign students did not appear on the educational scene in significant numbers until the 1950s, when, with little advance notice or proper preparation, their numbers first doubled and then trebled. Today, after more than three decades of continuous increase, foreign students are moving into the mainstream of educational development. It is, therefore, timely that the growth of the foreign student population be chronicled and its impact on the educational community scrutinized.

The purpose of this book is threefold: (1) to review on a broad scale some of the educational, political, financial, and institutional implications of the foreign student movement; (2) to examine ways in which existing procedures—such as admissions, advising, and planning—have been successfully adjusted or could be adjusted to cope with this rapidly growing segment of the student community; (3) to explore the future, seeking answers or suggesting ways to find solutions to problems that are now apparent in the scope and management of international educational interchange.

The book is designed to make some immediate, positive impact on the transnational movement of students and scholars. It offers instruction to the newcomer and discusses problems and improvements with the experienced practitioner. Thus, it describes practices and procedures that have proved to be most effective, for example, in the development of a comprehensive foreign student admissions process. It offers a variety of patterns of administration and shows how different institutions have organized the full range of their international educational interchange activities, including programs and services for foreign students and scholars and for United States students studying abroad, so that readers may determine which particular approach is best suited to, or can be adapted to meet, their own institutional needs. It illustrates existing faults, such as the lack of effective means of communication, which inhibit the achievement of optimum benefits and suggests ways in which improvements can be made. It demonstrates the inherent dangers in certain practices, especially those in the field of recruitment, and shows how they can be avoided and an acceptable recruitment program created. The basic information that is immediately required to achieve these purposes is contained within the covers of the book; the references and the instructions on how additional knowledge can be acquired provide the key to the further development of good practices and procedures.

The book is directed to a wide audience, including particularly those in college and university administration and among the faculty who have a major responsibility for institutional policy and the extent of its international activities, and may wish to be more knowledgeable about the foreign students on campus. It also anticipates a natural response from those who are dealing with foreign students or involved in the international educational programs at their institutions. Finally, it seeks to attract the interest of those in the wider educational circles and among the members of the community who have a concern for the foreign students in their midst and for the educational needs of world citizenship.

The book is sponsored by the National Association for Foreign Student Affairs (NAFSA), which, since its establishment in 1948, has been the primary source of the handbooks, guidelines, newsletters, and professional papers prepared for those who are engaged in all aspects of international educational interchange: the foreign student admissions officers, foreign student advisers, teachers of English as a second language, representatives of community organizations offering programs and services to foreign students, and the advisers to United States students on study abroad. Even in those early days, it was becoming apparent that the growing dimensions of the transnational movement of students and scholars were changing the very nature of the process and that the practices which had sufficed in a day when foreign students could be counted individually at the various institutions where they were enrolled were no longer adequate. The resulting obvious and urgent need for informed and authoritative resource materials was a major concern of the pioneers in the newly identified field of international educational interchange. Thus, within a year of its establishment, NAFSA (then known as the National Association of Foreign Student Advisers) produced the *Handbook for Counselors of Students from Abroad.* Identified as the "experimental 1949 edition," it was available in September of that year. It was a cooperative project, drawing on the knowledge and experience of those individuals in educational circles who were already committed to foreign student activities and, significantly, that of a number of representatives from national and international service and community organizations who foresaw international educational interchange as one of the critical elements in a developing global community. This "experimental 1949 edition," which is now something of a museum piece, was the forerunner of the hundreds of publications that have been prepared and distributed by the National Association for Foreign Student Affairs.

Because of the increasing attention given by educational authorities and the public media to the presence of foreign students in this country, NAFSA decided to complement its specialized materials, provided for those directly involved in foreign student affairs, with a book of more general interest that would examine the history and the current status of the transnational movement of students and scholars, giving particular attention to the massive flow of foreign students to the United States in the decades following World War II. The association therefore appointed an advisory group to oversee the project and commissioned its recently retired executive vice-president to work under the guidance of this group and recruit the necessary experts to write the various chapters. The advisory group, in addition to the current executive vice-president of NAFSA and the association's director of information services, includes a representative from the U.S. Information Agency, the government agency responsible for most of our international educational interchange activities; the director of the International Office of the College Board; and the president of the Council of Graduate Schools. The book is not the result of an extended and intensive research project. It is rather an accumulation of some thirty years of experimentation, observation, and rational review. The authors of the different chapters have drawn not only on the knowledge gained from their own daily experience but also on that of their colleagues in the field. Preparation has taken almost two years as the mass of available information and commentary has been sifted to provide, in one volume, a compendium of complementary discourse and practical reference.

The study properly focuses on the United States because the largest foreign student population is in that country. It also retains this perspective to permit prescription without presumption, for the inferences drawn and the recommendations made derive their authenticity from the experience of the various authors in their work with foreign students and scholars who are in, or are interested in, United States colleges and universities. However, the points of view are by no means parochial. All the contributors have traveled outside of the United States and shared their experiences and discussed mutual problems with colleagues on the international scene who are engaged in educational exchange and involved with foreign students in their respective countries. Thus, their comments are tempered by the knowledge and understanding that comes from a multinational insight into the total activity of international educational interchange.

The contents of the book have been ordered to follow the natural progression in the experience of those who seek educational opportunities outside their homelands, as seen from the vantage point of those who are directly involved in the transnational movement of students and scholars. Thus, the book starts with an overview of the past movement of students and scholars and an analysis of the forces that motivate the current vastly expanded international educational interchange and the circumstances in which this movement takes place, followed by an examination of what is happening to foreign students and scholars today. It describes the initiative that prompts individuals, in any country, to seek an education in a college or university outside their homeland and details the assistance available to help them achieve their goal. It examines the problems of those whose task it is to provide that assistance and the need that *they* have for an effective relationship with institutions in the host country.

Recognizing the degree to which, in its current dimensions, international educational interchange has moved into the forefront of educational planning, the second part of the book pays particular attention to the role of the institution. It begins by offering advice on methods of easing the financial pressures and restrictions placed on institutions and foreign students. It then examines recruitment and all that is involved in a deliberate attempt to attract and enroll foreign students. The ways institutions can respond to the outreach of the prospective foreign student and the action, or reaction, of the institution's admissions office are described. A model for foreign student admissions procedures and a listing of available resources are provided. Part Two continues with a cautionary review of the problems of alien status that students and scholars encounter while studying in a foreign country. Attention is then drawn to the way in which an institution copes with the totality of its international educational interchange activities, with the accompanying problem of budgetary implications. It examines the unique role that the foreign student and scholar, with the proper institutional encouragement, can and should play on campus as an international, intercultural educational resource. Part Two concludes with a review of the pressing questions, and possible answers, in the thorny issue of the costs and benefits of international educational interchange.

The authors in Part Three probe matters that, to date, have often been taken too much for granted. They ask whether the massive flow of foreign students to the United States in the past thirty-five years is circumstantial or whether it may be indicative of some more basic force or need. They question whether we are now moving to a plateau in the growth of the foreign student population and whether this should be seen as a natural result of changes in a global educational pattern. Alternatively, they suggest that a determined effort might now be made to relate more effectively the needs and growing resources of the developing countries to the advanced educational resources of the United States. They explore the redesigning of educational programs that such an effort would require. The section ends with a summary of the present status and a forecast of what might be achieved through the common efforts of the world community and its educational institutions.

The need for new assessment was underlined by Richard Lyman, president of the Rockefeller Foundation, in his speech to the 1981 NAFSA annual conference (subsequently reported in the association's summer newsletter). On the American scene, Lyman noted the paradox of a nation that has become increasingly involved in the rest of the world through massive increases in imports and exports and foreign investment in the United States and, at the same time, has suffered a catastrophic shortfall in its learning about and knowledge of other lands and peoples. Focusing on foreign students and their study in this country, he pointed out that the recently acceptable doctrine regarding the process of national development through the acquisition of the technology of the developed countries is now being seriously challenged by new nations that are reluctant to inherit all the problems that beset the industrialized nations. Placing these problems in the context of the complexities of a world that is reft apart by the struggle for its sources of energy and other natural resources, Lyman went on to define the contemporary quandary facing all those who are engaged in international educational interchange: "It would seem entirely predictable that the increased uncertainties and conflicting interpretations of what constitutes progress among peoples and nations can only complicate still further the already complicated working lives of foreign student affairs professionals. It has long been convention to recognize the potential for differences in objectives, as amongst universities in this country, the governments of other countries, the universities of other countries, and, last but of course far from least, individual students coming to this country or thinking about coming. In just about every one of these categories, there are now greater uncertainties than there were" (p. 189). Surely there could not be a more dramatic or opportune moment for the presentation of the current state of the art in international educational interchange—inspiring, one hopes, a further perceptive and skillful adjustment of existing procedures and programs to the emerging pattern of new directions and new opportunities in the field.

Acknowledgments

In addition to the chapter authors who collaborated in the production of this book, a number of other people have made contributions that were essential to the success of the project. First, there are the members of the advisory committee: Sanford Jameson (College Board), Michael Pelczar (Council of Graduate Schools), Mary Ann Spreckelmeyer (U.S. Information Agency), and John Reichard and Georgia Stewart (National Association for Foreign Student Affairs); all were most generous with their advice and counsel. Then there are the members of the staff of the NAFSA central office; their assistance in reviewing, revising, and updating the text was invaluable. Finally, there is Anna Corrales, without whose patience and secretarial skills the manuscript would never have reached the publisher. I am most grateful to them all.

Washington, D.C.   Hugh M. Jenkins
February 1983

Contents

The Authors

Hugh M. Jenkins, former executive vice-president of the National Association for Foreign Student Affairs, now serves as a consultant to that association. Educated in England, Jenkins was engaged in international service, first as a member of a Quaker relief team in wartime Europe and subsequently as the overseas secretary of the British Friends Relief Service. Jenkins moved to the United States in 1948, and entered the field of international educational interchange in 1951, when he was appointed director of the International Student House in Washington, D.C. In 1957 he was invited to serve as executive director of the newly formed Foreign Student Service Council, a position he held until his appointment in 1966 to the National Association for Foreign Student Affairs (NAFSA). Jenkins served first as executive director and later as executive vice-president of NAFSA until his retirement in December 1979.

In the course of his work, Jenkins has been an official visitor and delegate to national and international conferences in Europe, Africa, Latin America, and the Far East. Awards in recognition of his work in international education have been granted to Jenkins by the Agency for International Development, the International Communication Agency (now USIA), the International Society for Educational, Cultural, and Scientific Exchanges, and the National Council for International Visitors. He is an honorary member of the National Association for Foreign Student Affairs, the Pan American Association of Educational Credit Organizations, and People to People.

Alex Bedrosian is director of continuing education, New Jersey Institute of Technology.

M. Archer Brown is administrative director, National Association for Foreign Student Affairs.

George C. Christensen is vice-president for academic affairs, Iowa State University.

Kenneth J. Cooper is lecturer in the School of Education and research associate in the School of Engineering, Stanford University.

Joan H. Joshi is director of administration, International Center for Research in the Dry Areas (ICARDA), and former vice-president, Institute of International Education.

Robert B. Kaplan is professor of applied linguistics, Department of Linguistics, University of Southern California.

Ellen E. Mashiko is educational information officer, Japan–United States Educational Commission (Fulbright Program).

William S. Patrick is vice-president for student services, Georgia State University.

John F. Reichard is executive vice-president, National Association for Foreign Student Affairs.

Thomas B. Thielen is vice-president of student affairs, Iowa State University.

Valerie Woolston is director of international education services, University of Maryland.

Educating Students from Other Nations

American Colleges
and Universities
in International
Educational Interchange

Part One

Challenges and Opportunities of International Education Today

The current transnational movement of students and scholars bears the imprint of past events: the ancient gatherings of pupils around the great masters, the role of the early church in the dissemination of knowledge and the eventual establishment of the major educational centers of the Western world. By contrast the particular characteristics of the contemporary phenomenon are a massive educational interchange that brings its participants across cultural boundaries, adds training to learning and seeks relevancy as well as scholarship. For the international educational community the twentieth century is a time of transition.

The circumstances affecting the foreign student and scholar in the 1980s are vastly different from those faced by their predecessors. The dangers and hardships of travel have given way to the relative comfort of mass transportation, while the simplicity of study abroad has disappeared in a world beset by passports, currency controls, and immigration regulations. Overriding all these constraints is the determination of modern-day students and scholars who in unprecedented numbers seek educational opportunities outside their homelands.

1

Chapter One describes the magnitude of the current global movement of students and scholars and shows that as events of the past half-century have thrust the United States into the forefront of the world community its educational institutions have become the focus of foreign students from across the world. It tells about the awakening response on campuses and in communities in the United States to this rapidly growing responsibility. It points out how the movement is motivated by a variety of coexisting and sometimes competing national, institutional, and individual goals and incentives. Summarizing the impact of all these circumstances on the foreign student or scholar, the chapter concludes with thoughts about the need for a cooperative multinational approach to international educational interchange so that the optimum benefits may be obtained from this activity.

While the concept of study in a foreign country has been nurtured by the facility of modern international communication, many problems still face prospective foreign students. To meet their needs, in-country information and advising services have been established to assist in the search for a suitable educational opportunity in a foreign country. Ellen E. Mashiko, of the Japan–United States Educational Commission, with her extensive experience in both the receiving and the sending countries in educational interchange, discusses the functions and problems of those who offer this assistance. She describes a model information and advising service, explains the need for adequate liaison between the in-country services and the foreign universities, and points out the many ways in which the service can also be of help to the university. From her experience as a link between the student and the institution, she offers a prescription for improving the system of international educational interchange. Complementing this account, M. Archer Brown describes the circumstances in which United States students seek opportunities to study abroad. She notes the relatively unstructured development of United States study abroad activity and estimates its current dimensions. She defines the relationship of the institution to its overseas students and describes in detail, and differentiates between, the functions of advising students on study abroad and actually sponsoring or administering study abroad programs. She also outlines the means for the professional development of campus advisers and program administrators.

1

Growth and Impact
of Educational
Interchanges

Hugh M. Jenkins

During the past thirty-five years, there has been a fundamental change in international educational interchange, especially in the transnational movement of students at the college and university level. The increase in numbers; the difference in motivation, which to some extent has resulted in a change in the social background of the participants; the inclusion of new nations; and the intermixture of old cultures have combined to create an entirely new situation. New forces have come into play, and old forces have had an added impact, as national interests and multinational business incentives have cast the foreign student in a new role. Study abroad in the 1980s is no longer just a scholarly pursuit; it is also an instrument in national and international development. At the same time, colleges and universities are undertaking an intense examination of the resulting problems and benefits and an assessment of their effects on contemporary educational patterns. All this has brought us to the threshold of some

4

new approaches to international educational interchange and to a new look at the ways in which educational resources, wherever they exist, may be matched with educational needs, wherever they may be found. The purpose of this book is to examine current practices and procedures from the perspective of the participants in international educational interchange and to offer proposals for further development and improvement.

A superabundance of information exists on the subject of foreign students and educational interchange. Among the most relevant sources, *The Foreign Student in America* (Wheeler, King, and Davidson, 1925) summarizes the past history of student migration and of the early foreign student population in the United States. Information about the global foreign student enrollment and the current situation in the major host countries may be found, respectively, in the UNESCO *Statistical Year Books,* the studies made by various national organizations (such as the United Kingdom Council on Overseas Student Affairs in Great Britain and the German Academic Exchange Service in the Federal Republic of Germany), and the report of a conference on higher education reform sponsored by the Institute of International Education (see Burn, 1978). Early insights into the experience of foreign students in the United States are given in *Foreign Students and Higher Education in the United States* (Du Bois, 1956), while a later catalogue of research on foreign students in this country is provided in *The World's Students in the United States* (Spaulding and Flack, 1976). The statistics on foreign students enrolled in United States colleges and universities are presented and interpreted in the annual census, *Open Doors,* produced each year since 1919 by the Institute of International Education. In addition, there are the commentaries, studies, and guidelines published by the National Association for Foreign Student Affairs (NAFSA) since its establishment in 1948. The many characteristics of world higher education are recorded in *The International Encyclopedia of Higher Education* (Knowles, 1977), which also includes a most comprehensive account of international exchange (pp. 1505-1598). In light of all this existing information, this brief review seeks only to illuminate certain areas where it can be demonstrated that there is a need and a potential for new developments in programs and procedures.

To provide a minimal framework for our review, it may be safely stated that at this time the total world foreign student enrollment at institutions of higher education is over one million. To this basic group may be added the uncounted foreign students in elementary and secondary schools and those attending language schools and various technical institutions, who also contribute to the total impact of international educational interchange.

On a much smaller scale, the greater opportunities and available facilities for academic interchange also led to similar increases during the postwar years in the transnational movement of scholars engaged in research and teaching. Most recently, however, such interchange, at least in certain science and engineering fields, has in fact decreased (see National Research Council, 1982). Unfortunately, at this time there are no specific figures, or even estimates, of the number of scholars who are, worldwide, engaged in either short- or long-term educational pursuits outside their home countries. Many of the national and international organizations (such as UNESCO, NATO, the German Academic Exchange Service (DAAD), and the Council for International Exchange of Scholars) do keep records of the number of participants in the programs they administer, but this is only part of the picture. Some perception of relative numbers, in comparison with the foreign student population, may be obtained from random samples. In 1980 the Fulbright Program provided grants for 686 visiting scholars in the United States and 615 United States scholars abroad; in that same year, there were 895 transatlantic or inter-European exchanges in the NATO Science Fellowship Program. These examples, however, merely show the tip of the iceberg. The total interchange activity also includes an unspecified number of interinstitutional exchanges of professors and research workers, often arranged on a departmental or professional basis, and a variety of other programs in which individual scholarships are offered by international organizations, government agencies, educational institutions, and private foundations. Some idea of the extent of these opportunities for scholarly exchange may be obtained from *A Selected List of Fellowship Opportunities and Aids to Advanced Education* (National Science Foundation, 1980), which is almost exclusively devoted to exchanges at the postgraduate level and lists ninety-four scholarship or fellowship programs and provides a supplementary bibliography of forty-three other publications.

The problem of determining the number of foreign scholars in the United States is further complicated because, as is noted in Chapter Seven, the immigration status of foreign scholars, as distinct from that of graduate or postgraduate students, is hard to define. It is determined mostly by the fact that their scholarly activity does not involve registration in any formal academic program. This lack of precise designation sometimes means that they are included by implication in any discussion of the procedures or problems of international educational interchange. Thus, in the descriptions of the various aspects of this activity in this book, it may be properly assumed that where international scholars are not identified by specific reference they are included by inference.

While there may be uncertainty about the immigration status of foreign scholars in the United States, there is no doubt about the significance of the role they play in contemporary education. As teachers and scholars, they are an invaluable resource to colleges and universities in both the developed and the developing countries. Furthermore, the contribution of international visiting scholars is not limited to the campus where they may be located. In the United States, for example, their influence may be extended by participation in such programs as the Institute of International Education's International Faculty Lecturer Bureau or the Occasional Lecturer Program for Visiting Fulbright Scholars organized by the Council for International Exchange of Scholars. International scholars also play a most important role in the exchange of information and ideas at various conferences, symposia, and other professional gatherings that are part of the international calendar of educational activities. The roster of the participants in these events reveals an amazing traffic of thousands of scholars each year.

As individual contributors to the advancement of knowledge in their respective fields, as collaborators with professional colleagues in interinstitutional educational projects, and, among the younger group at the postdoctoral level, as the manpower for the furtherance of research and teaching, the visiting scholars make their impact on the international educational community in the twentieth century. Because of the level and quality of their educational role, their impact is quite out of proportion to their numbers when seen in comparison with the massive and recent growth in the foreign student population, which is itself a phenomenon peculiar to the postwar era.

In addition to the sheer magnitude of the foreign student population today, certain other factors have changed the nature of international educational interchange. The first is the breakdown of cultural barriers that once isolated educational development and the migration of students within their respective "civilized worlds." In ancient times, students' and scholars' travel and congregation was limited to their cultural orbits. Certainly this is no longer so, especially so far as the Western world is concerned. Even though it was to be many years before the term intercultural communication was to come into usage, intercultural contact was already well established by the beginning of the twentieth century, when the foreign student population in Western institutions included hundreds of students from China, Japan, India, Egypt, and the countries of Eastern Europe, Southeast Asia, and Latin America—although early reports and statistics make almost no mention of students from Africa. Nevertheless, even in those days, the traffic of students and scholars among various nations marked the emergence of a new pattern in international educational interchange—and the beginnings of the massive multinational, intercultural movement that exists today.

The second notable change, is the persistent acceleration in the postwar years of the flow of students—many of them from underdeveloped countries in Africa and Asia—to certain highly industrialized host countries, such as France, Germany, the United Kingdom, and the United States, which together accommodate roughly half of the current foreign student population. Nowhere has the upsurge in the foreign student population been more apparent than in the United States. In an un-interrupted rising curve which began immediately following World War II, the numbers have leapt from some 15,000 in 1946, to over 30,000 in 1951, reaching 145,000 twenty years later and still rising in the decade of the 1980s. In 1980-81, 311,882 foreign students were enrolled in colleges and universities in the United States, an increase of 8.9 percent over the number reported in 1979-80 (*Open Doors*, 1980-81, p. 2). While in proportion to the total student body, the percentage of foreign students in this country is not as great as in the other major host countries (in part because a much larger number of United States students continue into postsecondary education), the foreign student population in the United States is the largest in any country in the world, being approximately equal to the combined foreign student enrollment in France, Germany, and the United Kingdom. At this particular time and until indigenous resources are effectively available, the dominant factor in international educational interchange today is the desire of vast numbers of foreign students to gain access to the educational resources of the Western world.

Finally, in the years since 1945, forces such as the drive for modernization and the acquisition of new technology have changed the motivation of international educational interchange. In response to their need for national and economic development and their concern for equal educational opportunity, the new nations and developing countries have reached out to wider sections of their society to find the necessary trained manpower. Although students from the old and new elite and middle classes still constitute the bulk of the foreign student population, we now find increasing numbers of students from the rural areas and the poorer elements of society. The institutions where these students are enrolled are faced with an entirely new and sometimes difficult element in their educational activities and responsibilities. Thus, the contemporary foreign student population may be distinguished from that of earlier years by several significant features: it is relatively immense, it is intercultural, it is more universal in its representation, and it is Western oriented in its study programs.

This last feature has a special significance: The institu-

tions in which most foreign students pursue their studies abroad
have their origins in and are part of a Western cultural and educational environment. It is a condition that can have far-reach-
ing effects, both in relation to the necessary adjustment of
the students and the relevance of the education they may receive.

At this time the future transnational movement of students is uncertain and making predictions is a hazardous business. To date, despite all the apparent restraints, such as rising
costs, diminishing financial aid and restrictive employment policies, students have sought educational opportunities outside of
their homelands in increasing numbers and the flow of foreign
students to the United States in particular has grown annually
for more than thirty years. While the wealth and variety of educational opportunities in this country and the active interest of
many U.S. institutions in attracting foreign students will remain
influential factors, changing needs and the gradual advancement
of postsecondary educational resources in the developing countries will also have their impact on the transnational movement
of foreign students in the next decade. Thus, while it is safe to
say that the foreign student population in the United States will
continue to grow, it is likely that the rate of increase will slow
down. In these circumstances the enrollment projections of a
million or more foreign students in the United States in the
early 1990s (see *Foreign Students and Institutional Policy,*
American Council on Education, 1982, p. 44) may need to be
revised to a lower figure of perhaps half that number. The an-
ticipation of some continuing increase and the uncertainty as to
the rate or nature of the increase certainly justify the decision
to try to shed some light on the present problems and future
potential of this significant group of internationally educated
persons.

United States Students Abroad

While the major traffic in international educational interchange in the United States is in the flow of foreign students to
United States colleges and universities, there has also been a sus-

tained movement of United States students to other countries in search of some foreign educational experience. Reflecting both the autonomy of the institution and the independence of the student, there are no complete records of the many individuals who leave the United States each year for a variety of organized or self-initiated study programs in some foreign country. There are, however, a number of highly organized activities, both at the state and the institutional level—including independent programs and those planned by consortia or through other forms of interinstitutional cooperation—which are designed to provide United States students with a valid and acceptable study abroad program, one for which credit may be granted by the home institution. In addition, a variety of nonacademic, semieducational programs are available. Thus, it is often very difficult to determine what constitutes a genuine study abroad program or foreign educational experience. The existing record of those who participate in the college-sponsored study abroad programs during the academic year—29,819 students in 1979–80 (*Open Doors,* 1980-81, p. 65)—constitutes only a small part of the total study abroad activity. For many years those responsible on campus for advising United States students on study abroad and those who administer study abroad programs have been engaged in bringing some kind of order into this activity, seeking to establish standards and develop guidelines. As a result of their efforts, there are now a number of instructive publications (see National Association for Foreign Student Affairs, 1982b), as well as workshops and other training programs, to assist in the professional development of those working in this field.

Study abroad programs are now being increasingly recognized as an essential element in the total international program of the college or university. In a number of institutions, the programs for foreign students and those for United States students abroad are part of the combined responsibilities of an international office. At the national and international level, study abroad for United States students has its own forum in various conferences and workshops, and there is increasing communication among those who are professionally involved in this activity both in the United States and in the foreign countries where United States students are engaged in their study abroad. The response to this need in United States education and the development of new programs and relationships (such as the institutionally organized exchanges on a one-for-one basis), which are described in Chapter Three, are some of the more promising aspects of international educational interchange.

Foreign Students on United States Campuses

The history of the foreign student on the American campus goes back to references to the presence of students from other areas in the colonial colleges. For many years afterward—beginning with one Francisco de Miranda, who came to study at Yale University in 1784—foreign students came to this country as individual adventurers. Many of them are recorded by name in the annals of the institutions where they studied, often because they returned to make significant contributions to the national or educational development of their homelands. Although their numbers were sufficient to be recorded as statistics in the first years of this century (2,673 in 1904), they were still for the most part a rare and somewhat unusual presence on campus, noticeable perhaps because of their particular use of the English language or by a peculiarity in dress that made them a colorful, even exotic, addition to the student body. In these same years, a new figure appeared in the campus administration. Records show the appointment of a "foreign student adviser" in the year 1908. Today, with the vast increase in numbers and the governmental requirement that institutions play a role in the regulation of the admission and stay of foreign students in the United States, the foreign student adviser is to be found on every campus where foreign students are enrolled and, as will be seen in this book, plays a key role in the development of policies and procedures in foreign student affairs.

With the massive increase in numbers of foreign students in the United States and the inclusion of new types of students representing a wider section of society, certain problems became apparent in such areas as adjustment, English language proficiency, and finances. Although these affected only a proportion of the foreign student population, they were sufficiently persistent so that administrators and faculty became conscious, or were made uncomfortably aware, of the presence of foreign students in their institutions. Thus, instead of being seen as individuals, as in the earlier years, foreign students in United States colleges and universities tended to become identified by their problems and classified under the generic term "the foreign student." The error of this approach to thousands of different persons, whose only common attribute was the fact that they came from a foreign country, was soon recognized: "For the purposes of study, to treat a great variety of foreign students as a single category is a human and scientific monstrosity. Actually, those who come to this country to pursue their education are of an infinite variety of nationalities, temperaments, and backgrounds. If one is concerned with the processes and factors affecting them, it seems wise to begin with individuals" (Du Bois, 1956, p. 35).

For a number of years, and in some cases even today, the rising enrollments of foreign students outreached the institutional capacity to take adequate care of them. While the vast majority of these students made their own adjustment to life and study in the United States and so were unobtrusively absorbed into the campus community, those who were not so fortunate attracted the most attention. Then, too, various international crises, or conflicts in some foreign country (such as the war in Vietnam or the Biafra struggle in Nigeria), had an immediate and catastrophic impact on all the students of a particular national origin. Thus, the vast foreign student population in the United States continued to be regarded as the "foreign student problem."

Today, in the early 1980s—after years of experience and a great deal of study, with a much greater understanding of cross-cultural relationships and intercultural communication, with more efficient methods of evaluating and developing proficiency in the English language and more knowledgeable procedures for determining financial resources—the persons involved in foreign student affairs can be much more effective in dealing

with their responsibilities. Thus, foreign students now coming
to the United States may expect to find that, for the most part,
they are no longer treated as a stereotype, with a predetermined
set of problems, but, as Du Bois recommended, greeted as individuals who bring with them their own cultural heritage, have
their own capabilities, and pursue their own particular goals.

A rapid review of the distribution of foreign students at
United States colleges and universities over the years shows that
this has followed what in retrospect proves to be a very natural
progression. From the beginning and up to that great divide
World War II, there were no extraordinary features in the pattern of enrollment. There was merely a steady but—by comparison with later years—not extraordinary growth. The noticeable
factors influencing the attendance of foreign students at different institutions included personal acquaintance, the recommendation of foreign alumni upon their return to the homeland, the
reputation of certain institutions through the activities or writings of faculty, religious affiliation, and the initiative taken by
some institutions to enroll students from selected regions or
countries of the world. All these factors remain influential in
determining the institutional preference of foreign students
today.

The first major development in the pattern of enrollment
was concurrent with the first waves of the postwar movement
of foreign students to United States colleges and universities in
the 1950s. By that time the involvement of public and private
sponsors in foreign student programs and the focus on certain
fields of study resulted in a growing concentration of large numbers of foreign students in a relatively small number of institutions, so that "half of the foreign student population was concentrated in only forty-seven colleges and universities, each of
which reported an enrollment of four hundred or more foreign
students" (*Open Doors*, 1966, p. 6). This tendency has continued, so that by 1980–81 there were seventy institutions enrolling more than one thousand foreign students. Today, however, the rising tide of foreign student enrollment is reaching
further and further into the community of educational institutions. With the persistent growth in numbers, the foreign stu-

dent population is now dispersed among a total of 2,734 colleges and universities; thus, the relative proportion of the large concentration at a few institutions is steadily decreasing.

But this rising tide was not entirely without direction. Increasing numbers of foreign students were turning toward the community and junior colleges, not simply because it was often easier to gain admission to these institutions but also because for many students they offered the most appropriate level of study needed for their careers upon return home. At the same time, community and junior colleges were recognizing that they could fill an identifiable need, especially in the developing countries, for trained manpower at the middle level: "Foreign students are enrolling in United States community and junior colleges in record numbers. Students from Third World countries are playing a dominant role in this increase. Community and junior colleges find themselves offering studies appropriate to many foreign nationals—and many institutions are eager to render these services" (Diener, 1977, p. 14). The combined effect of both attraction and outreach has resulted in a marked increase in the enrollment of foreign students at these institutions, from a number that was almost negligible in the middle 1960s to 54,220, or 17.4 percent foreign student population, in 1980-81.

Several other factors have contributed to the current trend for foreign students to spread to a wide variety of institutions across the United States. Foreign students are more knowledgeable, since much more information and advice are available in the students' home countries about the educational resources in the United States. The objectives of their study abroad are more precisely defined both by the students and their sponsors. A number of institutions not previously involved in international educational interchange are now, for a variety of reasons, actively recruiting foreign students. As will be seen in Chapter Five, this particular development has been the subject of widespread discussion and concern. The difference between acceptable efforts to attract good students and a single-minded search to fill gaps in freshman classes has been drastically demonstrated by a number of unfortunate incidents in which the financial motivation has been obvious and the accompanying sense of educational responsibility conspicuous by its absence. A set of recruitment standards now provides guidance to those who wish to make a rational addition to the institution's educational activities by seeking and enrolling students from foreign countries (see Jenkins, 1980a).

Institutional and National Responses to International Activities

Faced with the presence of large numbers of foreign students, and stimulated by other interinstitutional relationships and the international experience of many members of the faculty, a number of universities and colleges began to give special attention to this new dimension in their educational programs. Indeed, no small part of the resource materials now available consists of copies of relatively recent intrainstitutional reports on their international activities. An example of how one major institution views its foreign students in the context of its total international involvement is given later in this book (Chapter Nine). In the introductions to other comprehensive institutional reports, one finds references to the need "to make adjustments in educational patterns that will prepare students for this changing world situation" (Michigan State University, 1980, p. 1) or to take a lead "in preparing students and citizens to live in an increasingly interdependent world" (Purdue University, 1979, p. 1) or to regard international activities as "spanning the globe . . . a national resource, in some cases a world resource" (Klitgaard, 1979, p. 27).

These institutional reviews probe every aspect of the international activity of the college or university, seeking the relationship between all the programs in every department and discipline and placing the role of scholarly exchange and the enrollment of foreign students in the context of their total international involvement. At the same time, some reach beyond the campus to examine the impact of these foreign students, and their accompanying families, on the local community. Equally important, the reports are by no means complacent but raise critical questions concerning, for example, the relative virtues of enrolling graduate or undergraduate students. They also note existing inconsistencies in the totality of the international dimension—for example, the underutilization of available foreign talent in an institution committed to international educational programs.

Today this concern is not only institutional but interinstitutional. The deliberations of the American Association of Community and Junior Colleges and the Council of Graduate Schools reveal an increasing attention to the international dimension of contemporary education and the relevance of the presence of foreign students at their member institutions, while many of the institutional associations have their own offices of international programs and international relations. At the national level, the President's Commission on Foreign Language and International Studies (1979, p. 22) includes among its findings the recommendation that "colleges and universities should . . . look more to the opportunity for encouraging international perspectives offered by the presence of foreign students and other visitors from abroad." Of more particular relevance is the fact that a special committee of the American Council on Education has just completed its investigation of the impact of foreign students on colleges and universities in the United States (American Council on Education, 1982). Thus, within the individual institutions and at the national level, the place of foreign students and scholars in United States colleges and universities is the subject of sophisticated and critical attention—a far cry from the days when they were considered only an unusual addition to the campus community.

This increased attention, derived from an accumulation of experience over the past thirty years, may now lead to further study at the international level to improve and develop in its global context the full potential of international educational interchange. Concurrent studies in the other major host countries also offer ample evidence that the time is ripe for such a multinational examination of this phenomenon.

Interest in the personal welfare of foreign students and, more recently, in the function of international educational interchange has not been confined to institutional administrators and the campus community. Although it has been more noticeable in the United States, where the pattern of organized or individual citizen participation has been prevalent for many years, there has been a similar, if nationally distinctive, involvement of nonacademic organizations in the other host countries. A by no means inclusive but illustrative list of such organizations and agencies would contain the British Council and the United Kingdom Council on Overseas Student Affairs, the Canadian Bureau for International Education, the French National Center for University and Student Services (Centre Nationale des Oeuvres Universitaires et Scolaires), and the German Academic Exchange Service (Deutscher Akademischer Austauschdienst). A newcomer to the field, reflecting the increase in foreign students in that country, is the Japanese Association for Foreign Student Affairs.

Focusing once more on the United States, community or national interest in foreign students was manifested as early as 1911, when the Committee on Friendly Relations Among Foreign Students (now the International Student Service) was organized under the auspices of the YMCA and YWCA for the benefit of students from other lands studying in the United States. In 1919 the Institute of International Education was established as a national organization concerned with student migration to and from the United States. Educational associations, such as the American Council on Education and the Association of American Colleges, also were taking an increasing interest in the foreign students enrolled at their member institutions and in the newly developing exchange programs. These pioneer organizations continue to take an active role in the search for new and better ways of managing the exchange activity, and the major national educational associations are also devoting considerable interest to this field. Private philanthropy was also making an early contribution as the first of the now famous International Houses, built through the generosity of Mr. and Mrs. John D. Rockefeller, Jr., was opened in New York in 1924.

The early efforts of a few concerned individuals to welcome and assist foreign students carried the seeds of what was to become a nationwide community activity. Keeping pace with the growing foreign student population, a network of independent groups—some informal, some highly organized—spread across the country, offering an increasing number and variety of programs and services to the foreign students and other foreign visitors in their community. Today there is some kind of community service group working with practically every institution that has a sizable foreign student enrollment. As will be seen in the description of institutional activities and organizations in Chapters Eight and Nine, colleges and universities look to these groups for many of the services considered essential for an acceptable foreign student program.

These community groups meet newly arrived students at the local airport, bus station, or railway station; organize and staff clothing banks or furniture loan services; offer assistance in finding off-campus housing; establish programs for foreign wives; and provide extracurricular educational programs, such as conversational English, visits to industry and government offices, and professional contacts. All these are supplementary to a home hospitality program that brings thousands of foreign students and visitors into the homes of interested families across the United States. These community services are organized at the national level by the National Council for International Visitors and by the Community Section of the National Association for Foreign Student Affairs. Through these organizations the members of the different groups across the country gather together for national conferences, prepare and distribute resource materials, and organize workshops and other training opportunities for newcomers and for the more experienced volunteers.

Paralleling the private initiative, there was within government circles a growing interest in the potential significance of the foreign students in this country, an interest that soon began to reach beyond those who were participants in the official exchange programs. By 1941 the attention being given to the foreign student population was such that the Department of State's Advisory Committee on the Adjustment of Foreign Students, originally established in 1936, proposed a national meeting of those who were actively engaged in work with foreign students. With the participation of representatives of the interested nongovernmental organizations, a conference of foreign student advisers was organized in 1942. As noted by Putman (1965, p. 6), this was the first of a series of meetings which resulted in 1948 in the establishment of the National Association of Foreign Student Advisers—now called the National Association for Foreign Student Affairs (NAFSA). With the creation of NAFSA and its consequent development (with the support of the Ford Foundation during its critical growth years), there was now a focal point for all those concerned with the foreign student population in the United States.

In its present form as the National Association for Foreign Student Affairs, NAFSA comprises in its membership foreign student admissions officers, foreign student advisers, teachers of English as a second language, advisers to United States students on study abroad, and the representatives of community and national organizations that offer services and programs for foreign students. It involves in its activities the representatives of educational institutions and organizations, of government agencies and of business and industry and, in recent years, of foreign governments. An independent professional association that derives much of the support for its programs from government sources (the United States Information Agency and the Agency for International Development), it provides training programs and consultation services, publications, workshops on new developments and contemporary problems, liaison with governmental and private agencies and organizations, and annual national and regional conferences for its approximately 5,000 members and others who are involved in international educational interchange.

On the national level, a significant number of organizations and associations are now involved in educational exchange —either directly, through the administration of programs and services, or indirectly, by participation in the deliberations regarding policies and practices. Acting together as the National Liaison Committee on Foreign Student Admissions (NLC) are the American Association of Collegiate Registrars and Admissions Officers (AACRAO); the College Entrance Examination Board (CEEB), more commonly known as the College Board; the Council of Graduate Schools (CGS); the Institute of International Education (IIE); and the National Association for Foreign Student Affairs (NAFSA). This committee has been responsible for the development of various innovative programs in the field: the Overseas Consultations and Workshops, which provide the latest information on United States higher education to those who are responsible for advising and counseling students in their home countries who wish to study in the United States; the Foreign Student Information Clearinghouse, a computerized service that helps foreign students find the most appropriate institution for study in the United States; and national colloquia on the education of foreign students in United States colleges and universities. The committee is an excellent example of public and private cooperation, since the various activities are designed and operated by the committee and the funding is provided by the U.S. Information Agency.

Another important manifestation of the concern of the wider educational community is the development within educational and professional associations of projects designed to examine their own relationship to the foreign student population in the United States. As already mentioned, the American Council on Education has established its special committee to investigate the impact of foreign students on higher education in this country. Similarly, the American Assembly of Collegiate Schools of Business has for many years been concerned with the international dimension and the exchange of students in its field. A new and especially auspicious example of the growing interest in the professional field is the appearance in 1981 of the *Guide to Chemical Education in the United States for Foreign Students,* published by the Committee on International Relations of the American Chemical Society. Conscious of this wider interest, the National Association for Foreign Student Affairs, following the pattern of self-regulatory initiatives prompted by the American Council on Education, has developed a new declaration of general principles for international educational interchange (see Appendix). With the encouragement of a num-

ber of organizations, agencies, and associations, NAFSA now
seeks national endorsement of this document as the accepted
basis for the maintenance and improvement of programs and
services in this area of activity in United States institutions.
Concurrent with these programmatic developments, a coalition
of the major United States exchange organizations, known as
the International Educational Exchange Liaison Group, is seeking to educate those who set government policy, the higher educational community, and the media by the promulgation of
statements concerning international educational interchange.

All the necessary elements are now present, both at the
national and the international level, for a concerted effort to
move beyond the adjustment of established procedures and the
improvement of existing programs. The next necessary step will
be to take an entirely new look at the goals of those who participate in international educational interchange, to review the
ways in which these goals may be reestablished in the light of
needs in coming years, and to indicate how these needs can be
most effectively met.

Conflicting Forces in International Education

The Individual. Whether because of intellectual curiosity,
academic inquiry, a certain restlessness, or a desire for professional advancement, the foreign student or scholar throughout
the ages has been self-motivated. Today, as in years past, most
of the men and women pursuing a course of study in a foreign
institution do not see themselves primarily as elements in a national development plan or economic training program, even
though some may use these as a vehicle for the achievement of
their goal to study abroad. Essentially they are marching to the
beat of their own drum and seeking to fulfill their own intense-
ly private life plan. In the same way, the sponsored exchange
program, whether publicly or privately supported, is by definition purposeful. However benign, there will be some religious,
philanthropic, economic, idealistic, or nationalistic intent; and
the program will be designed and participants selected in accordance with criteria that are compatible with the sponsor's

goals. The increase and outreach of sponsored programs in the years following World War II have affected both the dimensions and the diversity of the contemporary foreign student population.

Host Countries. One of the more significant of the various modern forces that direct the transnational flow of students and scholars is national interest. As far as the major host countries are concerned, this is either a direct descendant of earlier policies of colonial powers to extend their influence through educational relationships or an attempt by newer world powers to establish such relationships, especially with and among the developing nations. The distinction between domination and persuasion is hard to draw. From the perspective of the foreign student, the difference may well be in the eye of the beholder. The Patrice Lumumba University in Moscow was established in 1960 "in compliance with Leninist policy to render disinterested assistance to the peoples of developing countries" (Binyon, 1979, p. 7). In the United States, the Foreign Assistance Act of 1961 (from which the funds are derived for the Agency for International Development's participant training program) is described in its preamble as "an act to promote the foreign policy, security, and general welfare of the United States by assisting the peoples of the world in their efforts toward economic development and internal and external security." More compatible with the long-term goals of educational interchange is the Mutual Educational and Cultural Exchange Act of 1961, designed "to increase mutual understanding between the people of the United States and the people of other countries by means of educational and cultural exchange" (Statement of Purpose). In the pursuance of this goal, we have benefited from the powerful persistence of Senator Fulbright that this program which bears his name should be free from any political propaganda. Thus, in many countries it is a cooperative effort of both the United States and the foreign government. In any case, even conceding the existence of ulterior motives, it is generally acknowledged that the nationally supported exchange program, from the point of view of the host countries, is at its best a worthy educational venture and pragmatically a worthwhile form of national diplomacy.

Home Countries. The motivation of the home countries from which most of the students come, and especially that of the developing countries, is more single-minded and urgent. For them all, and particularly for the new nations, education is both an instrument for social equality and a means of national development. Vast and ambitious plans for economic progress call for a new cadre of skilled and semiskilled manpower. In these circumstances the need to call on the educational resources of the highly industrialized countries has resulted in some programs initiated entirely by the home country—notably the oil-producing countries, which have abundant financial resources. Other programs, involving countries without a supply of essential natural resources, are partnership activities supported mainly by the host countries. In all cases, in the area of study abroad, the long-term goal of equal educational opportunity has of necessity given way to the more immediate needs of national development. Thus, although there has been a widening of the circle of society from which the students have been drawn, we have yet to feel the impact of the total democratization of international educational interchange. In the awkward meantime, students who have come from the developing countries are subject to an extraordinary pressure to bring their study abroad programs to a successful conclusion as rapidly and efficiently as possible.

Business and Industry. For many years a number of major corporations in the industrialized nations have had their own training programs, tied to their foreign development projects. Many international contracts for new heavy machinery, new equipment, and new systems of communication and administration include a provision for the training of those who will be responsible for the operation and management of the foreign factory or service. As their local establishments proliferate across the world, representatives of the multinational corporations are to be found recruiting foreign students as they complete their studies in the host countries. The need was summarized by the leaders of business and industry and the educators who participated in a Special Brookings Panel on *International Dimension of Management Education.* In their report they call on business education "to develop broad understanding of multinational and transnational affairs in order to add a global dimension to teaching and research" (Brookings Institution, 1975, p. 3). Although this may be a concern which is acutely acknowledged in this particular field, it is equally applicable to almost every field of economic and industrial endeavor. Thus, the foreign student becomes part of the interdependency that characterizes present-day economic development.

The College or University. In every host country, the institution that enrolls foreign students has its own rationale, even though this may sometimes be by default rather than by explicit policy. In the United States, the reason may be harder to find in that there may be different motivations within the component schools or departments of the same institution. Some are more expedient, such as the need to fill certain classrooms, the unresisting response to applications from students who seek admission and have the necessary financial resources, or the opportunity for relatively inexpensive teaching and research assistance; some are more purposeful and derive from the intention to add an international dimension to the institution's educational programs; many are a combination of both.

There is a comforting universality about the commitment to international educational interchange that is to be found in the public declarations and documents of most colleges and universities. While few institutional administrations would claim that they are completely successful in fulfilling their expressed intent, that intent is at least on record and serves as a support for those who are directly involved in the institution's international educational activities. Out of the many statements of intent, one that is particularly concise and apposite was made by the president of the University of Southern California: "We believe that international education must be based on a campus recognition that international students are an important element of our total activities. We see the presence of foreign nationals as an opportunity to expand the vistas of our domestic students, and as a means of enriching most of our curricular and research activities" (Hubbard, 1978, p. 7).

Roles of Foreign Students and Scholars

As a result of the different forces that motivate international educational interchange today, foreign students and scholars are perceived in a variety of roles. During their period of study abroad, they appear to some simply as members of the campus community who happen to be foreign; to others they represent an educational resource for the enhancement of the institution's international educational activities, both on campus and in the community. In the world of commerce and industry, some will be seen as the future work force for international private enterprise, while in the home country others are identified and anxiously awaited as the necessary national resource for economic, social, and political development.

On completion of their stay in the foreign country, some students will return home to assume a role which has been the defined goal of their entire educational career and for which their study abroad was a specific preparation. Others may find that they are designated to play roles which they are reluctant to assume or which accrue without their knowledge or intent. Even when study abroad is a prescribed training for some developmental activity or national program, the individual participant is subject to the inevitable process of change that is part of education; as a result, roles that were once clearly defined and acceptable may become obscure or seen as a burden rather than an opportunity. The limited task of serving as an instrument in the transfer of technology may be transformed into the more complex and sensitive role of acting as an agent of change. The uncertainty about what the future may hold, or the lack of any assured position, may severely inhibit the foreign student from making the best use of the advantages derived from the opportunity to study abroad, thus depriving both student and society of the benefits of what is generally a long and expensive educational process. It is in these circumstances that the completion of the period of study abroad and the definition of the role to be played may involve anxious readjustment as the returning student seeks to adapt the knowledge and training acquired in a foreign country to the needs and opportunities of the home land.

The new roles and responsibilities of the foreign student and scholar today derive from and must relate to the fundamental changes that face them and the rest of their generation. In the lifetime of many of those who are now studying outside their homelands, and certainly in that of their immediate predecessors, the political and economic conditions of the world have, quite simply, been upset. The results at this particular time seem to exceed the management capacity of the expert and surpass the comprehension of the ordinary educated citizen. The political complexities have been described by Barnet (1981, p. 135): "With the collapse of the old colonial empires and the creation of scores of new nations, it is no longer possible for the fate of people in Asia, Africa, and Latin America to be settled in a few chancelleries of Europe. International politics, which was once a drawing-room drama, has become an extravaganza with a cast of thousands." Whether they like it or not, the foreign students presently enrolled in colleges and universities across the world will soon be called on to be members of that cast. At the same time, in the field of economics, interdependence has become a fact of life in which the ownership, acquisition, and disposition of the world's resources arbitrate the comfort and may eventually determine the right to life of everyone everywhere. Foreign students are themselves part of these resources, and many of them will be responsible for their management. The journey to the moon and the view of our planet from that vantage point have dramatized the oneness of our world and inspired all sorts of rhetoric about the global community. But, so far, it has been very difficult to identify the qualities that are essential to such a community, such as an agreement on common concerns and the encouragement of mutual interests. It is in this world, wrenched from the progression of previous centuries, and facing an entirely new set of conditions, that foreign students and the institutions in which they are enrolled must seek and find a viable response to contemporary problems. At such a time in the long history of the transnational movement of students and scholars, international educational interchange is no longer a matter of scholarly choice but a question of global survival. It is a crisis that calls for an examination of priorities, both in the development of the foreign student population and the focus of international education.

Foreign students have been recognized in each of the major host countries as a factor of major importance in contemporary education, and international educational interchange is seen as a significant element in international relations. Statements of government policy; the national calendars of conferences, workshops, and seminars on the subject; the immense bibliography; the particular attention given by major educational institutions to their international programs and the foreign students on campus—all provide ample evidence of a common concern. Emerging clearly from all the discussions, inquiries, and deliberations is the acknowledged importance of the individual participant in the transnational movement of students and scholars. Foreign students have been the subject of research and review in every stage of their development—as applicants for admission; in the classroom; as fiscal items in institutional budgets; as international links in educational exchange; and, in their subsequent careers, as administrators, industrialists, entrepreneurs, or educators. But the work that has been done to develop and improve the process of international education has been carried on—mostly in the major host countries, sometimes in binational projects—quite independently and sometimes almost in isolation. Few concurrent or cooperative steps in progressive development have been taken at the international level.

In a field where so many interests in so many countries are involved, this seems the proper time for concerted action. The precedents have already been set by a number of collaborative efforts at different levels of activity. The experiment in a statewide referral system for foreign student admissions, the intercountry workshops on the evaluation of educational credentials, the regional agreements on the recognition of degrees, and the computerized foreign student information service are existing examples of the value of joint effort and suggest that even more progress could be made if there is sustained and imaginative collaboration at the international level.

Reports and Recommendations

A great deal of valuable work has already been done to identify and evaluate the problems and achievements in work with foreign students. Recent examples are to be found in the report *The Overseas Student Question* (Williams, 1981), the follow-up to an earlier report, *Freedom to Study,* both of which are the result of lengthy and extensive research funded by the Overseas Students Trust in the United Kingdom. In the United States, the publication *Needs of Foreign Students from Developing Nations at U.S. Colleges and Universities* (Lee and others, 1981) is the product of a three-year research project conducted under the auspices of the National Association for Foreign Student Affairs and funded by the Agency for International Development. Another recent report is *Foreign Students and Institutional Policy* (American Council on Education, 1982), funded by the Andrew W. Mellon Foundation. All these reports contain a wealth of current information and sensitive comment. They demand some common and cooperative attention at the international level.

At this time, therefore, there is an obvious need and a unique opportunity for a series of multinational task forces or some other form of international collaborative endeavor to examine the problems revealed by these and other studies and to recommend viable solutions for consideration by the international educational community. Among the items that merit further scrutiny are the question of costs, of legal status, and of relevance, all of which are also to be found in this book. Of overriding importance, however, is not so much what happens in any particular country as how the policies and practices in different countries may affect the direction and flow of foreign students to other countries. It is in the interrelationships of international educational interchange—of individuals, institutions, and nations—that we may discover the ways to ensure the optimum benefit from this activity.

As noted, the topics that have been briefly reviewed and placed in historic perspective in the previous pages are the subject of a more illuminative examination in the remainder of this book. It covers the process from the time the prospective student explores the possibility of study abroad to the completion of the educational program in a foreign country. Out of their experiences, the authors have identified old and new problems and noted those practices and procedures that have proved of value. Because a study in any field of activity that deals with people can never be considered complete, this book seeks only to give the latest and sufficiently comprehensive information to those who may be marginally concerned with or intellectually curious about international educational interchange in the 1980s, while opening the way for future study by those for whom this is a prime interest.

2

Preparing Students
for Study Outside
Their Home Countries

Ellen E. Mashiko

There is a vast communication network that reaches the higher
education community and the student population in countries
across the world. Although it is incomplete, and some of its
connections are very tenuous, it carries a continuing exchange
of inquiry and information between education authorities, institutions, and individuals who are concerned with the transnational movement of students and scholars. Some of the most
important links in the network are those persons who provide
advice and information in their home countries to students
seeking to study abroad. In this task they are called on to serve
as interpreters for foreign educational systems and, in some
cases, as local outposts for those institutions in the host countries which are involved in international educational interchange. Many of the students and their parents who are explor-
ing the possibility of study in a foreign country turn first to
these information officers and counselors for advice and assistance.

Some of these resource persons are primarily concerned with binational exchanges and are related to such agencies as the British Council or the United States Information Agency (USIA). Others, such as the Documentation Center of the Colombian Institute for Educational Credit and Technological Studies Abroad (ICETEX), seek to serve as a focal point in their country for the entire range of international educational interchange. Whatever their role or goal may be, they have some common characteristics: they are for the most part inadequately financed; they are manned by an overworked but enthusiastic staff, either paid or volunteer; and they are faced with an almost impossible task as they strive to keep up to date with educational developments in countries both foreign and distant and to relate these developments to changing conditions in their homelands.

The following description of the process of educational interchange is offered from the perspective of those who serve in these information and counseling offices across the world. It examines the way in which they carry on their work, their needs and problems as they try to facilitate the exchange of students between their countries and the major host countries, and the possibilities of bringing some international order into this massive and growing multinational activity. The picture presented provides a key element in the understanding of international educational interchange. It is, in many respects, a projection of the concerns and problems described in other parts of this book. At the same time, by its complexity and involvement in detail (derived from carefully kept records), it conveys a sense of the particularity and immensity of the daily demands on the information and counseling office in a foreign country.

By definition, international educational interchange signifies that there are no "insides" or "outsides." Countries are labeled as host or home countries only in relation to the movement of the individuals who comprise this growing phenomenon. For purposes of this writing, the "outside" will be defined as looking at interchange from other than a United States perspective. Furthermore, discussion will be limited to the interchange of individuals for study and research at university-level institutions. There is no intention to discount or ignore the importance of interchange at other levels or through other avenues, simply a need to reduce to more manageable terms the diverse world of interchange.

Looking at the process of educational interchange from the "outside" presents difficulties and multidimensional challenges that have been neglected far too long despite the growing importance of understanding and working effectively with the increasingly large transnational movement of students and scholars. The process, while offering all the advantages of a plural system, appears to be disorganized, inefficient, and lacking in effective cooperative management. Emphasis in this chapter will be placed on the information and advising resources available outside the United States because these resources serve as articulators of American education and have significant influence on the vast number of prospective students and scholars. Little has been written about these resources, which represent a relatively untapped reservoir and are generally overlooked and unheard. In addition, there will be an examination of these questions: How do individuals select United States institutions? What factors influence their decisions? How can the system of interchange be improved?

Background

For purposes of clarity, information and advising services will be defined as the resources available to prospective students and scholars to help them determine whether educational opportunities in the United States will enable them to attain their educational, professional and personal goals, and whether it is practical to consider seeking these opportunities. The definition does not include placement and recruitment activities. Placement has been defined by Lockyear (1980, p. 21) as "that function in which an individual or agency attempts to gain admission for an individual student or group of students into a college or university," and recruitment as the "process which seeks to attract students to a particular college or university." Information and advising services may extend into placement "if the agency is free to recommend any appropriate institution in the U.S. . . . Unfortunately, the placement agency is typically tied in with a very small number of institutions and would not make any money if an institution not on its list were selected by the student. On the other hand, placement can be closely related to recruiting because the agencies frequently work with recruiters" (p. 22).

A comprehensive view of resources abroad is difficult to provide because there is no centralized pool of data available on information and advising services throughout the world. Focusing on the United States, we find that the Board of Foreign Scholarships (BFS), the twelve-member board appointed by the President of the United States to determine policies and procedures for the Fulbright Program, lists forty-one active binational commissions. Of this number, thirty-four binational commissions, created by executive agreements between the United States and other nations to administer the Fulbright Program, have made some provision for student advisory services on a regular basis, ranging from regular program staff handling inquiries as required to the hiring of one or more counselors. There are also private organizations, such as the Institute of International Education (IIE) and the American-Mideast Educational and Training Services (Amideast), which provide counseling services. The IIE has offices in Hong Kong, Mexico, and Thailand; Amideast provides counseling in capital cities with some outreach in Egypt, Jordan, Lebanon, Morocco, Syria, and Tunisia. When the United States International Communication Agency (USICA) was established in 1978, its purpose was "to encourage the sharing of ideas and cultural activities among the people of the United States and the people of other nations" (United States International Communication Agency, 1980, p. 2). To this end, the agency (now known as the United States Information Agency), through its offices abroad, provides advisory services in all countries where binational commissions and private organizations are not involved.

Another key difficulty is the unevenness of services provided. Staff members assigned to information and advising services differ not only in numbers but also in background and training. In 1976, in response to requests from overseas educational advisers for assistance in helping students prepare for study and living in the United States, the National Liaison Committee on Foreign Student Admissions (NLC) (see also Chapter One) published the *Overseas Counselors' Manual.* This was the first effort of its kind to meet the needs of advisers abroad—both United States citizens and nationals of the host country. These individuals are almost always hired in the country and then self-trained or trained by a more experienced staff member. The NLC has also sponsored overseas workshops through which experienced American educators and administrators have visited various countries to lecture, advise, and direct the establishment and/or improvement of existing services. However, because of lack of funding, the NLC has been unable to conduct these group workshops and individual consultations on a regular, ongoing basis and has not covered all the countries from which a significant number of students and scholars originate.

This leads us to a further difficulty, the lack of financial support of overseas information and advising services. In general, the commissions and other policy makers regard these services as an appendage to grant-giving and other programmatic activities, even though statistics show that the percentage of foreign students and scholars in the United States sponsored by the United States government has dropped to 2.3 percent of the total (*Open Doors,* 1980–81, p. 26). These information and advisory services, in addition to meeting a general need, are very important to students sponsored by the United States government, since most grantees are asked to select the institutions to which application will be made directly, or on their behalf, through exchange organizations such as the IIE. In times of diminishing funding of United States government grant programs, there is a tendency to look askance at information and advising services and in severe cases to consider the termination of such services in order to fund additional grants.

Change and diversity of needs throughout the world also contribute to the difficulty in looking at international interchange. While relatively little can be done to predict sociopolitical change and its impact on interchange, it appears that the diversity of needs between and within countries has been over-looked. In order to cope with the vastness of the "outside," we witness a propensity to group countries into areas, and areas into regions, even though there are great differences within these geographical boundaries. We also observe an inclination to merge countries by economic need, even though these countries differ socially, culturally, and by stage of development. It is cru-cial to look at individual countries because within a given coun-try are various sectors for which education in the United States may be sought.

As colleagues in education, it is the information and ad-vising services (and placement only when the student is free to choose any institution) that should be our focus, because those providing such services have as their main task the articulation of American education, followed by assistance in appropriate admissions and placement, and orientation for those individuals who actually depart for the United States. The challenge to these articulators and United States institutions is great, since most of the world still looks to the United States as a willing, although increasingly costly, teacher, trainer and partner in edu-cation. Furthermore, we can expect an increase in the numbers of foreign students and scholars in the United States; and these individuals will critically review and evaluate United States edu-cation and its response to international educational interchange. We also face the challenge of enhancing and balancing the flow of information between the United States and other countries, for even though labels such as interchange and exchange are fre-quently used, the flow of information and the sharing of profes-sional experiences about this important task are usually uni-lateral, moving from the United States to other countries. Even this flow is fragmented and at times completely lacking. When the current is reversed, the information is too often available only to a very narrow audience within the American educa-tional community. There appear to be no widely known and effective mechanisms, so the channels remain thin pipelines even though both the United States and the "outside" are inter-dependent. The important task facing the articulators and United States institutions requires a mutually agreed-upon effort as society faces an era of growing interdependence that is increasingly being expressed in the form of multilateral interchange.

Components of a Model Information
and Advising Service

In spite of the differences in the circumstances of various countries with which the United States engages in interchange, there are eight basic components of a model information and advising service. They are described here to familiarize American educators with the scope of services being developed abroad. Although these services already receive assistance and cooperation from a sizable proportion of United States institutions, it is to be hoped that this necessary help will be increased in the future.

Structure and Operations. The relationship between the model information and advising service and the parent organization is clear to users of the service as well as to United States institutions. There are no charges for basic services, such as access to reference materials and bulletins. When necessary, charges are minimal and clearly stated. In addition to handling inquiries from individuals who have easy access to its premises, the information and advising service is organized to assist those who are not in the immediate vicinity. General inquiries, particularly those from individuals in the early stages of planning for study or research in the United States, are handled through printed materials usually developed by the information and advising service and written in the local language if English is not widely used or sufficiently understood by the majority of the inquirers. Group sessions are held regularly for those who can participate, and form letters are prepared and sent with appropriate printed materials for inquirers who cannot. Inquiries from individuals concerned with specific aspects of study and research in the United States are responded to through individual advising sessions and correspondence. Communication by telephone is common. Consultation is available to the government and private sectors, particularly concerning the establishment and operation of educational interchange programs. Records of contacts with inquirers, including the current occupation of and information sought by these inquirers, are maintained to facilitate ongoing planning, to improve services, and to predict future trends. These data are shared with appropriate agencies in the country, with the information and advising services in other countries, and with professional international educational interchange organizations in the United States and other countries. Information on standardized admissions tests is available, and test bulletins are distributed. Staff members, whether employed on a full- or part-time basis or assisting on a volunteer basis, have all studied in the United States. They are given periodic opportunities to travel to the United States to attend professional meetings and to visit universities, colleges, other educational training sites, and educational interchange organizations. Furthermore, all staff members, whether from the United States or local nationals, are thoroughly familiar with the educational system of the country.

Resources. The model information and advising service maintains a library of current general and area specific reference books and the bulletins of a wide range of accredited institutions. Materials other than bound printed matter are filed according to field of study or function. Frequently used holdings are updated annually; less frequently used materials, biennially. The library is organized for easy use and is open regularly to the public. Staffed by personnel who offer assistance in identifying appropriate materials, interpreting and clarifying written material when necessary, and providing guidelines for planning, the library serves as the core of the information and advising service.

English Language and Orientation Programs. Since English language and orientation programs are sought by individuals in most countries, reference materials and program-specific materials are placed in the library and are updated annually or as new items become available. Staff members are prepared to offer guidelines on the selection of programs.

Predeparture Orientation. Orientation for individuals admitted to United States institutions is an integral part of the information and advising service's activities. Appropriate printed materials are developed to meet country-specific needs, and more general publications are made available. Group sessions are conducted by level—undergraduate, graduate, and scholar—and/ or by fields of study if there are large numbers of individuals participating. Recently returned students and scholars, as well as American students and professors, serve as speakers and panelists. Small-group discussion and other opportunities for participants to ask questions and raise issues are included in the program. If sufficient numbers of Americans living in the country are willing to volunteer, home visits are arranged; departing students and scholars and their families meet with these volunteers over a period of time to learn more about the United States, and how Americans live, think, and communicate. The volunteers and the departing students are matched according to common interests, academic background, or familiarity with the state or region to which the student or scholar will go. The home visit portion of the orientation program is a mutually rewarding experience, with the Americans learning more about the country and its people through close contact with an individual or a small group.

Recruitment. The policies of the model information and advising service in dealing with direct inquiries from recruiters, as well as from prospective students who have been approached by recruiters, parallel and support the joint statement on *Principles of Good Practice with Reference to College Admissions* (approved by the American Association of Collegiate Registrars and Admissions Officers, College Board (CEEB), National Association of College Admissions Counselors, National Association of Secondary School Principals, and endorsed by the American Council on Education), the College Board's (1978) *Guidelines for the Recruitment of Foreign Students,* and the recommendations and criteria for ethical recruitment made by the participants of a colloquium on foreign student recruitment (Jenkins, 1980a). In addition, country-specific guidelines and suggestions for United States institutions that wish to enroll students are available. Infringements of accepted practices are reported to appropriate authorities and professional organizations within the country as well as to those in the United States.

Liaison with Educational Organizations. Liaison is maintained with educational and professional organizations within the country and in the United States for further development of the service, overall coordination of international educational interchange, and staff training. Membership in professional associations is encouraged to facilitate the rapid acquisition of information and professional development.

United States Students and Scholars Abroad. The service provides information about educational opportunities in foreign countries through the initiation of correspondence and the publication of guidelines and institutional profiles. It prepares orientation materials for United States students who have been admitted to universities and for scholars who have been placed in academic research centers, conducts orientation sessions upon their arrival, and supplements the support services provided by the receiving institutions.

Staff. The eighth component, the staff, is ideally composed of both nationals of the country where the service is located—specifically, nationals who have studied in the United States and who have preferably completed a program of degree study in education, counseling, or other social sciences—and Americans with graduate degrees in education, counseling, or other social sciences. Those who are familiar with the educational system of the country, and who have sufficient language proficiency in the predominant language, are used to conduct group and individual advising sessions and to consult with educators, administrators, and others. Staff members who have worked at a United States institution of higher learning are especially valuable. Individuals who have successfully completed programs of study, who hold positive views of the value of international educational interchange based on their own experiences, and whose primary interest is education in its broadest definition are essential.

Survey of Available Resources

A questionnaire covering the eight basic components of a model information and advising service was mailed by the author to information and advising organizations in or representing the nine countries with the largest numbers of students in the United States. (The selection of countries was based on data available in 1978-79. The survey was conducted prior to the publication of data for 1979-80.) In rank order these included Iran, Nigeria, Taiwan, Canada, Hong Kong, India, Venezuela, Saudi Arabia, and Mexico; Japan ranked sixth and was also included, for a total of ten countries. In addition, the questionnaire was sent to six other countries: Belgium and Luxembourg (served by a single commission), France, Jordan, Malaysia, the Netherlands, and the United Kingdom. As was expected, Canada does not provide information and advising services to individuals who wish to study in the United States because of its geographical proximity and accessibility to United States institutions. While the position in Iran is subject to continuing change, the situation in 1981 was described as follows: "In Iran the major student advising activity was carried out by Amideast until they closed their office in Tehran in July 1980. Before the U.S. Fulbright Commission was closed, a relatively small number of students, especially Fulbright students, did receive advice. . . . Within the Ministry of Culture and Higher Education (formerly the Ministry of Science and Higher Education), the State Organization for Student Affairs (SOSA) had a staff responsible for advising students about educational opportunities in all countries abroad. . . . As far as anyone knows, there is presently no student advising activity of any kind available to students from Iran" (letter from F. E. Lockyear to E. E. Mashiko, May 7, 1981).

Of the eleven information and advising services that responded, seven are integral parts of binational commissions and four are private organizations.* No charges are made by three,

*The respondents were Margaret Nicholson, academic counselor, Commission for Educational Exchange between the United States of America, Belgium and Luxembourg; Charlette Soto, head, French Section and University Documentation and Counselling Center, Franco-American Commission for Educational Exchange; John Brohm, director, Institute of International Education, Hong Kong; Prem Parischa, evaluation, testing, and advising officer, United States Educational Foundation in India; Frederick E. Lockyear, consultant in international educational and training services concerning U.S. higher education, Kenmore, Washington (on

while eight charge for specific services and items such as photo-copying, postage for return mailing, and certain publications to help defray the cost of printing. One private organization charges for placement, certification, and translation services. In varying degrees, all the respondents handle inquiries by mail, telephone, visits to the office, and group and individual advising sessions. Branch offices are maintained by three information and advising services; the others provide periodic outreach programs. Where there are no branch offices, the most frequently mentioned other reliable sources of information in the country are the United States Information Agency libraries, government ministries of education, and university information centers. Staffing patterns vary from one to seven full-time staff members, and in combinations of full- and part-time staff. There are both United States and non–United States citizens in nine organizations; one single-person organization is staffed by an American; in the remaining organization, the entire staff is comprised of citizens of that country, who have all earned graduate degrees in the United States. One organization receives considerable assistance from eight volunteers. Library holdings of bulletins, reference books, and other related publications differ by country; but it is significant that eight of the eleven organizations subscribe to microfiche collections of college and university bulletins—indicating that inquirers have access to current information on a wide range of institutions. While all the respondents make available information on English language training programs, only four actively seek this information. Predeparture orientation sessions are conducted by ten organizations; nine disseminate specially prepared materials. Assistance to United States students in the countries is provided by eight organizations; all receive inquiries.

Iran); Ellen E. Mashiko, educational information service officer, Japan–United States Educational Commission; Alain McNamara, director, American-Mideast Educational and Training Services, Inc., Jordan; Terry Whiting, director, Educational Information Center, Malaysian-American Commission on Educational Exchange; Rene Greenwald, representative, Institute of International Education, Mexico; Julie Hu, student adviser, Foundation for Scholarly Exchange, Taiwan; Margaret McDonald, student adviser, United States–United Kingdom Educational Commission; Isabel Gouverneur, director, Educational Guidance Service of the North American Association of Venezuela.

Although this cursory summary of the eleven information and advising services does not convey the scope of programs conducted and the milieu in which each functions, the views of the respondents have been incorporated throughout this chapter.

How Foreign Students and Scholars
Select United States Institutions

There are countless ways in which prospective students and scholars begin their search. In the ideal case, individuals visit, telephone, or write to an information and advising service, which provides them with printed material describing the United States system of education and the admissions process. These materials are often written in the language of the country, to assure understanding of basic information. Individuals who live within easy access to the office are likely to be invited to participate in a group session during which audiovisual materials, such as the videotape recordings *If You Want to Study in the United States* (United States Information Agency, 1974) and *Student Life in the United States* (United States Information Agency, 1981), are shown. A staff member then reports on more detailed aspects of study in the United States, and a question-and-answer session follows. Individuals are then oriented to the use of the library and invited to individual advising sessions as needed. In a growing number of countries, individuals have access to the Foreign Student Information Clearinghouse, a computerized college and university selection service developed by the NLC. (Local processing centers for the clearinghouse are served in Brazil by the Foundation for Educational Credit of the Brazilian Association of University Graduates (Fundação APLUB); in Colombia by the Colombian Institute for Educational Credit and Technological Studies Abroad (ICETEX); in Europe by the Franco-American Commission for Educational Exchange; in Japan by the Japan–United States Educational Commission; in Mexico and Central America by the Institute of International Education, Mexican Office; and in Puerto Rico and the Caribbean by the College Board, Puerto Rico Office.) Upon completion of a simple, two-page form by the prospective student, this information is fed into a computer,

which produces a list of institutions that best fit the specifications given by the user. These specifications include twelve
items, such as field of study, location, college setting, available
funds, and religious affiliation. The clearinghouse appears to be
a useful tool in helping the prospective student focus on dis-
crete specifications that should be considered in the early stages
of planning, in providing an objective selection of institutions
that welcome applications from outside the United States, and
in shortening the time usually required in searching for appropriate colleges and universities. The prospective student then
turns to field-specific reference books and the bulletins of the
institutions shown on his or her report form to learn more
about the selections and subsequently to narrow choices further. For the adviser the clearinghouse is a helpful counseling
tool, provides information to expand the adviser's own knowledge of United States colleges and universities, and promotes
better-quality service. (Currently the data bank comprises over
1,600 junior colleges, four-year colleges, and universities.)

Prospective students are offered guidance throughout this
entire process. Before mailing inquiries they are assisted in evaluating the appropriateness of their plans, the extent to which
they meet specific admissions requirements, and the way a particular institution meets the needs and goals of its individual
foreign study program. As application materials are received,
prospective students call on the information and advising service
for answers to questions about institution-specific procedures.
Finally, as letters of acceptance are received, the students call
for advice in making their final decisions.

The criteria used by prospective students in selecting colleges and universities are related to academic, financial, environmental, and social factors.

The availability of a progam in a particular field of study
at the level sought is perhaps the most significant criterion.
Prospective students seeking admission to graduate schools will
have more specific purposes and may wish to study under a particular professor. The prestige and ranking of a department and/
or institution as a whole within the United States *and in the
home country* is often crucial. In countries such as Venezuela,

revalidation of United States degrees is essential for employment. In Japan individuals who are sponsored by their employers are sometimes permitted to study in the United States only
if they gain admission to any of a particular group of universities. Furthermore, the academic excellence and ranking of a university are important if a university student wishes to spend a
year abroad and transfer credit back to his or her home university, which may decide to accept such credit on the basis of
where it was earned. The decisions made by government ministries and agencies, employers, universities, and sponsors may be
based on a variety of factors, including regional and professional
accreditation, published lists and ranking studies, previous experience with graduates of United States colleges and universities, and the personal experiences of those individuals who are
directly involved in making these decisions. Institutions concerned with extending their international relationships, gaining
recognition in foreign countries, and bringing up to date the
available information about their educational programs can do
so by making contact with the organizations and agencies listed
as "Other Sources of Assistance" in Chapter Six.

The cost of study and living in the United States is a second important criterion that directly affects the movement of
students. Since students must accommodate their plans to the
limits of their *proven* financial resources, decisions about where
to study will be influenced by the differential in tuition fees
and cost of living in a particular country or, in the United
States, in different areas within the country. In Malaysia, where
students have traditionally gone to the United Kingdom, there
was a 100 percent increase in the number of students departing
for study in the United States from 1979-80 to 1980-81. "In
addition to Malaysia's own lack of facilities, interest in study in
the United States has increased due to (1) large increases in
British fees . . . [and] (2) increased awareness of U.S. degrees
and recognition by the Malaysian government as good students
return home and rise to increasingly important positions"
(Whiting response, 1981, p. 2). The increase in British fees also
led to growth in the number of individuals seeking admission to
United States colleges and universities from Hong Kong and

from foreign students in the United Kingdom, where over two thirds of the individuals assisted by the student adviser at the United States—United Kingdom Educational Commission are third country nationals. From another viewpoint it has been predicted that the number of students from Venezuela may decrease by as much as 50 percent "if U.S. costs continue to rise, Venezuelan universities improve and expand, and scholarships for study abroad are reduced" (Gouverneur response, 1981, p. 2).

Related to costs is the availability of financial assistance—a prime concern of students from developing countries (Lee and others, 1981). Even in the developed countries, academically and professionally outstanding students and young scholars may have no access to funds other than personal savings to permit further study and research. Whether based on need or merit, financial assistance is crucial to many individuals who simply cannot meet the rising costs of study and living in the United States. (In fact, as the statistics demonstrate, most of those students who do come to the United States have in some way or another gained access to the necessary funds from sources outside the United States.)

Environmental factors, such as the location and setting of the institution, are also considered seriously by prospective students and their parents and sponsors. Mass media coverage of various cities has intimidated students, especially younger and married students, so that they will not consider an institution in those cities, even though it may best meet their academic needs. Lack of information about lesser-known parts of the United States can also contribute to a prospective student's choice, as can the lack of on-campus housing for both single and married students.

Solicited and unsolicited advice from family, friends, and colleagues who may or may not have studied or lived in the United States also affects choices. Family pressures to study where there are many *or* few other nationals of the same country often play a larger role in the final selection than may be realized, as can religious affiliation, extracurricular activities, and cultural opportunities.

Prospective students have also referred to the completeness and clarity of printed materials and the promptness of correspondence with an institution as contributing to a positive view of a particular program, college, or university. The worst case occurs when an institution does not respond at all.

In the ideal situation, a prospective student is given the opportunity to learn about the United States system of education, educational opportunities, realistic options, and specific institutions, considering all the criteria mentioned with the assistance of a skilled, well-informed, and unbiased adviser. We have limited knowledge about students who avail themselves of information and advising services such as those surveyed. What may be of greater concern are the other ways, about which we have even less knowledge, in which individuals proceed to the United States.

As noted earlier, the United States Information Agency, through its numerous posts and branches, offers assistance in all countries where there are no binational commissions or private organizations. Generally understaffed, with periodic personnel changes and limited resources, USIA offices provide a wide variety of services in addition to advising prospective students about study in the United States. Local universities in some countries provide access to reference materials and bulletins; in India, for instance, sixty-five universities provide this service through university employment and guidance bureaus. However, such materials may be out of date or represent a very restricted number of colleges and universities. Enrolled university students and graduates frequently consult professors, some of whom may have studied, conducted research, or lectured in the United States. While these professors frequently offer valuable information to and make initial contacts on behalf of the students who consult them, procedural matters are often overlooked; and the individual, believing that admission has been granted as a result of correspondence between professors who know each other, may find that it has not. Along the same line, prospective students turn to friends and family in the home country and the United States for advice and sometimes receive negative or biased impressions.

Prospective students are being increasingly exposed to advertisements and direct mail approaches by commercial study abroad agencies. In many countries it is not uncommon to see advertisements in newspapers and magazines, special study abroad directories, subway and train posters, or posters on utility poles. Commonly run as independent businesses by nationals of the country, who often hire an American to lend credibility and assistance to the operation, these agencies may also operate in conjunction with, or be run by, travel bureaus, banks, insurance companies, English language schools, or preparatory schools. These agencies often use the names of specific United States institutions without the institutions' knowledge, and their advertisements imply that admission is guaranteed irrespective of test scores, previous academic records, and other usually required documents. In recent years such agencies have proliferated throughout the world and have, along with other third-party recruiters, come to the attention of the American educational community and foreign governments. For the prospective student, who may have failed to gain entrance to postsecondary institutions in the home country, who has less than satisfactory transcripts and low English language proficiency, the temptation to pay the usually exorbitant fees to the commercial agency and gain admission to a United States institution is great. For the uninformed, a persuasive commercial agent may convince prospective students and their parents that the only way to study in the United States is through an agent. Although an increasing number of individuals abroad have been exposed to the American educational system, there are still many who have no idea what is involved in gaining admission to and studying at an American institution.

In observing how prospective students approach the entire process of admission, we can discern several common mistakes. Insufficient time is given to deciding whether study in the United States is appropriate or practical. Educational opportunities in the home country or a nearby country are not explored, nor are future employment opportunities and the marketability of United States degrees. The length of time and the cost of study are not adequately assessed. English language proficiency and communication skills necessary for academic study and living are confused with rudimentary conversation skills. Parental pressures overpower individual choice. Study in the United States is viewed as a panacea for improving all aspects of an individual's life, and the attitude that somehow everything will work out all right is too prevalent. Even if an individual has carefully considered all aspects of study abroad, during the admissions process he may fail to consider whether the curriculum is relevant and whether an institution has answered the questions that he asked. (It may be relevant to note here that, as reported in Chapter Six, only about one quarter of the students who make their initial inquiry directly to United States institutions have any reasonable hope of even being considered for admission.) The prevention of these mistakes rests with the individual, the information and advising service, and United States institutions. More misunderstanding, distrust, and disappointment will be bred unless a concerted effort is made to improve the entire process of international educational interchange. Because the basic cause of all these errors is misinformation and misunderstanding, the solution may be found in a concerted effort by all concerned, first, to extend the outreach of their channels of information and, second, to increase the available resources of reliable information and knowledgeable advice.

Basic Issues as Seen from the Outside

Communication of United States Institutional Policies. United States institutional policies are frequently unknown, unclear, or communicated ineffectively—for instance, in publications that are more graphic than substantive. In some countries photographs of scantily clad students relaxing on campus definitely work against the institution. More important is a clear, concise explanation of the goals, priorities, and policies of the institution. An institution's commitment to education begins with clear statements that will be useful to prospective students, their parents and sponsors, alumni, and other educators and interested parties in the United States and other countries. If institutions are firmly committed to education, then there should be a natural concordance between policies for Americans and non-Americans and in the way these policies are communicated. Prospective foreign students and scholars are often interested in how Americans evaluate and select institutions and are curious to know how attendance at a particular institution may affect an American's future. At a time when reports of the financial crises of United States institutions and the recruitment of foreign students as a way of counteracting declining enrollments and depleting incomes become news in at least the more developed countries of the world, institutional policies are of utmost importance in developing, maintaining, and advancing the image and status of United States education abroad. Sound institutional policies, reflected in the relationship with prospective foreign students and scholars and the institutions from which they come, are a crucial factor in the efficient conduct of international educational interchange.

Foreign Student Recruitment. Recruitment practices have recently come to the attention of American educators and led to the convocation of a colloquium held at Wingspread in Racine, Wisconsin, in March 1980. The colloquium—as indicated in its title, "Foreign Student Recruitment: Realities and Recommendations"—made specific recommendations and proposed criteria (see Chapter Five) for the maintenance of ethical recruitment practices (Jenkins, 1980a). The "outside" has observed less than ethical recruitment practices in varying degrees. Of the eleven countries that responded to the questionnaire, only France and Belgium indicated little or no recruitment activity, which suggests that recruiters, particularly third-party agents, operate more actively in the non-European countries; the United Kingdom, with its relatively large population of foreign students, reported some activity. While attention has focused primarily on third-party agents who require fee-for-admission payments from the student and fee-for-enrollment payments from the receiving institution, representatives of institutions have also been observed recruiting students in less than ethical ways—for example, by illegally distributing blank but signed Forms I-20 (Certificate of Eligibility for Nonimmigrant Student Status), which may then be used for anyone, irrespective of eligibility. Such actions by a misinformed institutional representative tarnish not only his own institution's image but also that of American education as a whole.

Uninformed institutional representatives who have not taken the time or made the effort to become familiar with the educational system of the country and then comment on what is needed in that country are quickly written off by the educational and governmental community. To a prospective student, they are simply confusing. Institutional representatives must do their homework, ask appropriate questions, invite questions, and visit countries with more than numerical quotas for enrollment in mind.

The "outside" also finds it difficult to comprehend some of the requests of institutional representatives. For example, United States educators who request permission to recruit students on campuses of colleges and universities abroad will get nowhere. Common sense and respect for other educators and institutions sometimes become diffused when institutional representatives travel abroad, and this may make it difficult for the next visiting educator who arrives with other interests in mind. Some foreign institutions have been inundated with correspondence and visits from American educators to the point where letters remain unanswered and appointments are politely refused. Bluntly put, it is a buyer's market, not a seller's market, in many countries; and foreign individuals and institutions are particularly careful in what they select.

Most of the respondents to the questionnaire do not regard recruitment by commercial agents as an effective way of recruiting students under any circumstances. Charges usually paid by prospective students are characteristically high, the assistance given is minimal, and the information provided is misleading—either by inclusion or omission. Since these agents must rely on the income from fees paid by the prospective students or by the United States institution, there is no way to ensure that appropriate information and advising are given. Association with an agent, in general, will in the long run produce negative effects that will be difficult to counter even if a relationship were to be terminated. In most cases the "outside" regards a United States institution's affiliation with a commercial agent as an indication that the institution is second or third rate and in desperate need of students.

Information and advising services abroad are receiving an increasing number of inquiries from prospective students, their parents, and educational and governmental sources who are concerned about commercial operations. In some cases agents may be promising placement in an institution without its knowledge—which leads to the next warning. Institutions must exercise caution in responding to letters requesting information and publications from organizations abroad, even if there are references to "approval" by the local United States embassy or a professional organization. Embassies do *not* approve or certify agents, nor do local governments or ministries of education. An institution can verify letters from unknown sources by contacting professional organizations in the United States, such as NAFSA, and embassies, binational commissions, and ministries of education in the home country. Laxity on the part of United States institutions can lead to complex situations into which the institutions never intended to enter. To an uninformed prospective student with low English language proficiency and strong wishes to study in the United States, the fast-paced, smooth presentations by recruiters provide no opportunities for careful and thoughtful consideration. The temptation to accept a quick and easy method is too strong. In the end, the student and the receiving institution must bear the burden of creating a relevant and acceptable educational program.

Institutional Practices in Admissions. Admissions practices are generally perplexing to the "outside." Common inquiries and complaints concern the numerous forms, which sometimes are sent with no letter or instructions or with unclear or ambiguous instructions. Once documents are submitted, students often have no indication when admissions decisions will be made and when they can expect to receive a reply. The organizational structure and functions of the different parts of the institution are not made clear to the prospective student and may be even more confusing to individuals applying for permission to function as a visiting researcher or scholar. It is difficult to explain why one institution centralizes all services for foreign applicants while another is decentralized. Since changing the infrastructure of institutions to a uniform system is unlikely, it would be helpful if prospective students and scholars receive brief explanations of how a particular institution functions.

In summary, United States institutions, in their contacts abroad, should first explain the American educational system and then promote the commitments of the particular institution. The most powerful and convincing institution is one that responds promptly to individual inquiries and requests from recognized organizations, provides complete information in a clear and succinct manner, and takes students' questions seriously. The institution that exercises caution in replying to unknown organizations abroad protects itself and helps assure that its name will not be used indiscriminately. The well-informed institutional representative who travels abroad and who takes the time to answer questions about American education in general and provide information in areas where the inquirer seems to be uninformed before talking about his own institution encourages respect, trust, and good will, which in the long run will bring students and scholars to the institution and foster interchange.

Foreign Scholars. One group that has been given relatively little attention are the foreign scholars who conduct research and teach at United States institutions. Arrangements between individual American and foreign scholars seem to prevail over more institutionalized arrangements. While research and joint efforts may be effectively carried out in specific academic areas, institutions could foster greater use of these valuable resources to promote interchange on a broader scale. In addition to the existing Fulbright Occasional Lecturer Program of the Council for International Exchange of Scholars, the Institute of International Education (IIE) initiated in 1980 a new computer-based International Faculty Lecture Bureau. Visiting foreign scholars interested in giving occasional lectures and seminars at campuses other than their main assignment register with the bureau. United States institutions that wish to invite a scholar submit requests to the bureau and receive biodata of visitors in specified fields.

It is hoped that this new effort to meet the needs of both visiting scholars and host institutions will further increase these opportunities for mutually rewarding experiences that by nature have a potentially strong multiplier effect. This powerful multiplier effect of scholars through writing, teaching, and academic and professional activities cannot be overlooked and should not be wasted.

Diversity of the "Market" and Resources

Irrespective of the view we choose in looking at the "outside," countries are changing and becoming more differentiated. It is, therefore, a mistake to approach a given country or region in the same way. Table 1 illustrates the differences between and within countries by showing in percentages the current occupations of inquirers and information being sought in the eleven countries that responded to the questionnaire. Respondents also were asked to indicate their country's policy or stance toward study abroad; their responses indicate the differences. "A United States bachelor's degree is considered worth less than the Belgian near equivalent (license/licentiaat), whereas the master's degree does not really exist in most fields. Therefore, most students prefer to go to the United States for a graduate degree" (Nicholson response, 1981, p. 2). In France and Mexico, graduate students and specialists are encouraged to study abroad, as are individuals from Taiwan, although "it is becoming easier for graduates of junior colleges to study in the United States as transfer undergraduates. The government also seems interested in seeing that reasonably well-prepared students study abroad. Thus, [in Taiwan] the requirements for a student passport include a TOEFL [Test of English as a Foreign Language] score of 500, proof of having graduated from a postsecondary, government-recognized institution, and admission from an accredited United States school. The low rate (10 percent) of students who return is a continuing cause for concern. There is thus an effort to strengthen in-country graduate programs" (Hu response, 1981, p. 2). In Hong Kong, Japan, and the United Kingdom, there are no restrictions, and study abroad is widely

Table 1. Current Occupations of Inquirers and Information Sought in Eleven Countries.

Current Occupation	Belgium-Luxembourg	France	Hong Kong[b]	India	Japan	Jordan	Malaysia	Mexico	Taiwan	United Kingdom	Venezuela
High school student	3	2		2	6	42	75	28	0		66
Vocational/technical school student	2	2		0	3	7	10	1	0		0
Junior college student	0	0		5	1	1	0	0	7		0
University student	75	23		25	29	25	0	41	73		27
Graduate student	6	55		68	6	7	12	11	10		7
Employed full time	3	8		0	31	14	0	9	10		0
Educator	9	3		0	3	1	2	4	0		0
Parent/family member	2	4		0	1	3	1	4	0		0
Other	0	3		0	21	0	0	2	0		0
Total	100%	100%		100%	100%	100%	100%	100%	100%		100%

(continued on next page)

Table 1. Current Occupations of Inquirers and Information Sought in Eleven Countries, Cont'd.

	Belgium-Luxembourg	France	Hong Kong[b]	India	Japan	Jordan	Malaysia	Mexico	Taiwan	United Kingdom	Venezuela
Information Sought											
High school	2			0	2	1	2	2	0		0
Vocational/technical school	1			0	2	4	1	1	0		0
Junior college	0			0	7	7	2	1	0		0
University	22			2	31	49	93	20	17		66
Graduate school	66			98	39	39	0	30	83		83
English language program	6			0	11	c	2	40	0		e
Other	3			0	8	0	0	6	0		0
Total	100%			100%	100%	100%	100%	100%	100%		100%
Increase in the next 10 years by about	10%	20%[a]		20%	16%	15-20%	d	50%	30%	5%	50%[f]
Decrease in the next 10 years by about											
Remain about the same		X	X								

aAnnual increase.
bMajority of visitors to the office are secondary school students anticipating freshman admission.
cEnglish language program inquiries included in other categories.
d100% increase in 1980–81 over previous year; future increases difficult to predict.
eAlmost all Venezuelans who study in the United States need English language training.
fBased on continued increases in United States costs, expansion and improvement of Venezuelan universities, and reduction in scholarships for study abroad.

Note: Where no figures are given, information was not available.

accepted. In India "there are a number of restrictions on medical students going out, but otherwise there are no restraints. ... Students must have attained a certain level of educational achievement ... to secure foreign exchange [meaning, to obtain permission to purchase the dollars necessary] for study in the United States, but if financial assistance is obtained, this restriction is waived" (Parischa response, 1981, p. 2). "Although Jordan has a number of quality institutions of higher learning, both academic and technical, not all Jordanian students can or wish to attend these institutions. In these cases ... the government encourages students to seek higher study abroad" (McNamara response, 1981, p. 2). On the other hand, students in Malaysia are encouraged to study abroad because of limited opportunities within the country: "About 50 percent of those who went to the United States for academic year 1980–81 were financed by one of several Malaysian government agencies" (Whiting response, 1981, p. 2). While the Venezuelan government encourages study abroad at the two-year technical and graduate levels, and scholarships are provided by many sources, "revalidation of degrees obtained abroad still remains a problem except for graduate degrees in fields not offered in the country. Returning students must take courses and examinations in Venezuela to validate degrees and thus be accepted into professional associations and for employment" (Gouverneur response, 1981, p. 2).

The sampling of countries presented here does not take into account all the factors that contribute to the movement of students from these countries to the United States, and certainly does not include all the countries from which students and scholars come. However, the sampling demonstrates the differences between and within countries and could serve as one important baseline from which United States institutions can consider, plan, and carry out programs. Also helpful to institutional planning are the ten-year forecasts for increases and decreases in the number of individuals who wish to study and engage in other scholarly pursuits in the United States. Furthermore, in many countries there are multiple resources which prospective students and scholars can consult regarding plans for study and scholarly pursuits abroad; United States institutions can and should maintain contact with these resources.

English Language Programs

One category of information sought, English language programs, merits special attention. With few exceptions, most students traveling to the United States for enrollment in academic programs need some form of English language training. Many seek this training even if the receiving institution does not require further training. Prospective students at higher levels of proficiency seek programs of English for special purposes, that is, programs that are specifically designed to meet the English language needs of those who are studying in a particular field, such as management and economics. As noted in Table 1, almost all the students from Jordan and Venezuela need English language training; therefore, their numbers are "hidden" in the statistics for students seeking other categories of information. This holds true also for Japan, where growing numbers of individuals travel to the United States for English language study only, for periods as short as one month and as long as one year.

There are no data showing the total number of university-based public and proprietary English language training programs in the United States, and no form of accreditation to assist the prospective student in selecting an appropriate program from among the more than 400 programs available. *Guidelines for Selecting English Language Training Programs* (Center for Applied Linguistics, 1978) are available but do not reach the general audience of prospective students. The information and advising services are left with the task of guiding students—often with less than comprehensive information provided by the respective programs. While a lengthy discussion of the many concerns related to these programs is not intended, several points should be raised that are associated with international educational interchange.

English language training is an integral part of—and can constitute the whole—study experience of many foreign students in the United States. It is a rapidly growing activity, and it soon becomes evident to the "outside" that there are a number of such programs recruiting throughout the world, many both recruiting and disseminating information very effectively. Several respondents to the questionnaire noted that there was no need to request information on English language training programs because materials were received unsolicited; when information was requested, it was sent far more promptly than college and university bulletins.

A number of these programs are university-related or are located on campus; they are relatively, or in some cases almost entirely, independent operations. This gives rise to some problems. Some of the programs recruit through third party agents, particularly in-country commercial study abroad agencies. Some of these agencies capitalize on the university's name by implying that they represent the university as a whole or that admission to an academic program is guaranteed. At the same time, from the "outside" perspective, the university as a whole is identified with the quality and student experience of the English language training programs. The point to be stressed is that if a university conducts or is related to an English language training program, there should be a clear understanding as to whether admission to that program carries with it any provision for automatic transfer to an academic program. If admission to an academic program is implicit, then it is essential that recruitment and admission standards should apply equally to the university as a whole and to the English language training program. The university that permits "double standards" for its English language training program, either in the recruitment activities abroad or the actual operation of the program, will undoubtedly lose in the long run.

Prescription for a Better System

If we are to have an organized, efficient, cooperatively managed, people-centered system of international educational and cultural interchange, we must first excise notions of "inside" and "outside." (Although the theme of this book is international educational interchange, "cultural" has been included simply because both education and culture are inextricable components of international interchange.) There are host and home countries to aid us in assisting and managing the growing transnational movements of students, scholars, and professionals. The United States has the largest number of foreign students and scholars in its numerous institutions, and the largest core of professionals specifically assigned to assist students and scholars who study in the United States or, in the case of Americans, who study, teach, lecture, and conduct research abroad. It also has a great number of programs that prepare foreign students for academic study, a range of enthusiastic community-based organizations to welcome and help acclimate foreign students and scholars to American society, a dedicated academic community, interested government agencies, and concerned professional organizations. However, there are significant reasons for the United States to reevaluate its perceptions. There is no need to belabor the reasons for this reassessment: increasing global interdependence; managing the knowledge explosion; coping with world problems; changing transnational economic, political, and social trends; and diminishing financial resources. The recognition of the United States as "number one" has been challenged; "number one-ism" itself appears to be an outdated approach in relating to countries throughout the world. The report to the President from the President's Commission on Foreign Language and International Studies (1979, pp. 101-111) clearly outlines the current plight of the United States and offers specific recommendations on international educational exchanges. Burn (1980, pp. 143-155)—in describing the current situation, problems, and possible solutions—argues that a clearinghouse is needed.

The model shown in Figure 1 is offered as an internationally planned, organized, and operated scheme which from its inception will encourage open and mutual listening and learning from various sectors in all countries.

The model is based on these additional assumptions:

- Interchange may be bilateral or multilateral.
- Interchange need not be perfectly balanced, but reciprocity is essential.

Figure 1. A Model for an International Educational Interchange
Information Clearinghouse (IEIIC).

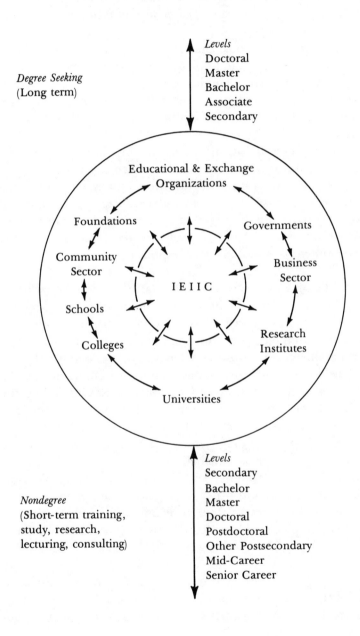

- Educational and cultural interchange differ and overlap.
- Interchange must be capable of meeting diverse but related needs as we move toward greater segmentation between and within countries.
- Because of continuous changes, we must not delude ourselves into planning and hoping for permanent impact.
- Short- and long-term planning are basic.
- The building of a network of individuals and organizations is fundamental between and within countries and across sectors.
- The strengthening of infrastructures within and between countries, and sectors within and between countries is vital.
- The proposed international educational interchange information clearinghouse (IEIIC) should organize the information flow, promote the sharing of expertise, coordinate programs, initiate programs, seminars, and research, and assist in the development of standards and responsibilities.

In the proposed system of international educational interchange shown in Figure 1, the *purpose and length of the sojourn* are combined into degree seeking (long term) and nondegree (short-term training, study, research, lecturing, and consulting). *Levels* parallel the purpose and length of the sojourn. In the degree-seeking category, it is unnecessary to comment on the associate, bachelor, master, and doctoral levels. Regarding the secondary level, an increasing number of secondary school pupils enter United States schools because of parents' transfer to the United States for employment or in many cases because these pupils and their parents believe that study abroad at these and lower levels is desirable. The National Association for Foreign Student Affairs and other organizations are giving increasing attention to issues related to secondary as well as elementary school pupils. The nondegree category is a potpourri and includes the very short (two-week) to one-year exchange programs of secondary and undergraduate students, one or more years of study and research at the graduate and postdoctoral levels, lecturing and consulting at the postdoctoral and senior career levels, technical-vocational training at other postsecondary levels, and mid-career intensive professional training programs. The combinations of actual length of the sojourn, type of activity, and level are multiple and too numerous to list.

The *channels* are the same as the *components of the outer concentric circle,* their representative offices or branches, and the information and advising services described in detail earlier. The schools, colleges, universities, research institutes, foundations, educational and exchange organizations, governments, and the business and community sectors are the resources and channels throughout the world which are cooperative members with full access to the international educational interchange information clearinghouse (IEIIC).

The IEIIC is not intended to be restrictive, exclusive, or regulative; it is intended to be a mutual and essential effort. The administrators and facilitators of interchange can and should serve as the models for interchange in other arenas of world affairs.

In a more short-term view, information and advising services outside the United States would appreciate and benefit from the following activities undertaken by American institutions:

- Greater support in providing current and complete information.
- The sharing of time by institutional representatives when they travel abroad to contribute to in-service training of staff members.
- Encouraging and actively supporting efforts to improve the standards, responsibilities, and services of United States educational institutions and organizations.
- Developing innovative programs to meet the needs of foreign and American students—for instance, joint doctoral degree programs that permit a student to complete dissertation research in one country and receive the degree from the home university, with faculty from both universities consulting and finally examining the student.
- Planning and carrying out new ways of articulating American education and responsible recruiting—for instance, through "study abroad fairs" in various countries.

- Feedback on the services provided by information and
  advising services abroad and how these services might better
  assist individual students and scholars, and the institution.

In our enthusiasm to improve the system of international
educational interchange, we must continually remind ourselves
that the individual students and scholars are not only the *raison
d'être* for our efforts but also valuable resources, and that it will
be of great benefit to include them in our planning and administering. We are *all* students and educators—listening, learning,
sharing, guiding, and working toward short- and long-term goals.
With this spirit, we can indeed bridge our differences.

3

U.S. Students Abroad

M. Archer Brown

The President's Commission on Foreign Language and International Studies (1979, p. 2) minces few words in its contention that a globally aware citizenry is crucial to this country's national interest—and to its very security: "National security . . . cannot safely be defined and protected within the narrow framework of defense, diplomacy, and economics. A nation's welfare depends in large measure on the intellectual and psychological strengths that are derived from perceptive visions of the world beyond its own boundaries. On a planet shrunken by the technology of instant communications, there is little safety behind a Maginot Line of scientific and scholarly isolationism. . . . The situation cries out for a better comprehension of our place and our potential in a world that, though it still expects much from America, no longer takes American supremacy for granted. Nor . . . do this country's children and youths, and it is for them, and their understanding of their own society, that an international perspective is indispensable. Such a perspective is lacking in most educational programs now."

The commission goes on to cite a number of facts that illustrate its concern for "Americans' scandalous incompetence in foreign languages" and "our dangerously inadequate understanding of world affairs" (p. 7). That "scandalous incompetence" and that "dangerously inadequate understanding" clearly inhibit the United States' conduct of its foreign policy, its ability to participate in international and bilateral trade agreements, and the degree to which its citizens are able to function in the real world.

Despite the seemingly arrogant national view that we tend to hold of ourselves vis-à-vis the rest of the world, there has been traditional, and sometimes substantive, support for the participation of our students and scholars in educational exchange activities. Support for these activities has developed from a wide variety of sources: state and private academic institutions, foundations, religious organizations, national nonprofit agencies, and the federal government itself. The participation of United States students in international educational programs and the nature of those involvements derive from our own historical perspectives and reflect a variety of methodologies and program philosophies. Therefore, the movement of United States students abroad cannot be equated easily with the corresponding presence of foreign students in this country. In fact, there are significant differences between these two equations in the exchange process.

Development of U.S. Study Abroad Activities

It is certainly safe to say that study abroad has existed as a practice as long as there has been a United States. Sons of wealthy colonialists were sent to European universities to compensate for the lack of educational opportunity at the relatively few institutions of higher learning at home. During the eighteenth and nineteenth centuries, the flow of students abroad—mainly from well-to-do families—increased; and study abroad was regarded as an essential component in a well-rounded education.

The twentieth century introduced a new element in study abroad—the institutionalization of study itself and the concept of group study abroad. In the 1920s the University of Delaware and Sweetbriar and Smith Colleges introduced the concept of spending a junior year abroad for undergraduate language majors and, in so doing, began a pattern of study abroad that is still very much in effect.

The numbers of students traveling abroad for educational purposes and the variety of programs in which they participated increased dramatically following World War II. These increases corresponded, as well, to an influx of foreign students to United States college and university campuses. A number of developments, both in the public and private sectors, were to have a profound impact on study abroad. The Council on Student Travel, for example, was established in 1948 by agencies in the private sector, to encourage and facilitate exchange-of-persons programs through the chartering of transatlantic ships, including reconverted United States troop carriers, to transport American students to Europe. These groups were primarily concerned with the resumption of secondary school and undergraduate exchanges following World War II, but only two years earlier the Fulbright Act (P.L. 584), a congressional initiative, launched a relatively large-scale international exchange of scholars and researchers as well as students.

The postwar period in general and the 1950s in particular saw the rapid development of area studies and language centers on United States college and university campuses; new bilateral agreements (even including some with the Soviet Union) provided impetus for exchange at various levels. Colleges and universities themselves began to form consortia—pooling their resources in order to provide increased study abroad opportunities for their students. The Associated Colleges of the Mid-West and the Great Lakes Colleges Association were in the forefront of consortial efforts and still in the 1980s represent this approach to the organization and continued development of study abroad opportunities. Since the late 1950s, National Defense Education Act (NDEA) Title VI funds have enabled a number of American institutions of higher learning to strengthen their international and area studies programs. The government's initiative in creating the Peace Corps lent further credence to the importance of experience abroad for young Americans. The numbers of United States students enrolled in foreign institutions increased from approximately 10,000 in the mid-1950s to more than 20,000 a decade later. During the same period, the number of United States students applying for passports rose dramatically from 60,635 to approximately 340,000. The financing of study abroad was assisted considerably by a favorable economic market and advantageous currency exchanges abroad and even, to a certain extent, by the availability of funds through private foundations.

For many supporters of educational exchanges, the passage of the International Education Act in 1966 was the ultimate (although unfortunately only apparent) recognition of the importance and respectability inherent in the study abroad experience, from a national perspective at least. The fact that the act was never funded by Congress presaged the rather stagnant period of growth in study abroad and educational exchanges in the 1970s. Less money was available in general from both the public and private sectors; United States universities began to face enrollment problems at home; foreign language requirements were dropped at many institutions; and the national turmoil associated with the Vietnam war as well as the heightened concern with domestic issues competed for student interests and energies.

Although some regard the 1970s as a gloomy period for educational exchanges, and although the statistics on study abroad seem to support that position, others point to a number of positive trends in educational exchanges. The options available to secondary school and undergraduate students, in particular, for study abroad or one of its related activities (traineeships, work-study) increased. In addition to the traditional junior year abroad model, opportunities were developed for study abroad during the interterm or for a trimester, semester, academic year, or summer period. Programs for upper-level secondary school students were expanded to include recent high school graduates; undergraduate programs began to include entering college freshmen as well as graduate students and faculty. United

States college- and university-sponsored programs began to provide more diverse curricula—including subject matter well beyond the traditional language, literature, and culture courses of the 1950s.

In addition, considerable efforts were made to expand study abroad opportunities beyond traditional European locations to non-Western countries. Colleges and universities, the major purveyors of education abroad, continued to develop international education centers on campuses; according to an informal and unpublished survey by the Council on International Educational Exchange, twelve such centers were reported in a mid-1960s' census; more than seven hundred were cited in 1974. In the 1950s and 1960s, formal academic programs were conducted primarily by four-year, private liberal arts institutions; in the 1970s there was a sizable increase in the number of state universities and two-year colleges offering study abroad options.

It is tempting to predict for the 1980s a significant increase in the number of students anxious to pursue part of their education in a foreign country. One can be hopeful that the impetus will come from a more clearly defined sense of national purpose and need in this area, as suggested by the President's Commission report. One can see the beginnings of positive reinforcement for the report through the National Council on Foreign Language and International Studies, established in 1980, and one can feel heartened by the fact that, despite the current trend toward budget austerity, a House education subcommittee unanimously supported a bill to create a new $87 million, annually funded, program to encourage the teaching of foreign languages in schools and colleges. The 1980s will surely demand greater cohesion in the support of the study abroad area, at all levels—governmental, institutional, and community—while still permitting and capitalizing on the diversity and special characteristics of the United States transnational student movement.

Numbers Involved in Study Abroad

For a number of reasons, it is extremely difficult to determine how many students are involved in educational pursuits abroad. The variety of programs available, as well as the broad range of program sponsors, contributes to the confusion that is symptomatic of any attempt to produce adequate statistical information. In addition, the bases on which statistics have been obtained by responsible agencies such as the Institute of International Education have changed from one decade to another, thereby making it impossible to compare the available statistical data. *Open Doors,* the IIE's annual census on participants in international educational exchange activities, reported on United States study abroad prior to 1973 by polling foreign academic institutions regarding their United States student enrollments. Between 1973 and 1977-78, there was no IIE census on study abroad, and since that time the census has reflected only those students studying abroad under the auspices of United States agencies and institutions. In the early 1970s, one could obtain some study abroad information from the World Studies Data Bank of the Academy for Educational Development, a now defunct activity that leaves an even greater gap in the data available for analysis.

The most general source of information available on the number of students traveling abroad and the purposes for which they go is available from the Passport Services Division of the Bureau of Consular Affairs, U.S. Department of State. According to these figures, 559,590 individuals designating themselves as "students" received passports in 1980, with 79,550 indicating that the object of their travel was educational. More specific data are available from *Open Doors* and from the information that can be compiled as a result of two IIE publications, *U.S. College-Sponsored Programs Abroad: Academic Year* and *Vacation Study Abroad* (which lists short-term programs sponsored by United States colleges and universities, private organizations, and foreign institutions). According to the 1980-81 *Open Doors,* 29,819 American students participated in academic year programs sponsored by United States colleges and universities in 1979-80. This figure is based on data collected for 794 overseas study programs. It is interesting to note that in the 1979-80 edition of *Open Doors,* slightly more programs were reported on for 1978-79 (804), but enrollments were estimated at 24,886, less than the current figure. The 1981 edition of *Vacation Study Abroad* reports on some 904 overseas study programs for American students but lists only those that are open to all students regardless of university affiliation; it therefore omits a sizable number of institutions that conduct programs abroad for their own students only.

In addition, none of the above sources concentrates specifically on secondary schools or national agencies that provide opportunities abroad, chiefly for students of high school age. The most recent figures obtainable from five of the major agencies working with secondary schools in the development of overseas programs indicate that over 11,000 students participated in secondary school exchanges in 1980–81.

Moreover, although the institute's sources include responses from some two-year institutions, the programs of only fourteen junior and community colleges are reported in *Vacation Study Abroad* and only two in *U.S. College-Sponsored Programs Abroad: Academic Year*. And yet this sector contributes significantly to participation in educational exchanges. A 1976 survey by the Council on International Educational Exchange of 631 two-year institutions indicated that fifty-nine schools sponsored 140 study programs abroad with a combined enrollment of over 3,500 students. These figures have certainly increased in the last five years, given the rapid development of two-year-college consortia, the majority of which include a study abroad component.

To the above-cited figures for summer and academic year abroad must be added the estimates of those students who study abroad through the auspices of private United States organizations that do not grant degrees or cooperate with degree-granting institutions; those involved in independent study and research, both at the undergraduate and graduate levels; and those directly enrolled at foreign institutions. The summer study abroad figures noted here would also be greatly expanded by the addition of those students participating in programs of experiential education, independent study, and special projects and the hundreds of combination work, study, and travel programs.

Given the five-year life span of a passport (before 1983), it would be reasonable to conclude that over 750,000 United States students work, study, or travel abroad or engage in a combination thereof in any given recent year. According to the data cited previously, it is possible to estimate that the number of students participating in two- and four-year college and university study programs and secondary school exchange programs is in excess of 75,000. Given the categories of study abroad for which no information is available (direct enrollment, independent research), it is not unreasonable to assume that at least 100,000 students engage in academic study abroad under more or less formal programmatic arrangements.

The figures cited above, or rather their inadequacy, indicate the necessity to document the not inconsiderable movement of United States students abroad far more systematically than has been done in the past.

Characteristics of U.S. Students Who Study Abroad

Motivation. A paper presented by two Thai students at a meeting of study abroad advisers at the University of Minnesota included the observation that "whereas the foreign student comes to the United States in fulfillment of a purpose, the United States student goes abroad in search of one" (Thavikalivat and Gongotena, 1977).

As is described in other chapters, most sponsored foreign students, particularly those from non-European countries, are motivated by their home governments or their home institutions to obtain a foreign education. United States students who study abroad are not fulfilling a governmental development objective. Nor, in most cases, are they motivated by the necessity to gain special technical knowledge not available in the United States. Nor are they reflecting their institution's commitment to international education. Nor, finally, do they believe that study abroad will contribute to their immediate career development or long-term professional goals (see President's Commission on Foreign Language and International Studies, 1979, p. 128; Henson, 1979; Hull, Lemke, and Houang, 1977). As noted in a recent overview of the transnational student movement, from the particular perspective of Great Britain: "For students . . . from highly industrialized countries for whom study abroad generally constitutes an enrichment rather than a dire necessity, the period of study abroad must often appear as an unwelcome prolongation of their course without sufficiently tangible recompense. That this feeling is in many cases a misapprehension is borne out by empirical evidence to the effect that meaningful study experience abroad tends to improve employment prospects, but feelings, subjective as they are, often die hard" (Smith, de Panafieu, and Jarousse, 1981, pp. 185-186).

Thus, although American students may have their own motivation to engage in educational activities abroad, the purposes for study abroad are not so clearly delineated by the home government or home institutions or encouraged by potential employers as is true of study in the United States by foreign students.

Length of Sojourn Abroad. Unlike the majority of foreign students in the United States, American students do not generally seek degrees abroad. This most assuredly gives them more flexibility in the selection of courses but also means that the overseas experience may not be as cohesive an academic package. The American student therefore generally spends less time abroad than the average foreign student spends in the United States. A United States undergraduate may be receiving credit at the home institution for a program as brief as six weeks during the summer, and rarely for longer than a year abroad. Numerous studies have indicated that American students acquire cultural sensitivity, as well as skills, in direct proportion to the length of time they spend abroad; the briefer the experience and the less time spent in planning and preparation, the less impact on the student. Some institutions sensibly view orientation and preparation as an integral part of the total education abroad program and permit several weeks or even a semester of orientation—sometimes for credit. American students going abroad to study certainly have far more opportunity for in-depth orientation prior to departure than counterpart foreign students in the United States, who receive the bulk of their counseling and orientation after arrival.

Geographical Distribution. The geographical distribution

of American students abroad also provides an interesting contrast to the Third World origin of the majority of foreign students in the United States. According to *Open Doors* (1980–81, p. 66), relatively few (34 percent) United States students study outside of Western Europe—primarily because these students lack the opportunity to learn the nontraditional languages before enrolling in course work abroad, and Third World countries provide few language support programs for foreign students. In addition, American colleges are often unable to establish institutional ties, or to maintain them without disruption, in non-Western countries; and, in any event, many of these countries lack university facilities and spaces. Possibly because of these drawbacks, a few institutional programs have been criticized for permitting a "ghetto effect" in their American study abroad programs, concentrating or clustering a number of overseas centers in certain prized European cities.

On the other hand, partly because of low-cost transportation options that were not available several years ago, many American students have become interested in traveling to non-European countries; and some universities, while not offering overseas study options in these parts of the world, have encouraged students to undertake independent study and research, with excellent results. Finally, the International Student Exchange Program, housed at Georgetown University and still in its pilot stages, has developed reciprocal agreements permitting a freer flow of students between United States, European, Latin American, African, and Asian institutions. One suspects that similar reciprocal agreements could be negotiated successfully to a greater extent than they are now between individual universities. For example, a number of United States institutions have actively negotiated with the appropriate authorities in the People's Republic of China for places in Chinese universities for their own students, in return for the reception and enrollment of sizable numbers of Chinese students and scholars.

Fields of Study. United States study abroad has traditionally focused on language and culture, rather than on the acquisition of specific knowledge in other fields. It is encouraging to note that this trend is changing and that study abroad is beginning to be seen as much broader in scope. *U.S. College-Sponsored*

Programs Abroad: Academic Year describes programs in sixty-eight specialized fields of study, excluding language, history, literature, and culture of the host country; *Vacation Study Abroad* lists seventy-nine specialized fields, with the same exclusion. *Open Doors* (1980–81, p. 71) provides an analysis of the study abroad programs offered in 45 different countries. Although most of the programs are in Europe, there are also listings in Asia, Latin America, Africa, North America, and Oceania. The programs are grouped into 10 fields of study, the largest number of programs being in the fields of social science, humanities, and the arts, with lesser groupings in education, science, business/management, and some in mathematics/computer science, engineering, agriculture, and health. Most of the fields listed in these indexes would lend themselves very well in a variety of locations to a combination of work-study, traineeships, and other nontraditional, extramural educational programs.

Age. On the average, United States study abroad participants are significantly younger than the foreign students who study in the United States. The majority of American students study abroad during their undergraduate years; and a substantial number, more than 11,000, participate in organized educational programs abroad during their secondary school years. At the same time, there has not been an appreciable increase in the number of individuals doing graduate work abroad; in fact, the numbers may even be diminishing. However, there is a basis at least at the lower end of the scale for building a continuum of international education from the early secondary school levels through the graduate years and beyond. Moreover, the upper age of students in undergraduate education is increasing to the extent that one third of all students in higher education are over the age of twenty-five. Thus the age range of United States students abroad is expanding. In his essay "Of Travel," written four hundred years ago, Francis Bacon noted that "travel in the young is part of education; in the elder, a part of experience." The strength of our current situation may be that the age range of those participating in international interchange can encompass both "education" in the formal sense and "experience" in the nontraditional sense of education.

Reentry/Return. Foreign students, particularly those from

developing countries, are frequently viewed as significant change agents in their home countries upon their return home. United States students are much less so, and yet they are a virtually untapped resource for strengthening the international dimension on the campus. As described elsewhere in this book, some institutions have made extremely effective use of returning Americans—as orienters for other students going abroad, as facilitators for foreign students recently arrived in the United States, and as energetic participants in the process of internationalizing their particular institutions. While the personnel involved with foreign students can be helpful only up to a point in easing the reentry transition anxieties of foreign students about to return home, they, together with study abroad advisers and directors, can be exceptionally effective in creating a different and more productive environment for our own returning students—for their own good and their institutions'.

Institutional Support for Study Abroad Activities

As has been noted previously, the support of higher education institutions for study abroad activities varies enormously. Some institutions—such as Goshen, Antioch, and Kalamazoo Colleges—consider the study abroad option an integral part of the undergraduate curriculum at the home institution. Still other institutions have issued landmark statements on their responsibilities and commitments to global education in their university communities. (The published statements of Iowa State University and the Universities of Kansas, the State of New York, and Wisconsin-Milwaukee provide particularly substantive reading in this regard.) For American students at some other United States institutions, however, study abroad can be an academic risk, depending on the posture of the particular home institution or the attitude of a particular discipline or department. A number of factors have traditionally contributed to some institutions' reluctance to encourage study abroad. These may include the perception that study abroad is a "frill" activity, appealing to the semiserious student; an unwillingness of United States institutions to evaluate and give credit for foreign study; an assumption that the only viable purpose of a study abroad experience is language acquisition; an unrealistic assessment of the cost of study abroad and/or its effect on enrollment; or, finally, a parochial attitude toward what the rest of the world would possibly have to offer a United States education and curriculum.

Whether or not an institution considers study abroad an important option for its students, it still must (1) define what is "educational" about study abroad in its own terms; (2) develop a policy that can be responsibly communicated to its own students, faculties, and administrators; and (3) consider the extent and means by which it will provide advice and guidance to those seeking to study abroad and/or administer its own academic programs abroad.

As Burn (1980, p. 76) has pointed out, "Attempts to measure systematically the effects of overseas study on students are ... fragmentary and insufficient." Any discussion of the educational value of study abroad at this time must therefore reflect conviction and commendation rather than research and data. Certainly, as Burn points out, existing studies and the information that is available support the notion that study abroad does provide a valuable experience. In the absence of hard evidence to the contrary, the proponents of this activity remain unshaken in their belief that it is a worthwhile and valuable educational endeavor.

Institutional Advising on Study Abroad. Advising students about the opportunities available for study abroad can be complicated by the fact that the options are as academically diverse as the institutions that sponsor or endorse them. What the various constituent parts of study abroad *do* have in common is the provision of a foreign experience that can be defined as educational in the broadest sense of the term. This "experience" may include any one of the following or a combination thereof: study at a United States college- or university-sponsored center abroad, regular enrollment in a foreign institution, or a combination of the two; independent study and research abroad, sometimes but not always connected to a foreign university; study tours (sometimes credited, sometimes not); study com-

bined with participation in voluntary service projects, traineeships, or seasonal work; living with a family as part of an exchange program (sometimes involving study, sometimes not);
and enrollment in special seminars focusing on a specific topic
or discipline.

Combined with a diversity of program patterns is the tremendous variety in the duration of the stay abroad. Study and/
or experiential programs are available for as short a period as
two weeks or for a summer, a semester, a year, or longer. Furthermore, the above activities may be sponsored by individual
United States academic institutions (secondary schools, two-
year colleges, four-year colleges and universities, consortia of
institutions, proprietary agencies (both United States and foreign), national nonprofit groups, commercial travel agencies, or
foreign educational agencies and institutions. What counts as an
educational experience worthy of the home institution's credit
depends, of course, on the attitude of the institution toward
transfer of credits in general. The multiplicity of offerings certainly suggests the necessity for an informed and coordinated
approach to credit evaluation and, in particular, considerable
interinstitutional cooperation between those advising the student on study abroad and those responsible for credit evaluation and credit transfer.

Fortunately, a number of resources are available to advisers who may be overwhelmed by the variety and multiplicity
of models of study abroad, as well as the broad range of spon-
sorships. The Spring 1982 bibliography published by the National Association for Foreign Student Affairs' Section on U.S.
Students Abroad lists more than one hundred readily available
and relatively inexpensive sources of information about all aspects of work, study, and travel abroad and makes extensive reference to the information available through national agencies
such as the Institute of International Education, the Council on
International Educational Exchange, and NAFSA. In addition,
advisory and coordinating services for United States students
going abroad are now provided on at least five hundred college
and university campuses; some estimates put the number closer
to 1,200. A NAFSA publication, *Study Abroad: Handbook for*

Advisers and Administrators (National Association for Foreign Student Affairs, 1979c), presents guidelines for the advisory process and recommends that for every 1,500 students there should be a half-time adviser and a half-time support staff member, in order to fulfill the following minimal advisory responsibilities, outlined in the *NAFSA Principles for International Educational Exchange* (National Association for Foreign Student Affairs, 1981):

- Clarifying objectives for wanting to go abroad.
- Identifying the quality, value, and appropriateness of a particular study abroad experience.
- Identifying opportunities that are educationally sound and culturally beneficial.
- Coordinating the evaluation of a student's educational background with admissions personnel of a foreign institution.
- Utilizing returning students in evaluating program opportunities abroad as well as the advisory services they received.
- Understanding the implications of a particular study abroad experience on graduation requirements, transfer credit, and financial aid.

In addition to assembling a resource library on opportunities abroad, the campus adviser should take advantage of on-campus and off-campus resources such as foreign students and foreign student advisers; staff in the admissions and registrars' offices; returned American students; language, history, and political science faculties; and the financial aid office. At one large midwestern campus several years ago, a newly appointed study abroad adviser discovered that there were more than thirty offices and individuals dealing with various aspects of her institution's international exchange activities, all unbeknownst to one another.

Regardless of who performs the major advisory function or where that function is placed administratively on a given campus (in academic affairs, in an international education office, in student affairs, or in the school of arts and sciences), certain basic guidelines should apply:

1. Institutional policies and procedures regarding study abroad have to be determined. The adviser must know what kinds of study abroad experiences will be considered for credit, the level of study abroad that will be approved, the length of study experience that will be permitted, and the documentation that will be required for certification of credit, conversion of foreign grades to United States equivalents, and so on.
2. If there are no existing institutional policies, the adviser will need to develop them, generally in conjunction with a broadly based faculty-administrative committee.
3. In addition to advising students on available opportunities abroad and advising faculty and staff on study and research, travel, and sabbatical leave opportunities, the adviser may also be an active participant in developing or directing study programs sponsored by the institution itself.

Institutional Sponsorship of Study Abroad Programs. "A study abroad program . . . is one of the more complex academic enterprises, which when oversimplified by the inexperienced can result in serious problems" (National Association for Foreign Student Affairs, 1979c, p. 29). Institutional policies and procedures have to be developed, both academically and administratively, in order to ensure the following generally accepted characteristics of a "good" study abroad program:

Well-defined academic objectives

Solid academic content at least comparable to that on the home campus

Carefully planned use of the resources of the study location abroad to create a unique educational experience that could not be achieved on the home campus

A meaningful degree of cultural immersion and interaction with people of the host country, even in short-term programs

Careful selection and orientation of participants

Provision for acquiring or improving language proficiency, if the language of the host country is not English

Firm but unobtrusive leadership to provide interpretation, guidance, and support to students when needed, and to handle administrative functions

Affordable costs, both to the sponsoring institution and the participating students

Carefully planned logistics, including transportation, class registration and scheduling, housing, meal service, and health service

A planned means of determining the effectiveness of the program

Desirable policies may include but not be restricted to

Centralizing program administration on campus

Viewing study abroad as an institution-wide activity, responding to the interests of as broad a cross section of students as possible

Establishing a broadly based advisory committee, responsible to institutional officers with institution-wide responsibilities

Selecting a variety of study locations and making available study abroad opportunities in a variety of subject fields

Providing adequate ongoing program supervision

Ensuring adequate financial support for the program, on the part of both the institution and the participant

At least one year in advance of the program, a number of programmatic decisions have to be made with regard to the above policies as they relate to

Program length and location

Scheduling (time of year and program activities)

Academic objectives and curriculum (fields of study, language of instruction, credit transfer)

Cultural components

Program size

Program supervision (the qualifications, duties, selection, and orientation of a program director)

Instructional patterns to be adopted (for example, arrangements with host universities or other institutions or for independent study)

Faculty (home institution, host institution, adjunct)

Personnel policies (salaries, local laws and customs)

Site evaluation; resources available

Program promotion and recruitment

Student selection (establishing qualifications according to academic level, grade point average, and language; screening for motivation, financial ability; determining criteria for applicants from other institutions if applicable)

Orientation (defining timing, length, and content)

Transportation (international, local, vacation, and field trip travel)

Housing (private homes, dormitories, off-campus apartments)

Meals

Health services

Local resources (library facilities, textbooks)

Reorientation of returned students

Evaluation of program (by students, directors, advisory committee)

Reciprocal arrangements with host institutions (faculty and student exchanges, joint research, and library exchanges)

Program costs and budgeting (including student costs, such as tuition, health and accident insurance, transportation, housing and meals; and institutional costs, such as program planning, printing, travel, salaries, orientation and evaluation, overseas tuition fees, space rental). [There are many patterns for funding study abroad. The preferred pattern is for overseas participants to receive the benefit of any institutional subsidy for educational costs that on-campus students enjoy. Study abroad can also be viewed, financially, as a self-sustaining component outside of the campus budget, paid for by the participants in lieu of tuition. A third alternative is to fund study abroad from instructional funds to the extent of the average cost of on-campus instruction, with any amount in excess passed on to the participant.]

Professional Development for Campus-Based Advisers and Program Administrators. Regardless of whether one advises or administers study abroad programs, there are a number of ways to avoid the pitfalls of inadequate preparation for the task and to develop, reasonably quickly, expertise in the area:

By extensive reading of the professional materials cited previously

By participation in local, regional, and national conferences and meetings, including those sponsored annually by NAFSA and CIEE, and occasionally by IIE

By applying for grants available for in-service training and campus consultations (NAFSA)

By development of professional contacts, not only through

national groups such as NAFSA, CIEE, and IIE but through cultural and information offices maintained by foreign governments in the United States and through direct contact with higher education institutions and international exchange organizations in other countries when possible through travel abroad.

Conclusion

Study abroad is a vital part of the interchange process, but it has its own particular characteristics, its own limitations, and its own opportunities. It reflects the individualistic nature of higher education itself and, especially at the undergraduate level, has only peripherially benefited from the support of the United States government, the private sector, and the business and educational communities. In fact, there may be some advantages in the current diversity of opportunities and motivations for study abroad: many goals can be pursued and a variety of results obtained. "We must recognize a potential conflict between those who feel that international affairs must be taught more diligently to preserve America's position in the world and those who espouse the need to find global solutions to human problems" (Tonkin and Edwards, 1981, p. 34). With or without a national policy or priority on global education for Americans, hundreds of thousands of students will continue to participate in overseas experiences which will take them out of the country and into the world—exposing them and educating them to the needs, concerns, and attitudes of a larger world. Their reasons for going abroad will be similar to those of their counterparts in the eighteenth and nineteenth centuries and will have as much to do with humanistic interests as material or national self-interest. The support and encouragement of educational opportunities abroad need not be the prerogative of a single body politic, public or private, but the importance of this interchange activity must be recognized and articulated as part of the larger issue of developing a national global awareness.

As the Office of International Education at Antioch College tells its students:

What's this kind of contact good for? It seems to help people put things in perspective. Other cultures tell us something about ourselves.

American students abroad get roughly the same deal as American tourists. They get what they ask for. [From the pamphlet "Out of the Country, Into the World," 1975.]

Part Two

Strengthening the Interchange Process in U.S. Institutions

The accelerated transnational movement of students and scholars affects a widening area of institutional management, and the massive flow of foreign students to the United States has prompted efforts to integrate this new international outreach into a coordinated pattern of institutional activity.

Although the opportunity to study in a foreign country is seen as a worthwhile investment of public funds and private resources, Joan H. Joshi notes in Chapter Four that public funds have been slowly diminished by inflation and the financial pressure of other domestic needs and that private resources have been increasingly burdened by rises in tuition fees and the cost of living. In these circumstances she offers advice on how foreign students may find the most education for the least cost and makes a number of recommendations on ways to ease the financial restrictions that threaten to stifle the growth of international educational interchange.

Chapter Five examines the whole question of the recruitment of foreign students, seeking to place it in the context of the best interests of the institution and the foreign student. The chapter emphasizes the prior need for institutional commitment to offer an educational program that will meet the needs of foreign students and to provide services necessary for their welfare while they are in this country. It provides information on how to construct and conduct an effective foreign student recruitment program; points out the danger areas; lists the resources available to enable an institution to develop and expand its foreign student activities; summarizes the abuses that have been identified by the United States educational community; and sets forth the criteria that have been adopted for an acceptable recruitment program.

Universities and colleges in the United States have adjusted to the needs of the postwar wave of foreign students and scholars by adapting existing procedures and practices. In the field of foreign student admissions, admissions officers have had to acquire a new expertise in the evaluation of foreign educational credentials and the determination of the admissibility of a student coming from an entirely different social, economical, and cultural environment. In Chapter Six, William S. Patrick discusses the ramifications of foreign student admissions and the development of a policy that can serve as a basis for foreign student enrollment. He provides a flow chart for the handling of foreign applications and notes the critical importance of determining that the student is proficient in English and has adequate financial resources. He discusses the ways in which the institutional process of foreign student admissions can be organized; offers insights into the significance of data collection; discusses the current multinational dimensions of foreign student admissions; describes the resources available within the United States and abroad to acquire and develop the techniques of credentials evaluation; and suggests ways in which the present practices might be improved.

In their life in a foreign country, students and scholars are limited by the framework of the national bureaucracy. Although for the most part this may not be obtrusive, nevertheless it exists and must be reckoned with. Alex Bedrosian, in Chapter Seven, provides some clarification of the complex and changing network of immigration rules and regulations that affect foreign students and scholars in the United States. He explains the significance of alien status, defines the role of student and scholar, and notes the restrictions that exist, especially concerning employment. He outlines the legal responsibilities of institutions that enroll foreign students and describes the role of the foreign student adviser in relation to his or her institution, to the government, and to the foreign student.

International educational interchange has affected more and more areas of institutional programming. Clearly, as Valerie Woolston notes in Chapter Eight, much time and effort can be saved if these activities are brought into one coherent organizational pattern. Noting that there are few standard operating procedures and that patterns and systems are designed to meet the particular resources and circumstances at each institution, she lists the required services and discusses the appropriate staffing needs for the administration of international educational interchange. She describes surveys of existing patterns of administration and suggests how an institution's commitment to the totality of its international education activities can be met most effectively.

International educational interchange provides the opportunity for sharing the cultural wealth of the world's peoples as they come together in classroom and community. In Chapter Nine, George C. Christensen and Thomas B. Thielen demonstrate how, with the encouragement of top-level educators and administrators, this opportunity can be made a reality as foreign students and scholars are recognized as a channel for cross-cultural communication. The experience of Iowa State University is offered as an example of the way in which an institution can provide the setting for the international members of a campus—foreign students and scholars and United States students and faculty who have lived and studied abroad—to make a unique contribution to the educational program of the institution and the off-campus programs in the surrounding community.

Current reductions in funding and the consequent imposition of budgetary restraints and priorities have forced the educational community to assess the costs and benefits of international educational interchange. It is an area in which there are currently more questions than answers and a conspicuous lack of consensus. The final chapter in this section of the book examines the effects of national, state, and institutional decisions and needs on the determination of costs and benefits. The author points out that the economics of educational interchange, especially the question of who is paying for what, has international implications, and he recommends that a multinational task force examine this complex subject.

4

Finances:
Finding the Funds
for International Study

Joan H. Joshi

The student or scholar able to contemplate overseas study without financial obstacle is fortunate and rare indeed. Among impediments to educational exchange, the problem of funding may be the one historical constant, although inflation and changes in the distribution of wealth and in currency relationships worldwide are altering characteristics of the issue with head-spinning rapidity. Therefore, it is extremely difficult to write of costs or sources of support without fear that assertions will become obsolete before the book is in print, and only the most intrepid would dare chart precisely the financial future of educational exchange. Nonetheless, we will attempt to review some of the fiscal principles governing international education in 1981–82 and to suggest several initiatives that might bring relief to subsequent years.

Costs of Study and Sources of Funds in the United States

Academic costs in the United States, unlike those in most other countries, can vary widely. Tuition at public institutions is generally far less than at private; two-year institutions tend to be less expensive than four-year; living costs are more moderate in the South than in the Northeast, on rural campuses than on those in metropolitan areas. A student with severe financial constraints can usually find a way to meet his academic objectives at a public institution in a low-cost area, and the availability of this option should be considered carefully in the initial stages of institutional selection.

With this variability of costs in mind, prospective students must be prepared to budget for the following items:

- Application fees, ranging from $10 to $50 per institution.
- Standardized tests of academic aptitude and/or achievement ($13–$28), plus the Test of English as a Foreign Language (TOEFL)–($23 overseas).
- Travel to and from the United States and fees charged to obtain a passport and visa.
- Tuition and fees (approximately $1,200 to $4,500 per academic year at public institutions; $3,500 to $8,500 at private institutions).
- Books, which can amount to more than $200 per year, with additional costs for supplies and equipment needed for studies in such fields as architecture and engineering.
- Room, board, and incidental expenses (for laundry, stationery, postage, local transportation, recreation), an amount which can vary with personal taste as well as with the cost of living in the area where the host institution is located. A minimum of $2,500 would currently be required for such expenses while the school is in session, but a budget of double that would be necessary at high-cost, urban sites.
- Extra clothing needed by students moving into a climate substantially different from that at home.
- Preenrollment medical exams and health insurance (Health insurance is essential, and annual costs range from around

$50 for single students to $250 for married couples plus $50 to $80 for children).

- Vacation expenses—that is, the costs of room and board, and perhaps travel, during the summer and the four to six weeks of holiday during the academic year when dormitories close.
- English language training, if the student is not prepared to enroll at once in an academic program.
- Dependent support, if the student will be accompanied. Students with dependents often cannot take advantage of subsidized campus housing and are forced to the higher-priced open market. There may also be costs for schooling or day care of children.
- Extra expenses for candidates for the master's or doctoral degree, including professional typing, microfilming, and binding, which can amount to $200 to $400.
- The continuing and probably increasing costs of most of these items for the entire period to earn the degree sought.

Information for prospective students in their home countries about costs and financial responsibilities for foreign students in the United States is prepared regularly by the College Board (CEEB). The latest edition of *Financial Planning for Study in the United States* was published in 1980.

The Institute of International Education (IIE) produces an annual report on *Costs at U.S. Educational Institutions,* which includes academic calendars, tuition, and fees at a great many schools and recommends for each an appropriate monthly maintenance rate based on the Bureau of Labor Statistics' annual review of family budgets in forty urban and five nonmetropolitan areas within the United States. Ranging in 1981–82 from $448 (in rural Georgia) to $635 (in San Francisco, with Anchorage off the top of the chart at $720), the rates are designed to cover room, board, and incidental expenses during term time and vacation periods for a single student. The 1981–82 recommendations averaged about 10 percent higher than those for the previous year. A similar increase in future years' recommendations seems inevitable at this time.

The costs of attending college in the United States have

more than doubled, in fact, in the past decade. Increases announced for the 1981–82 academic year hover around 15 percent and surpassed the rate of inflation, with figures for tuition, room, and board at some of the most prestigious private institutions soaring well over the $10,000 mark for the first time. School administrators point to spiraling costs of fuel, insulation programs, food, and equipment, as well as to modest faculty and staff salary increases in the 9 to 13 percent range. They fear that, despite changes in the academic calendar to lengthen winter vacation periods and reduce fuel needs, these factors will continue to push prices inexorably upward in the foreseeable future.

How do students defray these costs? The census conducted annually by the Institute of International Education provides an analysis of the sources of support for the 311,882 foreign students who were pursuing higher education in the United States in the academic year 1980–81. Over two thirds of the students for whom this information was reported paid for their education with personal and family funds. Nearly 16 percent were financed by their home governments or by a foreign private sponsor, while the college or university attended was the primary funding source for over 8 percent, the United States government or a United States private sponsor supported 4 percent, and 2.3 percent supported themselves from employment. These figures suggest that just under 15 percent of foreign student support comes from United States sources while just over 83 percent may originate from outside the United States. This balance has changed over the years. Data collected two decades ago showed that on the one hand home governments supported about 5 percent at that time, and only 41.7 percent declared themselves "self-supporting." About 30 percent, on the other hand, reported support from private organizations, more than double the percentage currently so assisted. To be sure, the year in question witnessed only 47,245 foreign students enrolled in United States institutions.

Personal and family support is complicated by fluctuating currency exchange rates, which make the calculation of the costs over several years for a full degree program extremely precarious. Furthermore, restrictions on the free exchange of currency by many governments of Third World countries have placed obstacles in the paths of their students. For example, until very recently the Brazilian government required persons departing for overseas to deposit a substantial sum in escrow, to be held without interest or inflationary correction until their return. In addition, a 33 percent tax was imposed on all money sent out of the country (for application fees, educational testing, tuition, room and board, for instance). Although the money was recoverable at the end of the year as an income tax credit, students were required to have funds available in the short term equal to one-third more than the already high academic and living expenses for a year of study. Even when official approval is obtainable, cash transfer procedures can frequently be tedious and time consuming, and they can fall prey to changing political circumstances—witness the plight of Iranian students during 1980 when commercial communications between the United States and Iran were interrupted as a result of the hostage crisis.

Support from United States academic institutions may take the form of a full or partial waiver of fees for tuition and/or room and board, of a cash fellowship, or of an assistantship involving some form of academic employment, usually teaching, research, or laboratory supervision for ten to twenty hours a week. Financial aid through a university is generally more limited for foreign students than for Americans, whose needs are given first priority. At the undergraduate level, scholarships are occasionally available from smaller liberal arts institutions eager to enrich their campuses through the addition of foreign students. In the arena of graduate education, field of study becomes a highly relevant factor, since much of the aid is controlled by individual departments. Financial support is rare for M.B.A. programs, for instance, and is limited for students in the humanities and the social sciences (with the exception of economics) and in the agricultural and biological sciences. In the physical sciences and engineering, research and teaching assistantships are available to well-qualified foreign students at both the master's and doctoral level, provided, of course, that they can demonstrate a reasonable level of English proficiency. Fear of insufficient English is one reason why most graduate schools are reluctant to risk assistantships with first-year students. Despite these limitations, the IIE's survey suggests that some 28,000 foreign students are receiving their primary support from the institution in which they are enrolled at the time of this writing, probably with a somewhat larger number aided by private rather than public institutions.

In recent years institutional assistance has decreased—or at least has failed to grow at the rate of growth of foreign student enrollment. Cutbacks in research funds and inflation have complicated the work of financial aid officers on United States campuses, who have been forced increasingly to grant larger but fewer awards from a shrinking coffer. Many institutions now limit tuition waivers because their value has increased so rapidly. Most graduate schools within university systems are required to cost out tuition scholarships they wish to grant and then make an equivalent amount available to the university. The future does not appear to offer much fiscal relief. Very severe reductions in federal aid to education as well as to research—reductions that will inevitably affect universities—are projected at the same time that questions are being raised about the propriety of "subsidizing" the education of citizens of other countries. The situation is compounded by the probable continuation, for the next few years at least, of an inflation rate that will weigh heavily on the labor-intensive education industry, operating in physical plants never designed for energy efficiency.

One innovative response to dwindling funds is a kind of barter arrangement now being negotiated. Some universities are signing linkage agreements, whereby students can be exchanged without a concomitant exchange of cash. The International Student Exchange Program (ISEP), administered out of Georgetown University, is based on the concept of bed-for-bed trade. A student from University X in the United States pays his full room, board, and tuition bill at home, buys an airplane ticket, then takes the place of a student from University Y abroad, who, in turn, has left a paid-up account. Although University X may send out no more students than it receives, its students may be placed at a number of institutions overseas, while incoming students may originate at different schools. ISEP provides the coordinating mechanism.

The United States government's rank as a direct source of financial assistance has likewise declined over time, from almost 5 percent a decade ago to just over 2 percent now. The flagship Fulbright Program, for example, supported up to 4,500 foreign students annually in its halcyon years. Since 1965 United States government contributions have remained essentially stable, with a 40 percent loss in purchasing power. In the academic year 1980-81, 2,300 students claimed Fulbright support, although over half received in fact only a travel grant under the program. While the Agency for International Development continues to maintain its programs for training foreign participants, the activities of the Office for International Training have also suffered from budgetary restraints and rising costs.

The United States Information Agency has lent support to the inmigration of foreign students by other than direct sponsorship, however. Its posts around the world serve as information centers for prospective candidates for admission to United States institutions of higher learning, while the Washington headquarters provides financial subsidies to a number of organizations that offer advisory services to independent students in the United States and overseas, train advisers, publish informational materials, collect data and carry out research on exchanges, and otherwise promote international education.

In response to a burgeoning demand for higher education which cannot be supplied by limited facilities at home, and often as a consequence of newfound oil wealth, foreign governments are sponsoring the study in the United States of large numbers of their young people. Notable are recent programs of the Venezuelan and Nigerian governments. Saudi Arabia also supports a large number of students in this country; and many of the Mexicans, Malaysians, Brazilians, Libyans, and Kuwaitis are here under official sponsorship as well. Rising costs in the United States, however, may restrict the number of students sent to this country under the sponsorship of their governments. This source of funds has proved to be not without its drawback as, again, currency fluctuations and politics hinder the smooth flow of funds. More important, since commitments have frequently outstripped the availability of cash, United States colleges have had to contend with long-delayed tuition payments, and the foreign students on their campuses have struggled to meet rent payments and buy food while awaiting tardy maintenance checks.

For the most part, home government support takes the form of direct grants to cover the expenses; but some students, especially those from Latin American countries, are recipients of loans obtained from local educational credit agencies. This "educredit," a concept pioneered by the Colombian Institute for Educational Credit and Technological Studies Abroad (ICETEX), operates much like the Guaranteed Student Loan Program available to domestic students. Repayment obligations commence when the student has returned to his home country to take up remunerative employment; repayment may be excused in whole or in part, however, when the position is deemed important to the country's economic development and is held for a specified number of years.

The opportunity to "work one's way through college" is not generally available to foreign students, and only 2.3 percent secure their primary support from employment. A few years ago, new and restrictive regulations regarding jobs were issued by the U.S. Immigration and Naturalization Service. At the present time, holders of the F-1 student visa may work on campus without INS approval, provided such employment, unless pursuant to an assistantship and thus part of the student's program of study, will not displace a United States citizen or permanent resident. But campus jobs carry such notoriously low wages that no student could sustain himself and meet his tuition bills from this source.

Off-campus employment for F-1 holders does require INS approval. At this time such approval is very difficult to obtain, especially during the student's first year in the United States, and it is granted only if the student can establish economic necessity brought about by unforeseen circumstances arising *subsequent to entry or subsequent to change to student classifi-*

cation. Work hours may not exceed twenty hours per week during the academic year, with full time during the summer and other vacation periods permitted. According to the INS, an F-1 student granted permission to accept part-time, off-campus employment must terminate that employment as soon as the unforeseen financial hardship ceases. He must also terminate his employment during any strike or labor dispute involving a work stoppage or layoff of employees at his place of work. Exchange visitors (J-1 visa holders) are affected by similar regulations, with the difference that approval for employment may be granted by the visa sponsor. Dependents of an F-1 student (holders of an F-2 visa) may not accept employment under any circumstances; dependents accompanying exchange visitors (J-2s) may apply to the INS to accept employment but only if such employment is needed for the support of the dependents and not for the support of the principal participant.

Designed, of course, to protect the jobs of American workers, these regulations, in the opinion of many, have caused hardship to foreign students without concomitant benefit to United States labor, since foreign students are often willing to accept jobs in low demand by Americans. The greatest hardship, however, falls on the incoming student, who must provide convincing evidence to a United States consular official that he has at his command sufficient funds to carry him through the entire academic program on which he has set his sights. Thus, access to United States higher education is unduly restricted to those from countries or families with the ability to pay, while the venerable American tradition of self-help is denied to the poor student from a poor country.

Although such detailed empirical data are not available, most foreign students in the United States, like most American students, have probably constructed for themselves a financial package that includes funds from a variety of sources. Some of the major United States scholarship programs—Fulbright and LASPAU (Latin American Scholarship Program of American Universities), for example—are based on this concept of financial packaging. Administrators of the programs seek to match fellowship funds, tuition waivers, and partial assistantships with the student's own resources in an effort to maximize the number of candidates assisted in the face of rising academic costs.

Costs of Study and Sources of Funds Abroad

Only a few years ago, foreign study and travel could represent a true bargain for the American student. The comparative decline in the value of the United States dollar and worldwide inflation have changed all that, as has the movement toward imposition of tuition charges pegged to the "real" cost of education in some countries. Certainly, however, some parts of the world remain a more economical choice than others, and costs can be heavily influenced by the nature of the academic arrangements made.

Undergraduate students frequently enroll in one of the programs sponsored by a United States college or university. The packaged costs of such a program usually match those of the sponsoring American institution and therefore vary, but remain substantial, especially with international travel costs added. Graduate students and a few of the more intrepid undergraduates tend to study independently abroad, which means that they must pay directly any tuition charged by the host institution and must buy their own room and meals "on the economy."

With an airplane ticket, a passport, and required visa in hand and paid for, the independent American must have set aside funds for books, health insurance, any remedial language training needed, thesis/dissertation expenses, and the almost mandatory vacation travel, in addition to maintenance and tuition and a possible fee charged by the home institution to cover accrediting of work done abroad.

Maintenance costs can vary widely from one country to another, but they are rising uniformly. Fulbright Commissions measure local living costs carefully in constructing their grant budgets; their 1981-82 estimates for monthly stipends range from a low of $300 in Colombia and Uruguay to $445 in Australia, $620 in Germany, and on to $922 in Japan, where housing costs in particular will astonish visiting American scholars until they experience some of the countries in the Middle East. An accompanying dependent will add 20 percent to estimated expenses. Long gone are the days when the United States dollar grew to two or three times its size when it traveled overseas.

Tuition and fees can be wholly subsidized, as they are at German universities. They can be partially covered by government subsidies and set at a modest rate. Or they can be calculated to equal or approximate the real, average cost of a study place at the host institution. While in some countries no distinction is made in the billing of local and foreign students, in others subsidies are restricted to, or maintained at a higher level for, students who are either citizens or permanent residents.

The United Kingdom, of course, is a case in point. For the academic year 1981-82, foreign student tuition was set at £ 2,500 (nearly $5,000) for arts students, £ 3,600 (some $7,000) for those in the sciences, and £ 6,000 (almost $12,000) for those in the clinical years of human or veterinary medicine and dentistry. Belgium has set tuition for students from developed countries at between $5,000 and $6,000, while students from the developing world are admitted for the same fee applicable to Belgians, roughly $300 per year. Canada's tuition for foreign students differs from province to province, but only four have failed to impose a differential. Quebec universities asked just over $4,000 for 1981-82, an amount calculated to represent 60 percent of real costs.

Tuition at medical schools abroad, which enroll a substantial number of American students, ranges from $800 per year in the Philippines and the Dominican Republic to between $4,000 and $6,000 in Mexico and Belgium. Where medical education is subsidized, as in Germany, study places for noncitizens are nonexistent or severely restricted.

No hard data exist on the overall number of Americans studying overseas or on the source of their financial support. We do know that approximately 30,000 are enrolled in study abroad programs sponsored by United States colleges and, in all likelihood, draw on the same financial resources for their overseas as for their domestic study. That is, these students—primarily undergraduates—can usually combine the accustomed personal and family funds with the financial aid that facilitates their enrollment at home: federal, state, and institutional grants or loans. And Americans enjoy a significant advantage over their foreign counterparts because the United States dollar, though weakened in relation to some, is freely convertible to any currency in the world. No authorization is required to transfer funds abroad; no restrictions are placed on amounts to be exchanged.

Although in most countries official permission to work is difficult to obtain, probably a good many students or their dependents do earn some money in the underground economy. The performance of household chores or handyman functions, baby-sitting, and English teaching frequently provide a financial supplement. Employment as a primary source of support, however, is probably relevant for an even smaller proportion of American students than for the 2.3 percent of foreign students who support themselves in this way.

Almost no special scholarship assistance is available to undergraduates. Graduate students and scholars, on the other hand, do have access to fellowships designated (or in any event, tenable) for overseas study. Exclusive of teachers, the United States government's Fulbright Program offers over 1,000 awards to some 125 countries. In addition, many other award programs exist. Large numbers of these awards are offered by foreign governments and foreign universities, alone or in cooperation with a sponsoring agency in the United States. Numerous organizations devoted specifically to exchanges between the United States and another country have their own programs, as do professional associations, which often provide grant support in particular fields of study. In addition, many corporate, community, or family foundations make grants to individuals for studying abroad. Even organizations that do not normally fund such activities—such as cultural, social, or religious community groups, ethnic clubs, or organizations and businesses—will sometimes be receptive to a request for funding from an individual interested in research related to their special needs. In addition, as with undergraduates, resources available to support domestic study (the GI Bill, government loans) can usually be redirected to defer educational expenses abroad.

Current Financial Issues

The fluctuating value of currency and the regulations inhibiting its free exchange will undoubtedly continue to affect traveling scholars in the foreseeable future. The economic conditions that have given rise to these obstacles, however, have engendered a much more significant and fundamental issue. As growth in an economy slows and money becomes scarcer for social programs of all kinds, there is a tendency to safeguard the continued existence of such programs by passing on to beneficiaries an ever larger share of their real or economic costs. This phenomenon has touched higher education generally; it has had a special impact on educational exchange, in the sense that opinion leaders in a number of countries (and in some states in this country) are asking why educational subsidies should continue to benefit students from other countries. After all, they argue, their first obligation is to educate their own, and funds for that purpose are already in short supply. Then, too, they continue, large numbers of students come from countries whose treasuries are overflowing with windfall oil profits. If higher education is a service those countries or their nationals wish to purchase on the international market, why should not that service find its fair market value?

These arguments led educational authorities in the United Kingdom to make the decisions described earlier, with the result that British universities lost an average of 11 percent of their foreign undergraduate intake in the academic year 1980-81. Graduate losses are calculated to be higher. Applications for 1981-82 are down 40 percent, while advisers on United States higher education in countries tied by long tradition to British education report a considerable upsurge in the number of students requesting information.

As will be seen in Chapter Ten, the argument over the costs and benefits deriving from the education of foreign students is by no means settled, and, indeed, the decision in the United Kingdom to pass full costs on to foreign students has not gone unchallenged. A crucial point from the point of view of the internationalists is the identification of the "real" benefits. They question the relative value of economic benefits (or costs) when compared to such other significant factors as the social responsibility of the developed nations to educate students from abroad, especially those from the developing countries, and the long-term benefits of such public diplomacy. Whether there are economic benefits, as maintained by some British educators, or actual losses, in that costs exceed benefits, as argued by Blaug (1981), these other considerations may be sufficiently important to affect the issue. Thus, although Blaug sees no *economic* reason for setting aside "the contributory principle of government expenditure"—a principle which states "Thou shalt not enjoy the services rendered by government if thou or thy parents have contributed nought to the public exchequer!"—he allows that a country might waive the principle "on other grounds by adopting a global, cosmopolitan approach to the problem of overseas students, thus entering into reciprocal arrangements with some countries where there is a basis for reciprocity and, as for the rest, treating the subsidy to overseas students as a special form of foreign aid" (Blaug, 1981, p. 86).

The battle rages while further studies are produced and while other countries—although not yet the United States—emulate the United Kingdom's policy.

A survey of public institutional policies toward foreign students, conducted by the IIE in mid-1981, provided little evidence of financial discrimination against foreign students. Despite much talk in state legislative halls about subsidizing the education of those who do not pay taxes, only 9 percent of 680 public institutions completing the IIE questionnaire charge foreign students a higher rate for tuition than is charged other out-of-state students. Even in these cases, the differential is relatively modest. The whole question of differentiated tuition and statewide surcharges for foreign students (as opposed to special charges designed to offset special services) is still subject to legal challenge.

The older issue of reciprocity in exchange is closely related to that raised by the full-cost protagonists. Countries hosting large numbers of United States students, often as participants in study abroad programs formally associated with local universities, have complained for years that far smaller numbers of their own students are given the opportunity to benefit from American higher education. France in a prime case in point. At last count in 1979-80, 3,726 United States students participated in 106 programs in France while a large (but uncounted) number enrolled as independent students, but only 2,570 French students were in the United States. Largely because the French authorities were unable to negotiate an acceptable accommodation with the 3,000 autonomous units in the United States educational system, it decided to impose centrally a variety of controls, including a requirement for formal application well in advance and the presentation of financial guarantees before visas are issued and limitations on the number of foreign students to be accepted.

Recommendations

Since fiscal constraints are likely to remain the paramount obstacle to exchange, it seems appropriate to consider a few ways in which they might be ameliorated. None are panaceas; all will elicit objection from one quarter or another. They are presented less in the hope that they will be implemented intact than that they will stimulate creativity in the fiscal arena.

Choosing a Lower-Cost Option. The prospective foreign student contemplating a period of study in the United States has hundreds of options before him. Most students, of course, immediately look toward perhaps six or a dozen schools with worldwide reputations. These include not only the most selective but also the most expensive institutions in the country, but they will not necessarily include those best geared to meet a particular student's goals, personal qualifications, or financial circumstances. Indeed, some of the finest institutions are publically supported and therefore more moderate in cost. First-class institutions are located throughout the country, as likely as not in areas where housing, food, and recreation costs remain relatively modest. A careful search should yield for most candidates a number of less expensive options that meet their academic objectives in every way.

For the undergraduate, one alternative is to spend the freshman and sophomore years at a community or junior college. These institutions, in most cases, charge the lowest tuition rates available and provide the general education courses required for admission to junior status at four-year institutions. American students under similar financial constraints increasingly begin their college years at two-year schools near their homes, then transfer to complete their bachelor's degree work elsewhere. For students seeking to enter a technical trade, such schools are far more relevant to their career preparation than most senior colleges, and the selection of a two-year terminal program might be the wisest choice.

Less ideal, perhaps, but a viable alternative for some nonetheless are correspondence courses taken at home to complete some portion of the degree requirements. New technology will lend increasing credibility to the concept of a University Without Walls stretching across national boundaries, but accredited United States institutions are already offering this option.

Finally, there is the possibility of carrying out thesis/dissertation research at home, with supervision handled either through correspondence or in cooperation with faculty of a home country institution, at which the student might be double registered. Living expenses away from home would thereby be eliminated, and tuition costs would be replaced by a minimal supervision fee. In point of fact, such an arrangement might be far more valid from an academic point of view than research in the host country, in that it directs the student to apply his learning to an indigenous problem.

Bed-to-Bed Exchanges. As discussed above, Georgetown's International Student Exchange Program (ISEP) is a matching service designed to trade students between colleges and universities in this country and participating institutions abroad. Students at both ends pay their accustomed fee for room, board, and tuition and then trade places for an agreed-upon period. Exchanges are not necessarily direct; through the medium of ISEP, students can go to the institution of their choice but their counterparts need not come from that same college or university, as long as each institution receives a student contingent from abroad as large as it sends out. The only "extra" cost students must bear is the international air fare and any imbalance in the value of money exchanged to cover incidental expenses. Because of outside supportive funding to cover ISEP administrative costs, no charge is made to member universities at present. In 1981, in two years of operations, ISEP had built up an institutional membership of 100 in the United States and 100 overseas and arranged the trade of 600 students—300 in, 300 out. Growing numbers will increase the program's flexibility, but officials indicate 90 percent of students are assigned to institutions of their first choice, with choice guided by detailed descriptions of participating universities and likely selectivity factors. The problems reported include such nitty-gritty as the number of meals per week covered at one end but not at the other. The more obvious one of fees paid by students at high-cost schools traded to highly subsidized institutions has led to complaints, but these are often stilled as students come to realize the difficulties they would have encountered in handling admissions arrangements independently, especially to courses of limited enrollment; in foregoing the support system provided by the program; and in ensuring the credit of their home institutions.

Some schools, of course, have negotiated such exchanges independently as part of linkage agreements with individual institutions abroad. This model largely avoids the problems of the transfer and fluctuating value of currency; it speaks to the issue of reciprocity and neutralizes full-cost arguments, and is worth serious consideration especially if undergraduate general educational exchange are the goal.

Changes in Regulations Regarding Employment of Foreign Students in the United States. Strong arguments can be marshaled to support a change in the current regulations of the U.S. Immigration and Naturalization Service limiting the employment of foreign students: unused study places are available in United States higher education institutions; in many countries there is a vast demand for higher education that cannot be met with current facilities at home; and American philosophical tradition esteems merit and personal effort over economic status. Even recognizing the current crisis in employment, the long-term advantages accruing from the United States' position as a leader in educational interchange may well justify such a change. Most restrictive is the stipulation that students cannot list income they anticipate from employment during the study period among their available resources at the time they face a United States consular officer to request a visa. They must instead have evidence that sufficient funds will be forthcoming from their families or home government or that the host institution has provided aid to cover all anticipated expenses for the duration of study.

But why should not students short on economic resources be given the opportunity to invest instead their energies, as long as they provide evidence of the will and ability to do so successfully and as long as their earning plan is realistic? Why should they not be permitted to take a position for which their skills qualify them—and to do so in the open market? Such liberality could be tempered by guidelines that reduce opportunities for students heading for cities or regions of high unemployment, that define the openings frequently available and indicate probable wages, and that limit employment to certain types of occupations in low demand by United States workers. At the very least, students should be permitted to enter with funding for the first year and a limited-term visa, renewable on presentation of evidence of satisfactory employment. Universities could be asked to help obtain and verify employment for their foreign students in need of such aid and, indeed, under current regulations, should be encouraged to increase campus work scholarships to students who cannot independently meet all their expenses.

In addition, INS regulations now make no provision for employment of any kind for dependents of students (F-2s). They should be revised to allow F-2s to work at least for their own support, just as is currently permissible for the J-2 dependents of exchange visitors.

Excursion-Rate Air Fares for Academic Year Study. At present airlines advertise numerous special fares to attract travelers to less used routes and to off-peak seasons, days of the week, or times of the day. Most such international fares are tied to specific periods, which the stay abroad must neither fall short of nor exceed. The Council on International Educational Exchange has urged that the international United States flag carriers establish a reduced fare for students certified as enrolled full time in an overseas study program sponsored by an accredited United States college, university, or secondary school. Specifically, the students would pay 50 percent of the lowest tourist excursion fare on their outward journey and 50 percent of the then existing lowest tourist excursion fare at the time of the return journey. The council suggests that such an arrangement would at least enable the serious full-time student to travel at the same cost as the casual tourist. Such a fare could, of course, be extended to all travelers enrolling full time in recognized institutions abroad.

Tuition Waivers Through Creative Accounting. If one argues, and a convincing case can indeed be made, that the United States educational system was created for and exists primarily to serve United States students, then each foreign student enrolled adds only marginally to the host institution's budget. On this basis a school seeking to enrich its campus life by enrolling foreign students, or to diversify the geographical and cultural areas represented, might well enhance this essentially educational benefit and satisfy its accountants by waiving charges to candidates from abroad above the level of marginal costs. Beyond simple numerical calculations, of course, lie the difficult-to-quantify but very real benefits to the primary constituents, the American students, that accrue from the presence of colleagues with differing economic, social, and political experiences. The contribution they make to the quality of the education offered the Americans could well translate waivers into sound educational investments.

The current fly in the ointment for some schools, however, is the fact that they are struggling to attract a breakeven number of primary constituents. These institutions, then, are forced to seek foreign candidates with the resources to pay a full share of costs based on average costing concepts. Since demographic projections suggest that this phenomenon will increase in frequency, many institutions will not have the luxury to develop the waiver policies suggested. For these, the negotiation of bed-to-bed exchange or changes in work rules to permit the foreign student to earn fees will be a more practical means to achieve an internationalized campus.

Educational Credit. Colombia's ICETEX has led the way to the establishment, in many countries of Latin America, of educational credit institutions to support domestic and foreign study. Although frequently modest and struggling, these institutions often provide crucial financing to complement a student's savings, a partial scholarship, or an employer's pledge of salary continuity to underwrite international study leading to acquisition of much-needed skills for national development. Operating with procedures not unlike the Guaranteed Student Loan Program in this country, applicants borrow the necessary sums at modest interest, and with interest usually deferred until completion of study. Repayment of the principal and interest, then, begins when the student has returned home to remunerative employment. In some cases repayment may be excused, in whole or in part, if the student accepts a position with his government and retains the position for a stipulated number of years.

This scheme has the merit of promoting national interests while opening opportunities to all those with the motivation and ability to seize them, without regard to their assets at the time of application. Once the revolving fund is established, its costs involve only administrative expenses, interest foregone by reason of subsidized rates or deferred collection, and erosion through default, although this problem has not become significant in Latin America.

In its *World Development Report,* the World Bank (1980) published the results of studies on the rate of return to education for wage earners. All support the idea that more schooling leads to higher earnings. One sample of thirty developing countries provides the "social" rates of return—that is, the increase due to education when costs, including foregone earnings as well as both public and private outlays, are compared with benefits, which are measured by income before tax. On this basis, the studies showed an estimated 12.3 percent rate for higher education, 15.4 percent for secondary education, while primary schooling yielded an astounding 24.2 percent. Even in fourteen industrialized countries sampled, secondary and higher education resulted in, respectively, 10.0 percent and 9.1 percent rates of return. These figures suggest that education can be looked on as a sound financial investment for nations and individuals—and for the international community as well.

The first proposal for a World Student Loan Bank dates back at least two decades, its purpose to provide an international structure through which governments, foundations, and academic institutions could join forces to open the educational opportunities of all countries to capable, deserving students of any country. A World Student Loan Bank might operate through the national educational credit institutions in the developing countries or might accept loan applications directly from students with the approval of their own governments. Its regulations and procedures could be designed to circumvent foreign currency exchange problems, to make needed funds available in the currency of the country where the host institution is located, and to permit repayment in installments in the currency of the country from which the students originate and to which they will return as employed adults. Interest could be subsidized, or charged at market rates, provided repayment of both principal and interest was deferred until earning began. Repayment could be divorced from the rate of exchange between the two currencies by the establishment of a repayment schedule based on a fraction of the annual earnings of the beneficiary over a stipulated period of years rather than on a fixed amount. Or indebtedness could be reduced by a formula designed to take into account the returned student's contribution to his country's development.

In recent years financial aid programs have been designed to ensure that no American student will be denied higher education of some kind for lack of funds. These programs have lowered one of the last barriers to equal opportunity and upward mobility in our society, surely for the benefit of that society as well as the individual. Can we benefit less in today's interdependent world by cooperating in efforts to open to the world's students the superb educational resources with which we are blessed in excess?

5

Recruitment:
Ensuring Educational
and Ethical Standards

Hugh M. Jenkins

There is no simple model for the recruitment of foreign students. Because the function of transnational recruitment and the process of communication across cultures cannot be mass produced, each recruitment program must be crafted to reflect adequately the institution's characteristics and project effectively its purposes in seeking to enroll students from foreign countries. The most important factors—those that will be judged most critically by the educational community both in the United States and abroad—are attitude and intention: How does the institution view the prospective foreign students? What motivated its entry into the field of international educational interchange? Specifically, the question is whether an institution is prepared to take the necessary steps to ensure that the students are properly selected for educational programs that will meet their needs or whether the institution is simply seeking to augment enrollment by a venture into a new market.

Although no model program can be provided, the following checklist of essential elements may be used as a guide for institutions that are interested in initiating or expanding the enrollment of foreign students.

- Appointment of a committee or task force to examine interest and feasibility and make recommendations to institutional authorities or governing body.

Assuming that the recommendation is positive and further exploration is approved:

- Examination of existing international resources and interest, either by departmental inquiry or campus questionnaire.
- Analysis of the institution's educational program, to identify the particular role it can play in education of foreign students.
- Evaluation of anticipated benefits that will accrue from enrollment of foreign students (including income from additional fees; increased use of facilities; economic advantage to local economy; and long-term impact of new contacts, new foreign alumni interests, and international status of institution both at home and abroad).
- Determination of resources that must be committed to the project (including costs of foreign travel, special publications, staff time, reception and advisory services, and fulfillment of legal responsibilities).
- Confirmation of institution's interest in following through on new or expanded international educational activities (if new, this step also entails submission of application to Immigration and Naturalization Service for approval for attendance of nonimmigrant foreign students).
- Identification of geographical/academic target areas.
- Formulation of plan for increased foreign student enrollment (including setting up admissions procedures and arrangements for reception and welfare of foreign students).
- Promotion of new activity (including development of contacts and preparation of publicity materials and travel itineraries for personal presentations).

Although the term *recruitment* is most often associated with the search for prospective students at the undergraduate level, aggressive enrollment practices are also found at the graduate level. The line between acceptable encouragement of suitable candidates and indiscriminate recruitment of applicants is in any case difficult to determine. It is even more obscure at the graduate level, where the process is more highly specialized, reflecting as it does the complexities of the organization and administration of graduate schools and departments in different universities.

In his report on a project designed to identify policies and practices in the graduate education of foreign students, Nelson (1975, p. 17) relates the reasons given by a number of graduate deans and academicians for admitting foreign students to graduate schools and departments: "To recruit the best available talent, to maintain the optimum number of students in the department, to fill the need for qualified research assistants (it being noted that foreign students can be obtained at lower rates than United States students), to implement a policy that ignores national origin and relates to the worldwide community of those engaged in a particular discipline, to extend a particular field of study by providing a nucleus of trained talent to develop new schools or faculties in foreign countries."

These comments suggest that each institution will have its own guidelines for the recruitment of foreign students at the graduate level. Universities that offer graduate academic and professional programs (such as law, medicine, engineering) undoubtedly have established their own international relationships and developed their own channels for the selection and admission of both undergraduate and graduate foreign students. At the same time, in some disciplines, the difficulty of evaluating the expertise and credentials of graduate students leads to problems in their selection and admission. Moravscik (1980, p. 20), in his comments on the needs of science students from developing countries, notes that in this field one solution to the problem of evaluating applicants could be the extension of oral interviewing techniques, which at that time were being used in only one discipline (physics) and only primarily in Asian countries. This approach, in which acceptable graduate candidates are identified by a qualified interviewer (generally a visiting professor) on a disciplinary rather than an institutional basis, is clearly a form of recruitment that can only be beneficial.

In the light of such special circumstances, the determination of any general rules concerning the recruitment of foreign graduate students becomes a very difficult task. However, mistakes and misconceptions that may be more immediately apparent in the recruitment of foreign undergraduate students are certainly not confined to that particular level of the educational process. Thus, while most of what follows in this chapter is presented in the context of the admission of undergraduate students, many of the problems described and the principles involved are equally applicable to recruitment at all levels.

Unethical Recruiting and Its Causes

A few well-publicized incidents of improper recruitment practice in the United States, stimulating further inquiries which exposed the existence and activities of a number of unscrupulous agents operating in foreign countries, have together served to give a bad name to the recruitment of foreign students. The existence of these blatant transgressions, which certainly demand stringent remedies, clouds what is in any case a very sensitive issue, since recruitment—a longstanding and respectable custom in postsecondary education in the United States—is not a practice that can be easily transposed to the international arena. Nonetheless, there is an increasing recognition that recruitment activities designed to reach foreign students, if conducted according to certain accepted principles, may constitute a useful and valid service that can benefit both the prospective student and the institution. At this particular time, therefore, foreign student recruitment must be seen as a relatively new development, one that merits cautious examination rather than an uncompromisingly negative approach.

The primary causes of unethical recruitment practices are not hard to find: they are the direct result of the pressures created in the foreign students' home countries and, more recently, at some institutions in the United States. In many foreign countries, both developing and developed, educational resources at the postsecondary level are insufficient to cope with the needs of the student population, especially in the fields of science and technology. Thus, students and their families and their governments look to some other country to find the opportunity that is not available in their homelands. In the United States, because of reductions in the number of high school graduates, many postsecondary institutions are faced with immediate and prospective declines in enrollment. Although this situation may be changed by other factors (see Scully, 1980b), the immediate reaction of some institutions is to look to the recruitment of foreign students to offset the shortage. These factors have created a climate of opportunity for pseudoeducational entrepreneurs working as "headhunters" on the international scene to catch the overflow of prospective applicants who cannot be accommodated by the legitimate agencies and organizations engaged in the process of international educational interchange. At the same time, a number of United States educational institutions have become involved somewhat carelessly, if innocently, in recruitment practices that are detrimental both to the students and, ultimately, to the institutions themselves.

Because of the attraction of the United States as a highly industrialized and technologically sophisticated nation and as a valuable source of education and training, many foreign students look to this country to find the solution to their educational problems. These prospective students and their families, overwhelmed by the complexity and decentralization of the United States educational system, or "nonsystem," are in urgent need of advice. Although there are legitimate public and private information and advisory services in most of the foreign students' home countries, these services are limited and insufficient to cope with the demands made on them. At the same time, the proper process of application, selection, and admission is of necessity time consuming, and there is a long waiting period before the student achieves the desired placement in a United States college or university. Thus, for the anxious and impatient foreign students, about to stake their own and perhaps their entire family's savings on this chance, payment of expensive and sometimes exorbitant fees for "guaranteed admission" seems a small price for an immediate solution to their educational dilemma. In particular, students who do not meet the generally accepted admissions standards consider the purchase of placement in this way well worth the initial investment. A purchased placement is also a great convenience for the person with no real intention of becoming a student. Unfortunately, as Lockyear (1980) demonstrates in his description of current practices in the recruitment of foreign students, the speedy result, obtained by short-cutting or eliminating the proper selection procedures, does not necessarily provide the desired solution. Often it only opens doors to more problems—either for the foreign student, who arrives on a United States campus to find that the reality is far from the promise, or for the institution that is committed to admit a foreign student who is in no way suited for postsecondary education in the United States. This kind of international educational traffic ultimately raises questions about the value of higher education in the United States and the validity of the degrees offered by its colleges and universities.

Despite these pitfalls, there are many effective channels of communication to ensure that the right student gets to the right institution for the right reasons. However, both the students and the institution must take certain essential preliminary steps. Prospective students must first be quite clear in their own minds why they need to study abroad. The educational institution, before reaching out to foreign students, must develop its own rationale for involvement in international educational interchange.

Effects of Admitting Foreign Students

Before undertaking a program for the recruitment of foreign students, an institution must be sure that it has a contribution to make to their education and is prepared to accept the responsibilities involved in enrolling them, in return for the benefits that will accrue to the institution. The institution must make this determination on what are essentially educational factors. The easy and somewhat naive assumption that the enrollment of students from foreign countries, provided they have the necessary financial resources, will be a profit-making venture may soon prove to be an error in basic bookkeeping in which profits and losses are confused with liabilities and assets. The invisible export represented by international educational interchange is not one that brings a quick and simple return, and the added stature of an internationally oriented educational program is an institutional investment that may not pay an immediate dividend.

It is only by taking a long view of the institution as a whole that one can make a valid judgment. The following are some considerations that might be included in such an appraisal:

- Does the institution want to prepare all its students for careers in which international sophistication is required for advancement? (If properly used as an educational resource, foreign students can contribute to an international dimension in the curriculum.)
- Does the institution wish to enhance its research programs through international interinstitutional projects? (The exchange of students and scholars will be an essential part of such a program.)
- Does the institution wish to establish a presence abroad? (Foreign students and subsequently foreign alumni will establish a vehicle for this.)
- Is the institution criticized for its parochialism? (Foreign students help to create an international campus community that will dispel that image.)

Finally, there is the opportunity to develop into a truly international institution with ample opportunities for United States students to study abroad and a constant transnational flow of students and faculty in a variety of fields. All this involves, and may begin with, the enrollment of foreign students.

Unless an institution is willing to be constantly on the defensive in educational circles, some kind of international activity is now mandatory. At the least, therefore, an institution can extract some advantage by making a virtue out of necessity; at the most, it can enjoy the full panoply of multinational relationships and international programs.

An institution may be so selective in its educational program and enrollment, however, that it regards the admission of foreign students as detrimental to its primary purpose. This may be considered a valid reason for deciding not to encourage enrollment from abroad. If an institution decides not to become involved with foreign students, this decision must be effectively enforced. Reluctant or haphazard acceptance of foreign students, failing a deliberate guiding policy and lacking an adequate control system over numbers or nationality, can result in serious problems.

Institutions that do opt for greater international involvement must implement that decision effectively, with an accompanying assignment of institutional resources. By taking the initiative, an institution can create a balanced foreign student population—which may, by design, be concentrated in one or two subject areas or distributed among all the various disciplines. In either case the participation of foreign students in the classroom may be used to develop and strengthen the international aspect of the educational programs offered by the institution.

Assessing Institutional Commitment

The college or university venturing for the first time into the field of foreign student education must carefully and comprehensively assess the commitment required. In the first place, requirements of the Immigration and Naturalization Service (INS) impose responsibilities on any institution where foreign students are enrolled. The institution must file an application to the INS for authorization and approval for attendance by nonimmigrant alien students. Before giving approval, the INS will require—in addition to proof of appropriate certification or other form of approval, as well as information about the plant and physical facilities, financial status, and educational resources—evidence that the school can provide advisory and consultative services for its students and trainees. Approval, when it is granted, involves compliance with reporting requirements—on the arrival on campus, or the failure to arrive, of foreign students who have been admitted to the United States to attend the school; on students' failure to carry a full course of study, as defined by the regulations; and on the termination of students' attendance at the institution. The extent of the legal requirements for institutions enrolling foreign students (described more completely in Chapter Seven) certainly entails the assignment of personnel with adequate time to fulfill these requirements, presumably in the role of foreign student adviser.

Institutional commitment will also entail organizing admissions procedures adequate to deal with the special problems of foreign student admissions. As noted in Chapter Six, in addition to the basic evaluation of foreign educational credentials, the institution must develop mechanisms to assure itself that the applicants have sufficient funds to live and study in the United States and are proficient in the use of the English language. If the applicant fails this last condition, the institution must provide, or ensure that the student arranges for, the necessary instruction in English. Upon arrival of the foreign students on campus, the foreign student adviser, in addition to the legal responsibilities noted above, must be in a position to organize the orientation and assistance in cultural adjustment that students from a foreign country will require at the beginning of and during their stay in the United States. The dimensions of such orientation are set forth in the guideline on orientation published by the National Association for Foreign Student Affairs (1980).

Constructing a Recruitment Program

Having determined its rationale and the extent of its commitment, the institution is now ready to augment its international educational activities by the active recruitment of foreign students. The next step should be an inventory of available recruitment resources, which will almost always reveal some degree of existing international involvement. An inquiry into the international experience of the campus community will, in the first place, focus attention on the potential contribution of the few foreign students already enrolled at the institution. It will also reveal those members of the faculty who have spent some time studying or teaching in a foreign country, and United States students who have lived, worked, or studied abroad. The inquiry may also disclose the names of forgotten foreign alumni who are now back in their home countries.

Although such an inventory may seem an obvious step, many institutions have never systematically explored their international resources. Even where such an inventory has been made, too often it has not been followed by a deliberate effort to harness these resources for the active development of the international activities of the institution. However small the number of persons on campus with international experience may be, their combined knowledge, outreach, and, most especially, their interest and enthusiasm can provide the nucleus for a committee or an advisory body. This group can prepare an inclusive institutional plan for further international activity and for the development of programs to increase the presence of foreign students at the institution and enhance their role as members of the campus community.

A number of resources at the national level can be utilized in the construction of an effective recruitment program. In the area of institutional relationships, every college or university belongs to one or more of the major institutional associations. Such organizations as the American Council on Education, the National Association of State Universities and Land-Grant Colleges, the American Association of State Colleges and Universities, and the American Association of Community and Junior Colleges have their own international liaison. They can provide a wealth of information on the changing educational needs and opportunities in foreign countries and offer contacts in countries around the world.

With the assistance of these national groups, the institution can match its own interests and resources with the objectives of students in different foreign countries and thus begin to identify those geographical and academic areas that should be targeted for recruitment. Information on current international activities and relationships in particular fields of study may also be obtained through contact with the various professional societies and organizations, such as the American Chemical Society or the American Assembly of Collegiate Schools of Business, that have acquired international experience, information, and contacts with professional groups in other countries. All these resources are accessible to any institution seeking to assemble the facts on which it may base its decisions regarding the extension of its foreign student activities.

Much pertinent information can also be provided by those organizations and groups of organizations more directly involved in international educational interchange. One such group of organizations is, of course, the National Liaison Committee on Foreign Student Admissions, which brings together the American Association of Collegiate Registrars and Admissions Officers (AACRAO), the College Board (CEEB), the Council of Graduate Schools (CGS), the Institute of International Education (IIE), and the National Association for Foreign Student Affairs (NAFSA). Both individually and in concert, these organizations have published a wide variety of studies, reports, and guidelines on all aspects of international educational interchange, some of which are designed to assist an institution engaged in various stages of the construction of a foreign student recruitment program.

Besides publications, these organizations can provide expert assistance in the form of consultants' services, seminars and workshops, and training for campus-based professionals in all phases of the institution's international involvement. Much of this activity is partially underwritten by the federal government in the form of grants from the United States Information Agency (USIA). A major source for these professional development programs is the Field Service Program of the National Association for Foreign Student Affairs, one of the programs made possible by the support of the USIA.

In constructing the best possible foreign student recruitment program, the institution must answer a series of self-imposed questions, including an examination of the institution itself:

1. Identification of fields of study and levels of study that may be offered most effectively to foreign students.
2. Determination of areas of interest in the development of international outreach—for example, institutional interest in area studies or opportunity to take advantage of existing or potential contacts in different countries.
3. Focus on appropriate environment—for example, climate conditions similar to those in particular areas of the world (especially in agricultural programs).
4. Availability of natural or industrial resources and, consequently, of relevant study programs—for example, mining, oil, heavy or light industries, or agriculture.
5. Physical attributes to be stressed—for example, small or large campus, urban or rural location, available dormitory accommodation.

The results of this kind of study will indicate what particular aspects the institution will need to communicate or emphasize in any recruitment program.

Other areas of investigation require information obtained from the expert resources outside the institution:

1. Current sources in the flow of foreign students to the United States. Certain countries, such as Taiwan, Nigeria, Canada, Japan, and Hong Kong, have long been the major sources of foreign students in the United States; however, the situation is by no means static (witness the massive influx of Iranian students in recent years), and changes in government policy may have both immediate and long-term effects on the flow of foreign students.
2. Current focus on areas of study. Despite the continuing attraction of engineering and business administration for foreign students, national manpower requirements and governmental development planning may create new needs that a country can meet only by sending students to study a variety of different subjects at educational institutions in the more industrialized countries.
3. Regulations imposed by some foreign governments, which,

through restraints on purchase of foreign currency, restrict study abroad to certain disciplines.

4. Possibility of developing interinstitutional relationships with certain countries.

5. Assessment of academic level of prospective applicants and general English language proficiency of students in different foreign countries.

The combined results of these inquiries and the matching of institutional interests and resources with the quantity, quality, and special characteristics of the demand in different countries will provide the institution with the basic information required to initiate its own foreign student recruitment program.

At this point, and as one of the first steps in foreign student recruitment, the institution may find it advantageous to request inclusion in the Foreign Student Information Clearinghouse. Operated by the National Liaison Committee on Foreign Student Admissions, this computerized program contains information on hundreds of colleges and universities in all parts of the United States. Prospective students complete a questionnaire about the characteristics of the college or university they are looking for, and the clearinghouse sends a response listing the institutions that most nearly meet these specifications.

The essential element in any recruitment program is communication. In a program directed toward students in a foreign country, both the materials and the means of communication must be very carefully crafted to make not only the maximum but also the optimum impression. Crossing cultural barriers, the written word must enable someone who is completely unfamiliar with higher education in the United States to determine whether the institution is suited to his or her needs and resources. The information provided in the usual college catalogue, prepared for an American audience, will not suffice. In addition to the general information designed to describe the institution, there must be practical information designed to inform the student on such matters as total expenses for the academic year, accommodation during vacation periods, possibility of financial assistance, shipping, shopping and banking, climate, the documents that must be included with the application, and the time required to process the application. For this reason many institutions, both small colleges and major universities, prepare special materials for their communication with prospective students from foreign countries. These materials, although designed specifically to inform and encourage the inquirer, can serve as instruments for recruitment in the best sense of the word. The College of Wooster provides an excellent example of such a pamphlet prepared by a small college, while the special airmail flyer used by Indiana University is representative of the approach that can be taken by a major institution.

Expanding Existing Activities

For many United States academic institutions, the question of involvement in foreign student activities has already been decided. There are virtually no large universities and very few smaller four-year or two-year colleges that do not have some foreign students on campus. For these, therefore, the question of recruitment is mainly one of how much and in what ways. Among these institutions, however, are those that previously have been somewhat passive, or even reluctant, in their response to the attraction of foreign student enrollment. For these, just as in the initiation of new programs, any deliberate expansion of existing foreign student activities—especially the active participation in recruitment programs—will demand the same assessment of interest, inventory of resources, and appraisal of costs. Past experience, both of the institution itself and of the United States educational community, will provide guidance for future planning. For such institutions the increase in foreign student activity should be on a gradual basis, with the governing factors being the interests and resources of the institution rather than the manpower needs of some foreign development program.

However, by responding to requests from developing nations or from various national or international sponsoring agents, a number of colleges and universities have moved rapidly from relative isolation to relatively large-scale involvement in international educational interchange. In developing activities through this channel, institutions should give special attention to certain potential problem areas. Of these the most important is overcommitment to any one national group of foreign students. The two most obvious disadvantages of such a policy are (1) the danger of creating a special-interest group that can be a disruptive element in the campus community and (2) the risk that some domestic or international crisis affecting the political or economic status of the group will create a crisis of major proportions for the institution. Such problems have a dynamic of their own: Domestic crises create emotional stresses, which are increased by news, or lack of news, from the students' home country. If there is a breakdown in financial arrangements, the stress is further increased by the immediate embarrassment of lack of funds for ongoing expenses. These problems are in turn reflected in academic failure, which may lead to loss of immigration status, a legal problem that may lead to deportation. Such accelerating difficulties are manageable when only one or two students are involved, but the impact of this type of crisis on a group of students will quickly exhaust institutional resources of time and energy (and certainly deplete whatever emergency financial resources might be available). In extreme cases this may create a situation in which the only viable solution is the premature return of the students to the home country.

Institutions should take precautions when contracting with national or international sponsors for programs involving the admission of groups of students. Such contracts may be made with an individual sponsor or a group of sponsors and may be negotiated by an individual institution or through a consortium or group of institutions. In any case, the final decision on the admission of each individual student in the group must remain with the institution, the contract must specify a timetable for the payment of tuition fees and living expenses, and the contract must include provision to reimburse the institution for the extra services required to administer and supervise the foreign students during their period of study.

While the negotiation of such contracts may present no problems to the experienced administrators of large universities, smaller institutions, particularly community and junior colleges, may provide the educational programs most suited to the immediate needs of the developing countries. Thus, an institution with little previous international educational experience may be faced with the opportunity to provide an educational program for a national or international sponsor. In such circumstances the institution should seek the advice and counsel readily available from its own institutional association or from the organizations and associations, already mentioned, that are the experts in the field.

Conducting a Recruitment Program

The most desirable way to conduct a foreign student recruitment program is through direct participation of faculty and administrative staff. These are the individuals who are truly familiar with the institution and can respond to all the questions about its educational programs, its physical aspects, its environment, and other matters of concern to the prospective students and thus assist them in deciding whether it will be most appropriate to their needs. To be truly effective, however, the recruiter must be not only knowledgeable about the United States educational system but also at least intelligently informed about the educational system of the foreign country. The recruiter must never seek to "sell" the institution or accept a student who is less than adequately prepared for postsecondary education in the United States. An ill-informed or insensitive representative of a United States college or university can have a negative impact, as Ellen Mashiko graphically describes in Chapter Two of this book.

Recruitment by members of the faculty or the administration can be planned on an individual basis, and in this case itineraries may be arranged and recruitment opportunities developed simply by seizing every opportunity to establish contacts in the target foreign country. These opportunities may include encounters with foreign educators at national or international conferences, contacts made by foreign alumni, direct communication with selected secondary schools in the target areas, international liaison services of some of the associations consulted when the recruitment program was constructed, and contact with foreign embassies in the United States or with United States embassies in foreign countries. The institution may develop outreach at different levels, to be approached separately or jointly. For example, a promotional visit at the presidential or faculty level may be sufficient of itself, or it may be followed up by visits of admissions officers who can complete the recruitment process.

Various group programs, or college recruitment tours, enable representatives of a number of different United States institutions to make school visits in selected countries. One such program is arranged by the European Council of International Schools. Although the primary target of such tours are United States-oriented schools, the student body at these institutions is international, and interested students from other institutions may take advantage of the visit, so that the opportunity is presented for the recruitment of foreign students.

Even if direct participation by institutional personnel is impossible, an institution still can maintain direct control over its recruitment activities by working through the international, binational, or foreign domestic organizations that offer educational advisory or counseling services to the student seeking to study outside the homeland. Many of these supplementary resources are well known among the community of admissions officers; and, as an institution gains its own experience abroad, it will develop its own list of reliable overseas contacts. Typical of such organizations are the information offices operated by the United States Information Agency across the world; the student advisory offices of the binational Fulbright Educational Commissions; the overseas offices of United States organizations such as the Institute of International Education and the American-Mideast Educational and Training Services; and the home country organizations—such as the Colombian Institute for Educational Credit and Technological Studies Abroad (ICETEX)—responsible for study abroad opportunities for their own students. In cooperating with these or similar organizations and agencies, the United States institution is accountable for reviewing any publicity to ensure the accuracy of what is said about it, and for retaining the authority to make the final admissions decision.

Contacts in foreign countries can be made through the use of independent profit-making recruiting agencies. However, such a step introduces a new element—namely, that of a business enterprise rather than an educational service—and thus requires special precautions on behalf of the institution. This is not to imply that the motivation of making a profit and that of providing an educational service are mutually exclusive. In fact, there is a very fine line between a nonprofit educational service and an educational service provided as a business venture, in that many of the organizations serving binational or international educational interests must charge a fee to cover the expenses involved. The basic question, and one that the United States college or university is responsible for determining, is that of ethics—of honesty in responding to the student's needs and in maintaining the institution's educational standards. The situation is further complicated by the fact that it is almost impossible to control the practices of an agency or individual prepared to go to any lengths in order to "make a sale." Consider, for example, agencies that place advertisements stating: "Guaranteed admission into all fields of study" or "Regardless of your academic qualifications or career goals, you can study in a U.S. University, College, Trade, or English Language School approved by U.S. Gov't" or "Guaranteed admission for all ages and levels of study and training in all parts of the U.S.A." Clearly, the college or university that engages even indirectly in such activity is doing a disservice to itself and, by implication, aiding in misleading some foreign student who seeks an educational program in the United States. Other advertisements—for example, one that reads "An Admissions Officer with full authority to grant an acceptance into 12 accredited U.S.A. universities and colleges will be in Manila"—may even further implicate a United States college or university that has surrendered its admissions responsibility to a third party.

These admittedly extreme examples demonstrate the risks taken by a United States college or university when it moves into the field of third-party recruitment. Even an agency with a base of operations in the United States still may use, as part of its recruitment activities in foreign countries, promotional procedures that would be unacceptable in the United States. Because of the difficulties inherent in a relationship established with a recruiting agency, an institution new to the field of international educational interchange should take the following precautions:

1. Before formalizing the relationship, the institution—with the assistance of the Foreign Student Recruitment Information Clearinghouse—should conduct a thorough review of the agency's activities. This service is operated on behalf of the National Liaison Committee on Foreign Student Admissions by the National Association for Foreign Student Affairs, 1860 19th Street NW, Washington, D.C. 20009.

2. The institution should never sign a contract with a third-party recruiting agency without ensuring that there is an appropriate escape clause to permit withdrawal if arrangements do not work out satisfactorily. While some commission or fee payment by the institution may be established in the contract, the institution should be aware of fees that the recruiting agency may be charging the prospective student for the same service.

3. The institution should ask for a full statement of the services offered and the fees requested by the recruiting agency. Here again, the Foreign Student Recruitment Information Clearinghouse may be able to help in obtaining the information.

4. The institution should ask for the names of other clients of the agency and should check with them to be sure that they really are clients and that they are satisfied with services provided.

5. The institution can make inquiries to the United States embassy or the appropriate authority within the foreign country (for example, the ministry of education), to ascertain whether the activities of the recruiting agency are known and considered acceptable.

6. In every case, if an institution decides to use the third-party recruiting agency, it must insist that it will review and approve all statements about the institution and that it will retain the final and absolute authority for the admissions decision.

Having taken all the necessary precautions, the institution that is seeking for the first time to make contacts with the educational community in foreign countries to recruit foreign students may find that the local knowledge and expertise of a reputable recruitment agency will be most valuable.

Avoiding Errors and Maintaining Standards

The increasing dismay and concern of the United States educational community over the growing incidence of malpractice in foreign student recruitment led, in 1980, to the organization of the Wingspread colloquium on foreign student recruitment. The thirty-nine participants in the colloquium included college and university presidents, deans, admissions officers and foreign student advisers, overseas counselors, members of the educational media, and representatives of consortia, professional associations, and government agencies with interest in international education. At the close of their deliberations, the participants unanimously approved the following statement (Jenkins, 1980a, pp. 56-57):

We believe it important to identify those abuses in the recruitment of foreign students which are of common concern. We consider them detrimental to the welfare of foreign students and to the reputation of higher education in the United States.
1. The use of placement agencies that charge institutions a per capita fee.
2. The recruitment of foreign students without prior consideration of and commitment to providing necessary campus services.
3. Failure to represent the institution properly in advertising, publications, informative materials, and personal interviews.

4. The use of inadequately trained foreign admissions officers.

5. The improper delegation of admissions authority.

6. The misuse of immigration forms with regard to a student's academic qualifications, English language proficiency, and financial resources.

7. The practice of granting admissions to English language programs to foreign students who are college bound, without regard to their academic qualifications.

8. The practice of granting foreign students admission to English language programs that do not qualify as full-time intensive programs and are therefore not in compliance with Immigration and Naturalization Service regulations.

9. The practice of promising and/or implying that admission to intensive English language programs constitutes admission to an academic degree program.

Criteria for Ethical Recruitment

To eliminate the abuses cited, institutions that recruit foreign students should:

1. Provide enough candid and pertinent information that a foreign student unfamiliar with United States practices in higher education may make informed academic judgments.

2. Avoid contractual arrangements with agents who require fee-for-enrollment payments.

3. Develop an admissions policy for foreign students which requires that admissions judgments be made by institutional personnel who rule on other admissions, is based on a system of written criteria, and is applied in competition with other applicants.

4. Seek a match between the needs and aspirations of the prospective student and the educational opportunities the institution affords.

5. Accept the commitment to provide effective educational opportunity for foreign students and establish appropriate institutional policies governing foreign student recruitment, admissions, support activities, specialized programs, and curricula.

6. Provide realistic estimates of costs for tuition, educational expenses, subsistence, and related fees and of the extent to which financial aid or scholarships are available to foreign students.

7. Restrict evaluation of foreign academic records to personnel who are trained and competent in interpretation of foreign educational records.

8. State clearly to students admitted to English language programs the extent of commitment made for their further education in the United States.

Describing recruitment as part of the process of directing foreign students to the appropriate United States institution and noting that "students—and the opportunity to study—are far too valuable to be dealt with in a haphazard or irresponsible manner" (p. 58), the colloquium recommended that a clearinghouse for information on foreign student recruitment be established. In October 1981 the Foreign Student Recruitment Information Clearinghouse was created with funds made available by the United States Information Agency.

6

Admissions:
Developing Effective
Selection Practices

William S. Patrick

The admission of foreign students to institutions in the major host countries will reflect the policies and procedures of their respective educational systems. In the United States, with its pattern of relative autonomy among the over three thousand institutions of postsecondary education, the foreign student admissions officer must deal directly with a very diverse collection of applications from across the world. Some will provide recognizable evidence of academic qualifications; others include credentials that are much more obscure and hard to evaluate; and many will indicate an obvious inadequacy for admission to any college or university, either abroad or in the applicant's home country. All of them are part of the transnational movement of students and scholars, which continues to grow and move further into the mainstream of educational development.

The dimensions of the situation may be observed from a brief comparison of the statistics on foreign students in the

United States in the years 1955-56 and 1980-81, as noted in
the Institute of International Education's annual census, *Open
Doors*. In 1955-56 there were 36,494 foreign students from
132 nations and political areas; data from 1980-81 show a foreign student population of 311,882 from 184 different countries and territories. The significance of the change is illumi-
nated by the listing of countries in the continent of Africa,
which shows not only an increase from thirty to fifty-five countries of origin but also some revealing changes in nomenclature
as names like Gold Coast, Belgian Congo, and Northern Rho-
desia are replaced by Ghana, Zaire, and Zambia. Of equal importance is the fact that the number of institutions reporting
foreign students on campus grew during this same period from
1,630 to 2,734. Included in this latter figure are a significant
number of junior and community colleges, where, in 1980-81,
54,220 foreign students, or 17.4 percent of the total foreign
student population, were enrolled.

In the face of a rising demand and guided by institutional
policies, admissions officers will be determining the distribution
of foreign students in United States colleges and universities. In
so doing they will be called on to make decisions affecting the
personal plans of each individual applicant. The goal of the admissions process was defined in the 1970 edition of the NAFSA
guideline on responsibilities and standards: "to assure, insofar as
possible, that foreign students are selected intelligently, placed
appropriately, and provided with the bases for potential success" (National Association for Foreign Student Affairs, 1970,
p. 6).

Application and admission, the basis of any agreement
between the student and the institution, assume a special significance in international educational interchange, when the variables are numerous, the risks relatively high, and the contract
calls for such a massive investment of individual resources and a
corresponding commitment on the part of the institution. Admissions policies are a reflection of the goals and purposes that
each institution, from the junior college to the graduate school,
sees as its distinguishing features. They determine the character
of the student body and protect, preserve, and enhance the in-

stitutional identity. It is in this context that the admission of foreign students and scholars may be seen in its proper perspective. On the one hand, there is a necessary selectivity, which must take into account the student's academic status and educational requirements and the relationship of these factors to institutional standards and resources. On the other, there is the opportunity for widening the "universe" of the campus community to encompass students and scholars who are the product of a variety of educational systems and cultures and the prospective managers, consumers, and suppliers in a global economy in which the United States, like any other host country, has a vital national interest. To achieve the full potential of international educational interchange and provide a defensible rationale for the presence on campus of foreign scholars and especially of foreign students, institutions must make basic decisions concerning admissions. What kinds of foreign students will be accepted? How many? Will the emphasis be on graduate or undergraduate status? Will the institution's educational programs be internationalized? For institutions that are actively seeking foreign students, the time has come to take a more positive role, moving from a haphazard reaction to applications received to a deliberate encouragement of applications from specific countries and in particular fields of study. For foreign students or scholars and their sponsors, such a clear indication of the institutional interests will provide a welcome guide in the process of identifying the college or university to which they should direct their application for admission.

Admissions Personnel and Procedures

There is substantial variation among institutions in the operation of foreign student admissions procedures. Some institutions make use of a committee on foreign student admissions; others assign the task to a member of the admissions staff or to the foreign student adviser's office. Those with a great many applications may appoint a special foreign admissions officer; those with only a few may use a foreign admissions consultant. In some state systems, a centralized foreign admissions office will deal with applications to the campuses within the system. The most recent development has been the establishment of an admissions referral service—as, for example, that operated by the Ohio College Association for the seventy-two public and private colleges and universities constituting its membership. In addition, it is becoming an increasingly common practice to involve in the admissions process not only the admissions officer and the admissions committee but also the foreign student adviser, the teacher of English as a second language, the registrar, and the financial aid officer.

Although the process of dealing with foreign student applications, from initial inquiry to final admission, will vary from institution to institution, the basic elements remain the same. The model shown in Figure 1 is adapted from one presented in 1981 at a beginners' workshop on international admissions, sponsored by the American Association of Collegiate Registrars and Admissions Officers (AACRAO). It illustrates the more sophisticated processes that may exist in institutions with a long history of foreign student enrollment, which are to a large extent built on this elementary plan and may be outlined in the following six stages:

1. *Initial inquiry* and positive or negative response—the latter because of an obvious failure to meet minimum standards or because requested programs are not available.
2. *Further exchange of information*—the dispatch and return of preapplication form (which will be accompanied by additional facts about the institution). This provides another checkpoint at which the admissions process may be terminated without either side's becoming involved in the burdensome process of formal application.
3. Continuing interest on both sides leads to provision of *application*—with which some institutions may send supplementary letters defining academic requirements in relation to educational systems in different countries and areas (country form letters).
4. When application form and fee, plus all necessary supporting documents, are available, the institution will make an

Figure 1. General Model of Foreign Student Application:
Flow Chart.

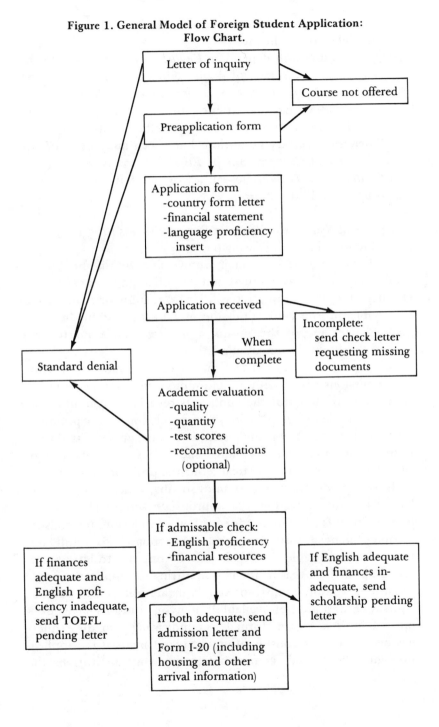

evaluation of educational credentials and determine the admissibility of applicant.

5. Admissibility will depend on *English proficiency* and *financial resources*; in case of doubt, admission may be offered conditional on further documentation of English proficiency (which may be attained through special study in the United States) and/or availability of scholarship funds.

6. When all necessary conditions have been met, *letter of admission* and *Certification of Eligibility for Nonimmigrant Student Status* will be sent, together with housing and other arrival information.

The principles and procedures of this admissions process are further examined in the following pages.

Initial Inquiries. A major university within the United States may receive as many as 20,000 initial inquiries each year. Of these less than a quarter will be from students who have a reasonable prospect of admission and thus merit further correspondence; and of this group, again less than a quarter will eventually receive letters of admission.

Coping with this avalanche of correspondence presents the admissions office with an enormous administrative and human problem. Some of the applicants reveal an apparent inadequacy in academic preparation, some seek courses or programs that are not available at the institution, some are confused both in information and inquiry, and some confess to a total lack of financial resources. In practical terms the problem may be dealt with by a predetermined system of sorting, which will place the letters in three categories for appropriate action: (1) a simple letter of regret; (2) requests for further information, referrals regarding financial assistance; and (3) responses to candidates most clearly suitable for admission. To respond to letters that reveal an obvious reason for not admitting the applicant (either because minimum admissions standards are not met or because courses desired are not available), many institutions have developed a short aerogram form letter indicating that the request has been given due consideration but regretting that the application must be denied. Unfortunately, in many institutions the admissions office does not have the resources to respond personally to every letter and must therefore deal with only the most promising prospects.

Even where careful and efficient management may solve the administrative problem of dealing with these letters, there remains the need to respond to the global human problem that they reflect. By the most rudimentary and conservative calculations, there must be hundreds of thousands of young people who make some unsuccessful attempt to find an opportunity to study outside their homelands. Among these seekers of knowledge who have demonstrated at least an unusual determination, there must be many who have the potential for further training and education but who at this time are not discovered or recognized and thus become a neglected human resource. Providing what at best can be only a pro forma response to their initiative must be seen as a temporary expedient in a situation that calls for a permanent solution.

Imaginative planning, more cooperative binational or international financial aid programs, more communication between the foreign university admissions office and national agencies that could provide educational credit or practical training in the homeland, and the use of computers for appropriate referrals—these are some of the ways by which these young people could be given encouragement and directed to the most suitable educational or training resource. Eventually the international educational community will have to develop a comprehensive educational plan to meet this need—perhaps by assigning the responsibility to a multinational task force or international agency.

Information and Application. If the initial inquiry provides the basis for further action, the channels for the subsequent exchange of information must be designed to ensure that both the foreign applicant and the institution are provided with all the relevant facts as expeditiously as possible. The sequence should be planned to ensure that either party can make appropriate decisions without necessarily completing the full admissions process with its burden of fees and the submission and verification of all the documents involved. For this reason many institutions have prepared a *preapplication form* designed to elicit the basic educational and personal data about the applicant before initiating the full application procedure. (Institutions that have not developed their own preapplication form may use the standard Preliminary Application Form available from the Institute of International Education.) Complementing this need to ascertain essential data is the need to provide applicants with adequate information about the institution, so that they, too, may decide whether they wish to proceed with the admissions process.

In developing this transnational information outreach, most United States colleges and universities are reluctant to engage in an indiscriminate mailing of catalogues abroad, both because of cost and labor and because the catalogues are designed primarily for United States students. To overcome these problems, institutions may provide airmail pamphlets designed specifically for use in foreign countries. These documents will contain the following essential general information:

- Description of institution and its environment.
- Requirements for admission of foreign students.
- Programs of study, degrees offered.
- Academic calendar.
- Statement of all expenses—tuition fees, cost of room and board (for the full twelve months), books, supplies, and incidentals.
- Information on housing facilities.
- Visa and other legal regulations.
- Employment regulations and opportunities.
- Available special foreign student services.

For those students who may wish to follow through with a formal request for admission, there will also be information on application procedures and the amount of time required for processing, deadlines for submitting applications, testing requirements, English language proficiency requirements, financial requirements, and a preliminary or regular application form. Some institutions prefer to combine the preliminary or preapplication form with a fairly brief information sheet and then send out the complete set of application materials subsequent to a review of the preliminary application. Others send out a more comprehensive pamphlet about the institution and enclose the regular application form and fee voucher, so that students who so desire can proceed immediately with the collection of required documents and submission of the complete application. The alternative options may be determined on the basis of relative costs (or perhaps the availability and use of advisory services in the applicant's home country), but in any case the prime consideration is the avoidance of unnecessary time and trouble on the part of the student in submitting, or the institution in reviewing, an application that is patently inappropriate. With the relevant facts available, the foreign student is in a position to decide whether the institution will meet his or her particular needs. If an application is then submitted, the transnational interchange between individual and institution moves to the next stage in the admissions process.

Although the facilities now available impose some severe restrictions in the initial contact between a prospective student in a foreign country and the institution in the host country, new developments in the field of telecommunications may soon enable institutions to project information almost instantaneously to any part of the world. The existing computerized Foreign Student Information Clearinghouse may be the forerunner of a new era in information sharing.

Evaluation of Educational Credentials. Once the application and all the necessary supporting documents have been received, the college or university must determine whether the applicant meets all the institutional requirements and that the educational goals are compatible with the institution's program of study. At this point the institution must recognize the significance of the word *foreign,* for two peculiarities about the enrollment of students from another country must condition the foreign student admissions process. The first is the fact of displacement. When admitted, the student will have to leave his or her home country and, in addition to tuition fees, make a considerable investment, both financial and emotional, in order to travel and relocate in a foreign country; once implemented, therefore, the admissions decision, although not irreversible, involves special problems if an error has been made. The second is the fact of transition between two entirely different educational systems and the need to find the appropriate level for the student to move from one system to the other. Since only institutions in the United States accept credits from foreign institutions, the consequent question of placement is a unique function of the admissions officers in colleges and universities in this country.

In any case, in the primary determination of admissibility of a foreign student, all the supporting documents—the transcripts, certificates of prior schooling, and letters of recommendation—must be construed in the context of a different educational system and a different cultural perspective. The evaluation of educational credentials is in essence a matter of interpretation. It is a complex and sensitive procedure, some of the finer points of which are examined by Haas (1979) in his article "Undergraduate Transfer Credits from Abroad." Unfortunately, owing to the urgency of some individuals' desire to obtain admission to a foreign university, the problem is further complicated by the use of forgeries in which credits may be added or names changed. In their pamphlet *Forged Educational Credentials—A Sorry Tale* Fisher and Dey (1979) provide tips on how to recognize forgeries and sources of verification of documents that seem suspicious.

One important point must be noted about the transfer of credits from one educational system to another. Foreign students will often find that in the process they have lost ground in their academic progress. This is inevitable because, while academic credits can be transferred, academic programs in different countries are not identical; thus, the academic achievement must be adjusted to the particular program requirements of the receiving institution.

As in any interpretive task, the necessary tools are the reference sources. For the admissions officer in the United States college or university, the first task is to acquire the primary resource materials and make contact with centers of continuing study in the field of credentials evaluation. Fortunately, a great deal of work has already been done in this field, and information is constantly being brought up-to-date by experts familiar with educational developments in different countries across the world. In the April 1981 issue of the *World Higher Education Communiqué,* the Institute of International Education (IIE) provided a bibliography and a list of sources for further information, which have been summarized in a special reprint entitled *Evaluating Foreign Students' Credentials* (Institute of International Education, 1981a). The Admissions Section of NAFSA also publishes a bibliography, *Foreign Student Admissions, Credentials Bibliography* (National Association for Foreign Student Affairs, 1979a), which offers much but not all of the same information in a different format, with some additional material. A recent addition to the list is the third edition of the AACRAO/AID publication *Bibliography of Reference Materials for Evaluating Foreign Student Credentials* (American Association of Collegiate Registrars and Admissions Officers, 1982). The two principal agencies for the dissemination of new and revised information needed to evaluate foreign education credentials are the American Association of Collegiate Registrars and Admissions Officers (AACRAO), with its continuing distribution of timely analyses of foreign educational systems in the World Education Series, and the National Association for Foreign Student Affairs (NAFSA), with its publications and emphasis on professional development opportunities for international admissions personnel. Together, AACRAO and NAFSA sponsor overseas workshops on the admission and academic placement of students from different countries. Reports produced by the workshop participants contain recommendations for placement of students from countries covered by the workshop.

In its entirety the current information on the evaluation of educational credentials requires not only a bookshelf but a sizable library. It continues to grow each year as educational systems change or are reorganized and new resources are discovered or developed. It is, therefore, not rational to attempt in any way to encapsulate the requisite knowledge in a few pages of general comments. For the newcomer the *Do-It-Yourself Evaluation of Foreign Student Credentials* (American Association of Collegiate Registrars and Admissions Officers, 1966) remains an excellent introduction for the acquisition of the necessary skills in credentials evaluation. Further assistance can be obtained in the guideline on *Selection and Admission of Foreign Students* (National Association for Foreign Student Affairs, 1978), which lists (pp. 22-23) the following as the *general* principles or factors to be considered in the evaluation of a prospective foreign student's academic background:

1. The country's educational system.
2. The type (academic, technical, and teacher training) of secondary and/or postsecondary school the applicant has attended. (If reliable information about the applicant's particular school(s) is available, that, too, should be taken into consideration.)
3. The meaning of the applicant's records, marks, certificates, or degrees in his or her own country.
4. The applicant's academic potential as judged by achievement in the home country's educational system. (For example, would the applicant be eligible to enter the appropriate level for such training in the home country, assuming space, political conditions, and the like, would allow?)

With these factors in mind, the guideline suggests that the following questions may be helpful in the development of criteria for evaluating an applicant's potential for a successful educational experience:

1. Does the institution offer a program suitable to the applicant's educational objectives; if not, can such a program be developed, arranged, or suggested elsewhere?
2. Does the applicant appear to have the necessary qualifications for the field being requested? (Here one should consider equivalent diplomas, degrees, and certificates, as well as course work and perhaps work experience that would give the applicant appropriate background.)

3. Is the applicant sufficiently proficient in the English language to pursue proposed academic objectives in competition with United States students in the field? Will the student be able to communicate effectively both in and out of class? Has the English ability been adequately confirmed through secure tests? If deficiencies are evident, can the institution either provide the student with the necessary training or arrange for intensive English language training at a special institute?

The process of evaluation is illustrated in the Credential Analysts Worksheet, which is used by the Academic Advisory Services of the Office of International Training, Agency for International Development, Washington, D.C. (see Exhibit 1).

In the final analysis, however, the evaluation of foreign educational credentials is much more than a matter of documentation. Perhaps one of the most useful single pieces of advice is that which appears in the *Do-It-Yourself Evaluation of Foreign Student Credentials*: "It is tremendously important to be aware of your applicant as a whole person—a personality of known age, interests, ambitions, traits, and background" (American Association of Collegiate Registrars and Admissions Officers, 1966, p. 6).

Admissibility: English Language Proficiency. Next to the academic capability and level of scholarship of foreign student applicants, the most important consideration is their proficiency in the use of the English language. The guideline on *English Language Proficiency* (National Association for Foreign Student Affairs, 1977), in its general orientation to problems related to English as a second language (ESL) in colleges and universities, describes the required proficiency: "Foreign students studying in colleges and universities in the United States need not only oral communication skills for daily activities but also highly developed listening, speaking, reading, and writing skills for academic purposes" (p. 1). The guideline also notes that "proficiency in using the kind of English encountered in the college classroom is vital to students if they are to be successful in reaching their academic goals" (p. 1).

Exhibit 1. Credential Analysts Worksheet.

1
CREDENTIAL ANALYSTS WORKSHEET (CAW)

This report is furnished by the Academic Advisory Services, Office of International Training, AID, Washington, D.C. It has been prepared with the assistance of AACRAO-AID professional credential analysts. **See previous page for explanations and interpretations.**

A.				
GENERAL	Mr. ☐ 1. Name Miss ☐ _____ Mrs. ☐ Last (caps) First Middle		2. ( ) Age Mo. Day Year Birthdate	
	3. Country 4. Participant Number 5. PIO/P Number			
	6. Desired Starting Date	7. Degree Objective Bachelor ☐ Other ☐ (specify) Master ☐ Doctor ☐	8. Major	9. Specialization

	10. Academic Credentials c. Missing credentials (if any):
	   a. Complete_____☐
	   b. Incomplete, but sufficient
	      to proceed _____☐			

B.		
SECONDARY EDUCATION	11. Name of Secondary School (if known):	13a. Number of years of elementary and secondary education which are standard in the country where participant received education ____

	12. Type of Secondary School d. Other ☐
	   a. General_____☐ (specify)
	   b. Vocational-Tech. ____☐
	   c. Teacher Training ____☐
		13b. Number of years of elementary and secondary education which are standard in the country where participant received postsecondary education ____

	14. Name of Certificate or Diploma Earned (if known): ☐ Documented ☐ From Bio Data (not documented)	15. Date Awarded_____ Month Day Year

C.					No. of Years	
POSTSECONDARY EDUCATION	16. Postsecondary Institution(s), Dates of Attendance, and Country Where Located	Certificate, Diploma, or Degree	Major	Date Awarded	Actual	Standard
	a.					
	b.					
	c.					
	d.					
	17. Highest Degree, Title, Diploma, or Certificate Awarded (in indigenous terms):					

AACRAO-AID PROJECT. Revised April 1981.   (Continued on page 2)

Exhibit 1. (Continued)

2

D.	18. Listed below are (1) the academic credentials on which this report is based, (2) the grade averages, verbal ratings, rank in class, or other indices of quality, and (3) grading scales, if available, given in indigenous terms.	

QUALITY OF CREDENTIALS

CREDENTIALS	QUALITY RATINGS	GRADING SCALE DESCRIPTIONS

19. Number of Years Since Last Enrolled for Formal Study____	23. General Comments

E.	20. Appropriateness of Previous Course Content for Proposed Program of Studies in U.S. a. Appropriate _____ ☐ b. Somewhat appropriate _____ ☐ c. Inappropriate _____ ☐
	21. Quality of Participant's Academic Record as Viewed in Country Where Participant Received Education a. Superior _____ ☐ b. Above average_____ ☐ c. Average _____ ☐ d. Inadequate _____ ☐
ANALYSIS	22. Recommended Level to Begin Study in U.S. a. Preuniversity _____ ☐ b. Undergraduate-First Year_____ ☐ c. Undergraduate-Second Year___ ☐ d. Undergraduate-Third Year_____ ☐ e. Undergraduate-Fourth Year____ ☐ f. Master's with deficiencies _____ ☐ g. Master's without deficiencies __ ☐ h. Doctor's _____ ☐ i. Not qualified _____ ☐ j. Undergraduate level, nondegree _____ ☐ k. Graduate level, nondegree ____ ☐

Date_____ 19_____
Month   Day   Year

In considering the admission of foreign students, therefore, the institution must quickly determine its policy regarding applicants who may not have the necessary language proficiency. There are three options. The first is to refuse to admit these students. The second is to offer conditional admission to the student reaching the necessary level through attendance at an intensive English institute. This choice would be used by an institution that does not have its own intensive English institute; it gives the student some assurance that if he or she does pay for the necessary English courses, the investment will not have been made in vain. The third option is to admit the student to the institution for a program that includes preliminary intensive English courses. There are a number of crucial economic and academic questions relating to the feasibility of an institution's developing its own intensive program in English as a second language (ESL). Institutions wishing to explore this possibility may request the assistance of an ESL consultant from the National Association for Foreign Student Affairs. In any case, within the admissions process, there is clearly a need for some means of testing those students for whom English is not the native tongue, in order to determine their proficiency for academic purposes.

The most commonly used instrument for measuring proficiency is the Test of English as a Foreign Language (TOEFL), sponsored by the College Board (CEEB) and the Graduate Record Examination Board, which is offered by the Educational Testing Service in Princeton, N.J., and administered in practically every country in the world. Interpretation of the test scores will enable an institution to determine whether admission should be unconditional or subject to further improvement in English proficiency. Recognizing the common usage of TOEFL, the NAFSA guideline on *English Language Proficiency* (1977, p. 4) provides a general interpretation of the TOEFL scores:

Everyone using TOEFL should be familiar with the *Manual for TOEFL Score Recipients* [now *TOEFL Test and Score Manual*, 1981] available from Educational Testing Service. The guidelines given below are not intended to be rigid. For example, a student with a test score slightly below 450 may be admitted if a good semi-intensive program is available, there are

English support courses, and his other documents indicate that he would be a good risk.

Below 450   Admit only to an intensive English program. May give conditional admission.

450–500   Admit only if there is a semi-intensive program available. If none available, refer to a qualified intensive program.

500–550   Admit only if English support programs are available.

550 and above   Admit with no restrictions. EXCEPTIONS: Graduate students in fields which require near native proficiency—such as journalism, literature, library science, and business administration—should have TOEFL scores of 600 or above.

For schools wishing to grant conditional admissions, a TOEFL gain study done by the American Language Institute at San Francisco State University has indicated that a mean gain of about 41 points can be anticipated in an intensive course of 300 hours. This study is available through Educational Testing Service.

Despite the general acceptance of TOEFL, institutions are advised to use the test results as a guide rather than a determinant (it is not a pass-fail examination). To assure that there has been no misinterpretation of the English proficiency, many institutions require that all entering students take a placement test on arrival on campus. The NAFSA guideline lists a number of available tests for this purpose, should the institution not prefer to create its own test.

Admissibility: Financial Resources. Inadequate financial resources have long been recognized as a primary source of problems for the institution and the foreign student. Despite all evidence to the contrary, the illusion remains that funds from one source or another will become available in the United States, once the student has arrived in this country. In actual fact, scholarship funds, never very abundant, have greatly diminished in recent years. At the same time, the regulations regarding, and generally forbidding, foreign student employment have been interpreted much more strictly. For these reasons those who administer the regulations governing the entry and stay of foreign students in the United States—the United States consulate in foreign countries and the Immigration and Naturalization Service (INS) in this country—have become increasingly cautious in their assessment of the foreign student applicant's financial resources. Because the initial responsibility for determining the financial resources lies with the institution that admits the foreign student, the INS presumes that the institution has available, and can produce on demand, the statement of financial resources provided by the student applicant.

There is always an element of uncertainty in seeking to establish the precise financial status of a person or a family from a different country with its own national economy. With this in mind, the National Association for Foreign Student Affairs created a model statement—Verification of Finances of Foreign Applicants and Financial Certificate—to be completed by foreign students seeking admission to a United States college and university. On one side the document displays the particulars of the applicant's plans for education in the United States; type of visa; whether single or accompanied by family— if so, number of dependents; and the length of proposed study program in the United States. It also indicates the various items of expense that must be anticipated, in addition to tuition fees, for the academic year plus the extra maintenance during the summer. The other side provides for the statement of assured support for the first year (noting the amount the students will have with them on arrival) and for the projected support during subsequent years of study. The form requires the certification of a bank official and, if scholarship funds are involved, of the sponsoring agency. This form, which was adapted in part from the Declaration and Certification of Finances of the College Scholarship Service of the College Entrance Examination Board, was prepared by NAFSA so that it could be copied by institutions for their own use—including the appropriate figures for fees and living expenses at that institution. The form specifically warns the applicant that as a general rule sources of support may not include employment. The current document most widely used is the Foreign Student's Financial Aid Application and Declaration, with accompanying guidelines, available from the College Scholarship Service of the College Board.

Whatever the method used by the institution to verify the financial resources of the applicant, the information requested must be quite specific. In completing the Certificate of Eligibility for Nonimmigrant Student Status (Form I-20), the institution must certify the following:

This school estimates the student's average monthly costs to be the following:

Tuition and fees	$——	
Living expenses	$——	
Expenses of dependent(s)	$——	
Other (specify)	$——	TOTAL $——

This school has information showing the following as the student's means of support, estimated on a monthly basis:

Personal funds of student	$——	
Family funds from abroad	$——	
Funds from this school (Specify type)	$——	
Funds from another source (Specify type/source)	$——	
On-campus employment, if applicable	$——	TOTAL $——

In reviewing this certificate when providing the student with the necessary visa for travel to the United States, the United States consul in the home country will certainly request assurance that the financial report is accurate and that the student does indeed have access to the funds required for study in the United States. When the student arrives in this country, there will be a second review by the Immigration and Naturalization Service officer at the port of entry.

Admission. Once the admissions decision is made, it must be transmitted to the foreign student. This final process also has its own imperatives. Because of the uncertainties of communication, it is essential that all the necessary documents—including the forms for application for a student or exchange visitor visa, and the information and instructions regarding date of arrival, registration, housing, and the like—be assembled by one source within the institution and sent to the student in one package, together with a covering letter listing the contents. Only in this way can confusion be avoided and the student feel confident that all the required documentation is in his possession. On receipt of this package, the foreign student will apply to the United States consulate for a visa to enter the United States and, subsequently, be admitted by the Immigration and Naturalization officer at the port of entry.

Data Collection

Statistics are used more and more as a basis for institutional and national policy and presumably, when they are available in sufficient detail at that level, will also influence international policies in educational interchange. For this reason the development of uniform methods of data collection, both within and among institutions, has become imperative.

In the United States, the prime mover on the national level in obtaining and providing information about foreign students has been the Institute of International Education (IIE), which prepares *Open Doors,* the annual census of foreign students in the United States and overview of study abroad programs sponsored by United States institutions. The institutional and individual data forms distributed by the IIE to every institution listed in the *Education Directory: Colleges and Universities* display in detail the different kinds of information currently being sought. The data provide information required by national organizations and associations and government agencies. They also meet the needs of scholarly research, public information, employment, and such institution-oriented activities as follow-up studies and alumni activities.

Admissions officers and registrars have a central role in institutional data collection. The Interassociational Committee on Data Collection (1982, p. 1)—composed of representatives of the National Association for Foreign Student Affairs, the Institute of International Education, and the American Association of Collegiate Registrars and Admissions Officers—summarizes the need for accurate and uniform data and defines the basic data elements as follows:

Accurate data on an institution's foreign student population are required by many administrators on college campus.

Admissions officers need data about currently enrolled students for regular bookkeeping, and to predict success and establish standards for future admissions.

Institutional researchers furnish data used in setting overall enrollment figures to institutional administrators.

Foreign student advisers must develop appropriate student support services, act as liaison between foreign students and the Immigration and Naturalization Service and other federal agencies, the community, and the local media.

Registrars require supplemental data for institutional planning, including curricula and housing.

Data element groupings should include:

Personal data
Immigration information
Admissions information
Language proficiency information
Financial information
Academic information
Follow-up information

As colleges and universities seek to define their proper role in international educational interchange and to determine appropriate admissions policies, the acquisition of accurate and comprehensive data on foreign students is being added to the computer programming by which institutions maintain the necessary information about their operation and activities.

The Foreign Student Admissions Community

As in any other field of specialization, the whole question of the admission of foreign students and the evaluation of foreign educational credentials has created its own community of experts and its own network of information exchange. The concerns and interests of these admissions specialists are now appearing on the agenda of a widening circle of organizations. For example, the College Entrance Examination Board includes the discussion of international admissions in its various regional meetings and summer institutes. The two national associations most involved, the American Association of Collegiate Registrars and Admissions Officers (AACRAO) and the National Association for Foreign Student Affairs (NAFSA), have been particularly active in establishing standards in their respective fields of activity. Both associations, in addition to providing essential resource materials, offer three other vital services to those responsible for foreign student admissions. They bring together in conferences, workshops, and study groups the hundreds of admissions officers across the country who are dealing on a daily basis with the full range of applications from foreign countries; they present a forum for the interinstitutional discussion of persistent problems and the confrontation of unanticipated crises; and they offer that irreplaceable benefit both to the novice and the experienced practitioner, a readily available channel of communication for advice and assistance in case of need. Membership in these two associations and the opportunity to participate in the conferences, workshops, and other professional development opportunities which they provide should be considered as part of the operational expenses of the institution's foreign student admissions activity.

The cooperative quest for sophistication and enlightenment has been further developed in the United States by the efforts of various interassociational entities. For instance, the National Council on the Evaluation of Foreign Educational Credentials reviews and approves the various placement recommendations for student applicants from foreign countries. The National Liaison Committee on Foreign Student Admissions (NLC) —including, in addition to AACRAO and NAFSA, the College Board, the Council of Graduate Schools, and the Institute of International Education—provides a recognized and respected national sponsorship for a number of activities related to foreign student admissions at the national and international level. Two of these activities are operated for the NLC by the College Board. They are the Overseas Consultations and Workshops, a program designed to provide up-to-date information on higher education in the United States to those responsible for advising and counseling prospective foreign students in their home countries; and the Foreign Student Information Clearinghouse, the computerized service that provides information on United States colleges and universities in response to foreign students' needs. Two are operated for the NLC by NAFSA. These are the National Credentials Evaluation Project, which mobilizes the resources of expert foreign admissions officers in a program designed to provide credentials evaluation advice to those institutions enrolling seventy-five or fewer foreign students and which do not have their own foreign admissions specialists; and the Foreign Student Recruitment Information Clearinghouse, which is described in Chapter Five. All these activities are supported by the United States Information Agency. The increasing mutual recognition of degrees awarded in different countries suggests that the coordination among the community of admissions officers and credentials evaluators will become increasingly transnational. Although there must be differences as admissions officers in Great Britain, France, or Germany evaluate the educational preparation of a foreign student against the standards and requirements of their own educational systems, mutual interests and common problems certainly justify a continuing international examination of the way foreign students and scholars are admitted to institutions outside their homelands.

Other Sources of Assistance

In the foreign students' home countries, a number of agencies and organizations may serve as intermediaries in the collection of credentials and the assessment of financial resources and individual capability. As described elsewhere (Chapter Two), they offer counseling and information services to applicants, but they can also be called on to serve as the overseas informant and adviser for the admissions officer. These intermediaries include governmental agencies, such as the foreign missions of the United States Information Agency; the binational Fulbright Commissions; private agencies, such as the overseas offices of the Institute of International Education; area-oriented organizations, such as the American-Mideast Educational and

Training Services (Amideast); and, where they exist in the foreign students' home countries, organizations that are also engaged in international educational interchange, such as the Colombian Institute for Educational Credit and Technological Studies Abroad (ICETEX). Although there is no single list or directory of all the binational or national organizations that are engaged in international educational interchange, information about organizations in different countries may generally be obtained from the IIE, NAFSA, or the United States Information Agency. Another, more direct, approach would be a letter addressed to the cultural attaché at the United States embassy in the country concerned, marked for the attention of the student adviser. One new source of information would be the European Region of UNESCO. The United States, having signed the UNESCO Convention on the Recognition of Studies, Degrees, and Diplomas in the states of the European Region (which includes the United States and Canada), is now participating in the discussions of the Regional Commission, which should lead to an increasing flow of information among the countries in the region.

Institutions that have been engaged for some years in international educational interchange will also have their own contacts in foreign countries, either through interinstitutional relationships with foreign universities or through foreign alumni. Utilizing all these resources and exercising considerable foresight, the experienced admissions officer will quickly begin to develop his or her own list of international correspondents who can be called on to amplify, clarify, and verify the information received in the foreign student's application file.

Nearer to home there are also a variety of resources that may be mobilized to make a perceptive evaluation of foreign student applicants and their credentials. Some generic information may be obtained from the international organizations that have offices or their headquarters in the United States, such as UNESCO or the Organization of American States, or solicited from the foreign embassies in the United States. Specific assistance may also be obtained for a reasonable fee from a number of private evaluation services or, for the institution that is newly engaged in foreign student education, from the National Credentials Evaluation Project, already mentioned, which is offered without charge by the National Association for Foreign Student Affairs. More particular and more detailed evaluation may be found on campus, among foreign students or scholars from the applicant's home country or from faculty members who have been students and/or teachers in that country.

The admissions office itself, however, should contain a library of reference and resource materials that will enable the admissions officer to begin to assemble the information on which evaluative decisions may be made. The library's primary resources should be augmented by the individual acquisitions of the concerned and inquisitive professional (including the record of admissions decisions made on students from different countries and institutions and the follow-up information regarding their subsequent progress or problems).

Transfers

Mobility between colleges and universities during the course of study is more prevalent among students in the United States than in other countries. Thus, admissions officers may frequently be faced with requests from foreign students who wish to transfer from another United States institution. If these students have an F-1 visa classification, they must obtain the authorization of a designated school official and report to the Immigration and Naturalization Service when making a transfer from one school to another. Although specific procedures may change from time to time—and new regulations proposed in 1982 are expected to be finalized in 1983—the essential requirements remain the same; namely, that the student was pursuing a full course of study at the school he was last authorized to attend and will pursue a full course of study at the school to which he intends to transfer. In general, such transfers are not permitted until the student has completed at least one full term at the institution named in the original request for a student visa. Also, many institutions may require a letter in which the foreign student adviser at the foreign student's initial institution gives pertinent information about the student and his situation at that particular college or university.

Apart from these special requirements that must be fulfilled by the foreign student seeking a transfer, the admissions process is very similar to that used with applications received directly from the home country. The receiving institution will wish to make its own evaluation of the student's credentials from the homeland and satisfy itself that the student is proficient in the English language and has sufficient financial resources. The institution will also require the official transcripts from the United States institution previously attended, indicating courses taken, examinations passed, and diplomas awarded, if any. With all this information in hand, the institution will then issue its own certificate of eligibility, which the student will require when requesting permission to transfer.

Some in-country requests for admission—for example, those received from students who have completed an intensive English course at another institution; those received from students who have completed a first or higher degree in the United States and wish to continue in a graduate program; or those received from students who wish to transfer from a junior or community college to a four-year institution, often in the same state educational system—are relatively simple and follow a logical progression. Other in-country applications may be more sensitive—for example, those received from students who wish to transfer because they cannot obtain the educational program they seek at the institution to which they were first admitted, or because they have not been successful in their studies at that institution, or because the particular "environment" at that institution is causing undue stress. Admissions officers may also be confronted by "walk-in" applications from students who came to the United States to review various options prior to making any specific request for admission. In such cases special attention must be given to the visa regulations, since students in this category frequently enter the country on a visitor's visa and must subsequently obtain permission to change to a student status. Such changes in visa status once a student has arrived in the United States are not readily granted and are carefully scrutinized by both the admissions officer and the Immigration and Naturalization Service.

In recent years a new problem has arisen because many of the increasing number of foreign students enrolled in elementary and secondary schools in the United States seek to continue their education at a postsecondary institution in this country (see National Association for Foreign Student Affairs and U.S. Department of Education, 1980). Because the admission of foreign students to a secondary school does not necessarily involve the same comprehensive evaluatory procedures that should be required for admission to a college or university, the admissions officer needs to exercise special caution in dealing with these applications. They may require an examination of records that combine previous education in the student's home country and the United States institution. The fact of attendance at a secondary school in this country does not, of itself, allow the assumption that the student is sufficiently proficient in the English language to cope with an academic program at the college level.

In summary, in-country applications for admission by foreign students may be more complicated than those received directly from the home country, although the task of evaluation is obviously simplified by the opportunity to determine the applicant's capabilities through personal interviews and academic examinations, if necessary.

Conclusion and Recommendations

In most host countries—that is, those in which a large proportion of the world's institutions of higher education are to be found—the admission of foreign students today is an extension of traditional admissions processes. Within the existing framework, adjustments have been made to accommodate the idiosyncrasies entailed in accepting students from foreign educational systems, and careful thought has been given to ensure an appropriate academic placement. Long-term studies are now being made of the relationship of admissions decisions to subsequent academic performance and the correlation of determinant factors to degrees of success and failure. While this evaluation of current procedures is both timely and necessary, a more fundamental question is whether adjustment of itself is sufficient or whether a new or revolutionary approach to the admission of foreign students and scholars is needed so that international education may become a more effective means of solving the vast and urgent problem of educating world citizens for their role in a global community.

Some glimpses of a new approach are now apparent: an application referral system among certain United States institutions, to ensure that foreign students are directed to the institution that most precisely meets their needs; the computerized information clearinghouse that provides guidance to foreign applicants in their home countries; the exploration of binational arrangements by which vacancies in one country's universities can be utilized to meet the needs of another country; and the agreements now being developed for the international recognition of degrees or certificates awarded. Other efforts might include:

- Finding ways to respond more positively, perhaps through a system of referrals to national organizations in the home country, to the thousands of student applicants who are ineligible for admission to a foreign university.
- Providing more immediate and effective channels of communication for information in the field of international educational interchange.
- Increasing on the international level interassociational cooperation and coordination in the evaluation of credentials and determination of equivalencies.

By working together in national or multinational task forces to examine their respective needs, resources, and practices, such groups could identify and eliminate many of the impediments to the free flow of international educational exchange. While not restricting the individual initiative that is an essential element in educational endeavor, these groups could create an organized approach to foreign student admissions on a global scale that is possible today and will be an absolute imperative in the years to come.

7

Alien Status:
Legal Issues and
Institutional Responsibilities

Alex Bedrosian

"The foreign student is a *foreign* student; this fact should be borne in mind." This clarification, at first sight redundant, is deliberately recorded in one of the earliest authoritative and comprehensive reviews of the significance of the rapidly increasing flow of foreign students to United States colleges and universities (Committee on the Foreign Student in American Colleges and Universities, [1963] 1979, p. 7). Although for many, and for most of the time, alien status is not obtrusive, it is nevertheless an important fact of life, requiring specific procedures and compliance with certain regulations. In times of national or international crises, or when unanticipated personal problems arise, the alien status of the foreign student or scholar assumes quite different and sometimes menacing proportions. Simple inconveniences become major difficulties, and the solution so easily accessible in the home country can be bewilderingly complicated. In the field of international educational interchange, the conditions in which they may enter and stay in a foreign country for educational purposes set the parameters for the transnational movement of students and scholars. These conditions are determined primarily by the concerns and requirements of the host country but to some extent also reflect the interests and needs of the home country.

Laws Governing Immigration and Educational Exchange

Over the years human migration from nation to nation has become progressively subject to the interests of the receiving country, as expressed in the laws governing immigration. The need for manpower, the desire to protect the employment opportunities of indigenous workers, the fear of cheap labor, and the concern for racial imbalance—all have served as governing factors in the historical development of national immigration legislation. Today the primary intent of all such legislation is to determine who may enter and remain in a country as part of its population growth and to specify the conditions in which the nonimmigrant alien may be admitted for specific purposes and a limited period.

Following the global pattern, the basis of immigration law in the United States has been, and remains today, the control of the number and kinds of persons admitted for permanent or temporary residence. The *Adviser's Manual of Federal Regulations Affecting Foreign Students and Scholars* (National Association for Foreign Student Affairs, 1982a, pp. 3-5) offers an excellent introduction to United States immigration law. Historically we see that while the United States has traditionally been viewed as a magnet attracting to its shores individuals looking for a better life for themselves and their families, in recent times a higher priority has been set on limiting population growth than on encouraging or facilitating the entry of more residents or workers. Thus, although in the early days all were welcomed, progressively restrictive policies were adopted in the 1880s to exclude some groups and later to limit the total number of persons who could come for permanent residence. The National Origins Quota System, a temporary quota law, limited the number of aliens of any nationality who could immigrate to 3 percent of the United States residents of that nationality living in the country in 1910 (United States Commission on Civil Rights, 1980, p. 9). Such policies contained discriminatory provisions favoring immigration from Northern and Western Europe and excluding all but a very small number of persons of Asian origin. In 1924 students were admitted according to a special immigrant classification, thus being exempted from those early limitations (sec. 4e, Immigration and Nationality Act, May 26, 1924). Classified as nonquota immigrants, they were admitted for a temporary period if they were at least fifteen years of age and accepted by an academic institution in the United States (8 *Code of Federal Regulations* 125, 1944). In 1965 the National Origins Quota System was abolished, and most of the discriminatory provisions of the law were eliminated.

The flow of aliens to the United States for permanent or temporary residence is currently regulated and controlled by the Immigration and Nationality Act (INA) of 1952 and its subsequent amendments. (Further revision of the act is currently under consideration, and new legislation may be enacted in the 98th Congress.) The act provides for the annual admission of a specified number of nonimmigrants to reside permanently and for an unspecified number of nonimmigrants to come temporarily for specific purposes and within specific limitations of those purposes. The act also drops the age requirement, classifies students as nonimmigrants (sec. 101(a)(15)(F), Immigration and Nationality Act, 1952), and removes all restrictions on the kinds of schools that can be approved for attendance by nonimmigrant students (Bernsen, 1981).

The Immigration and Nationality Act of 1952 is administered and enforced within the United States by the Immigration and Naturalization Service (INS) of the Department of Justice; outside the country it is administered by the Department of State through its various consular offices. In the United States, the Department of Labor is also involved because of the requirement that many immigrants and some nonimmigrants must obtain a labor certification to ensure that they will not deprive United States citizens or permanent residents of employment, and that their employment will not depress wages or adversely affect the working conditions of United States citizens. The daily operations of the three government departments involved in administering immigration law are governed by regulations promulgated by these departments and incorporated in the *Code of Federal Regulations.* All regulations must be consistent with the act and with the Constitution of the United States. Changes in these regulations reflect the national and foreign policy objectives and priorities of successive government administrations as well as the attitudes of lawmakers and the American public in response to national and international developments. (Information and advice about such changes are regularly provided to its members by the National Association for Foreign Student Affairs, either through the *Newsletter* or, when necessary, through special mailings.)

Since 1946, with the passage of Public Law 584 (the Fulbright Act), the United States government has encouraged educational exchange activities. In 1948 the Information and Exchange Act (known as the Smith-Mundt Act) provided the important authorization for the expenditure of United States currencies for this purpose. The various amendments to the legislation in succeeding years were brought together in the Mutual Educational and Cultural Exchange Act of 1961. While this act encompasses a wide variety of cultural and educational activities, it also provides further clarification of the status of foreign students or scholars in the United States, especially in regard to the conditions of their entry and stay in this country. In particular, the act defines the "exchange visitor status," whereby students, trainees, teachers, professors, research scholars, or international visitors are brought to the United States under the sponsorship of an agency or organization approved by the director of the Exchange Visitor Program of the United States Information Agency.

Foreign students or scholars first encounter United States immigration regulations when they apply for permission to enter the country for study or other educational pursuits. This is provided in the form of a visa, the stamp placed on a page of the passport. The two most common nonimmigrant student categories are the F visa classification (for the unsponsored student) and the Exchange Visitor or J classification (for those sponsored by the United States government, their home government, or another sponsoring agency). Other classifications include, for example, the members of families of diplomats serving in the United States, or scholars who have come for extended visits. Each is governed by different regulations and identified by an appropriate visa category, the one common factor being that they have come to this country for a temporary stay and not as permanent residents. A brief but very comprehensive description of the various immigration classifications and the relevant visa regulations is to be found in the *Faculty Member's Guide to U.S. Immigration Law* (Smith and Baron, 1980). Through a proposed rule of May 28, 1982 (which, it is anticipated, will be finalized, but possibly modified, in 1983), the Immigration and Naturalization Service is seeking to create a third nonimmigrant student category. The proposed M visa classification is to be used by students attending vocational or nonacademic institutions other than language-training programs. The proposed rule further narrows the F classification to pertain only to students attending "colleges, universities, seminaries, conservatories, academic high schools, elementary schools, and other academic institutions, and in language training programs." In addition, new immigrant classifications for students differentiate between the student (F-1, J-1, or M-1 visa category) and the student's spouse or child (F-2, J-2, or M-2 visa category).

The responsibility for determining that a person is qualified to apply for admission to the United States in a particular immigration classification is vested in the United States consular officer in the foreign country. For the prospective foreign student or scholar, this presents the initial substantial hurdle to be cleared in the journey to a college or university campus in the United States. In the first place, the unsponsored foreign student must be in possession of a Certificate of Eligibility for Student Status, Form I-20, issued to the prospective student by a school which has certified that to the best of its knowledge he is qualified academically, linguistically, and financially to attend the school and profit from instruction there. The sponsored student or scholar, too, must present a Certificate of Eligibility for Exchange Visitor Status, Form IAP-66, issued by the sponsoring agency.

In their attempts to secure visas to enter the United States for educational purposes, the prospective nonimmigrants, in addition to providing adequate evidence to substantiate their qualifications and acceptability, must also satisfy the consular officers that they have a residence abroad which they do not intend to abandon on completion of their studies. Of necessity, this determination is made on the basis of available evidence, political considerations, and subjective criteria of various kinds. In those countries where research shows that prospective student visa applicants are less likely to return, the consular official has a difficult task in determining whether the applicant is in fact planning to do so. Standards used in making these determinations appear to vary widely from one consular post to another; and, since decisions to deny visas are final and not subject to review, applicants have no recourse upon denial. As will be seen later in this chapter, the National Association for Foreign Student Affairs has included in a position paper submitted to the Select Commission on Immigration and Refugee Policy a number of suggestions for improving this situation.

Even when the foreign student or scholar has obtained the necessary visa, this only brings him to a United States port of entry, where he must then seek admission into the country. At this point the Immigration and Naturalization Service (INS) takes over the responsibility for the implementation of the regulations. Thus, the student or scholar must once again present all the evidentiary documents, and the immigration officer will determine whether in fact the applicant is qualified in all respects to be admitted into the United States. Two major concerns of the INS, both in the initial examination and in subsequent reviews, which consequently must be of equal concern to the foreign student or scholar, are (1) the opportunity for employment, which, in particular, the unsponsored student may need, or be tempted to undertake, in order to supplement limited financial resources; and (2) maintenance of status for the duration of stay in this country.

Regulations Governing Employment

Because unsponsored students account for the largest proportion of the foreign student population, the regulations governing this group are of primary concern to those working in the field of international educational interchange. While the sponsored students are subject to many of the same regulations, there are significant differences, especially with regard to employment. The assumption of the law is that, as a general rule, the student will not need to be employed and therefore will not be taking jobs away from United States workers or students. Permission to undertake employment is viewed, therefore, as an exception to the general policy. Briefly, such exceptions are:

1. Employment as a research or teaching assistant or in connection with a fellowship, such employment being considered as part of the student's educational program.
2. Other on-campus employment, if such employment will not interfere with the student's ability to carry a full program of study and will not displace a United States resident.
3. Temporary employment for practical training, generally granted on graduation and not to exceed twelve months duration for unsponsored students and eighteen months duration for sponsored students, if the employment is related to the student's course of study and/or future employment in his home country and if the student can demonstrate that comparable training offered in the United States is not available in the home country.
4. Employment necessitated by an unforeseen change in the student's financial circumstance, which arose *after* admission to the United States and which makes it necessary for him to work in order to help support himself. [For further details see Smith and Baron, 1980.]

The variations in government policy and in the consequent regulatory implementation are clearly illustrated in the history of the official attitude toward employment. Although, as noted above, there has never been a statutory provision for foreign student employment, benevolent administrators found that the silence of the statute was not necessarily an inhibition. Thus, in 1944 the regulations provided for employment on the basis of economic necessity, although not for practical training. Two kinds of employment based on economic necessity were provided for. The student who had some means but insufficient income to cover necessary expenses was allowed to accept employment to cover those expenses. The student without any means was permitted to work to meet necessary expenses. A few years later, the benevolent attitude toward foreign students reached a peak when the INS decided to authorize school officials to grant students *summer* employment permission annually, after first consulting the Department of Labor each year as to the potential impact on the labor market. In the early 1970s, however, the problem of unemployment, especially among the young, became a matter of domestic concern in the United States; and so, in 1974, the INS announced the discontinuance of the summer employment program. At this time, therefore, any foreign student seeking employment must make a direct application to the INS and must comply with the basic requirement that such employment is needed because unforeseen circumstances have diminished or eliminated the original sources of financial support. It should be noted that the proposed regulation changes would prohibit such employment for the F-1 student during the student's first year in the United States.

In general, the principle that foreign students may not seek employment also applies to the sponsored or Exchange Visitor student. However, in some instances the sponsor can grant permission for off-campus employment if an "urgent need" has arisen, and practical training for a period not to exceed eighteen months. Holders of the new M visa may not accept off-campus employment except when employment for practical training is authorized, the terms of which are uniquely defined by regulation.

Regulations Governing Status and Length of Stay

In principle, unsponsored foreign students may remain in the United States for the period required to fulfill their educational program—provided they continue to pursue a full course of study, as defined by the INS. The length of the program may be extended to include further study, such as that leading to an advanced degree, or authorized practical training. In all these circumstances, however, the student must first attend the school designated in the original Form I-20 used to gain admission to the United States; any subsequent school transfers require the authorization of a designated school official and must be reported to the Immigration and Naturalization Service. On completion of their studies, the students' status as nonimmigrant students is terminated. Unless they request and obtain a change in status, they are required to leave the country during the thirty days following completion of the full course of study. However, they may immediately seek readmission to the United States for the purpose of study—provided they can, once again, fulfill all the necessary conditions. This absence of any impediment to the readmission of unsponsored students (with F or M immigration classification) has been subject to question, and the new legislation may contain provisions requiring these students, on completion of their studies, to return to their home countries for a period of two years before being eligible for reentry into the United States. Such a change, if effected, may possibly dissuade some foreign students from seeking educational opportunities in this country.

Exchange Visitors or sponsored students must, by definition, have a sponsoring agency, which may, or may not, provide financial support. In determining the status of their students, such sponsoring agencies have considerable authority in such matters as the definition of a full program of study, whether students can change their fields of study, extend their stay, or transfer to another school or sponsorship. Sponsored students may not change their educational objective in the United States; they may not switch from one category of Exchange Visitor to another; and, if they wish to change to the less restricted category of an unsponsored student, they must go outside the United States, apply for a new visa, and (if they obtain the visa) reenter the country in the new status. On completion of their period of study or sponsored program in the United States, certain groups of Exchange Visitors or sponsored students are required to live in their home countries for a period of two years before they are eligible to apply for reentry into this country in some other status.

Holders of the new M visa, who are generally unsponsored, are admitted to the United States for the period of time necessary to complete their course of study (plus thirty days within which to depart) or for one year, whichever is less. School transfers generally are not permitted after the student has been in M-1 status for six months. In addition to these restrictions, M students are not permitted to change their educational objectives, nor are they permitted to change to an F-1 immigration classification.

The difference between the status of the foreign graduate student and the foreign scholar is sometimes difficult to define. As a general rule, it may be determined on the basis of enrollment and registration. Those nonimmigrant aliens who are not enrolled or registered in a formal academic program but are engaged in scholarly activity (such as teaching, conducting research, or gathering material for a book) at a university, college, research institute, or hospital are normally considered to be foreign scholars. The particular visa category and consequent status of the foreign scholar will depend on the proposed length of stay and the long-range plans of the individual concerned. The categories include the Visitor or Business visa (B-1 or B-2), for short-term programs; the Exchange Visitor visa (J-1), for those who may be in the country for a period up to three years and have definite plans to leave the United States at the end of their academic stay; and the Temporary Worker of Distinguished Merit or Ability visa (H-1) or the Trainee visa (H-3), for those whose initial visit may be for three years but who are considering remaining in the United States for an indefinite period beyond their initial plans.

As in employment, the regulations regarding status and the way in which they are implemented reflect the current concerns of the United States government, both in domestic and international affairs, and also the prevailing climate of public opinion. In 1976, for example, questions about the propriety of the presence of large numbers of foreign doctors in the

United States led to the imposition of special restrictions on foreign medical graduates coming to the United States as exchange aliens for postgraduate medical education or training. Those seeking this opportunity must now pass a special qualifying examination. The term of medical residencies for foreign medical graduates in the exchange program has only recently been extended from two years to a maximum of seven years; however, foreign medical graduates are not permitted to obtain waivers of the requirement to return home for a two-year period, which other participants in the Exchange Visitor programs normally may obtain on the basis of no-objection letters from their home government (sec. 601, Immigration and Nationality Act, Oct. 12, 1976).

The focus of government attention regarding the status of students has been, understandably, on the largest group in the foreign student population—the unsponsored students. This concern has most recently been intensified by public reaction in the United States toward Iranian nationals in particular and, by implication, toward foreign students in general. The history of governmental action in response to the various stages of the Iranian crisis—beginning with the violent demonstrations against the Shah which took place in California in 1979 and continuing through to the release of the United States hostages in Iran in 1981—provides a compelling argument for the need for effective long-term policies and procedures in the administration of the laws affecting foreign students and scholars. Of greatest significance was the impact on the regulations affecting the status of foreign students in the United States. In 1979 the existing regulation requiring that all students make an annual request for the extension of their stay in this country was altered to permit students to be admitted for "duration of status," eliminating the need for annual renewal and authorizing students to remain in the United States as long as they were pursuing the educational objectives for which they were originally admitted. Although this was in the best interests of the government, in that it relieved the already overburdened Immigration and Naturalization Service of an unnecessary bureaucratic chore, the service withdrew this privilege of "duration of status" in March 1981 and

reinstated the time-consuming requirement for annual renew-
als. This action, affecting all foreign students, was the direct
result of the government's frustration over the problem of locat-
ing and initiating deportation procedures against those Iranian
students who were deemed to be in violation of the terms of
their student status. Now, recently proposed regulations again
recommend a return to "duration of status."

The problems that face foreign students or scholars as a
result of their alien status in the United States are exacerbated
by the frequent changes in regulations and by the fact that regulations are administered by the various district officers of the
INS throughout the United States. Instructions from the INS
central office are interpreted and applied in different ways by
the different district officers, and these offices are for the most
part overworked. Foreign students are, after all, only a very
small part of the total responsibilities of the Immigration and
Naturalization Service; consequently, they must suffer long de-
lays in the processing of routine requests. Matters of urgent importance to the foreign student, such as a request for transfer
to another institution for valid educational reasons, may lie for
months unprocessed at the local INS office. In the meantime,
because of the imperatives of the academic calendar, the student may have enrolled at the new institution; if so, he or she is
deemed to have violated the conditions of status and may be
subject to adverse action by the INS. As a result of experiences
such as this, many foreign students are left with unfortunate
memories of their stay in the United States—a stay that was academically satisfactory but encumbered by regulations that
seemed designed to inhibit rather than encourage the fulfillment
of their educational programs.

Foreign Students and the U.S. Legal System

In order to place the position of foreign students or
scholars in the proper perspective and to evaluate the impact of
alien status on their life in this country, it is appropriate to review the legal framework that encompasses all individuals in the
United States. In his article "Law Concepts and Legal Rights,"
Smith (1977-78, pp. 44-46) notes that laws, both in this coun-

try and elsewhere, regulate individual and collective conduct in order to ensure a reasonable balance between personal freedom and the requirements of an orderly society. He observes that American law has grown over a long period of time into a necessarily complicated body of law involving the Constitution, federal statutes, common law, state constitutions, state statutes, local ordinances, court decisions, and various regulations issued pursuant to the laws. Like most other people, the foreign student or scholar pursuing an educational program in the United States is generally unaffected by and indeed unaware of this vast legal network. Thus, it is neither necessary nor would it be possible to provide a comprehensive analysis of concepts of law in this chapter. What is appropriate is a brief discussion of some relevant principles.

One of these principles is the rule of law; we are governed by laws, not men, and the law is supreme. Once the law is established, it must be observed by all; the law can be changed only by appropriate legislative procedures. The law protects us all from arbitrary actions of government and law enforcement authorities. Because the federal Constitution is the highest law in the land and all other laws have to be consistent with it, any laws or actions of the legislative or executive branches of the government which are not consistent with the Constitution can be challenged in court and nullified. This is the way in which our body of laws undergoes a continuous process of testing to ensure that it conforms with the principles set forth in the Constitution.

The Constitution guarantees due process of law to all persons, including aliens in the United States. Due process requires that orderly procedures be followed in the enactment, administration, and enforcement of the laws. The Constitution also guarantees to each person equal protection under the law. This means that the law applies equally to all, regardless of wealth, position, *or status,* and that one may not be discriminated against on arbitrary or capricious grounds. Some laws with a rational basis apply only to certain groups of people, such as the laws governing immigration, citizenship, voting, and residence in a particular state or city. These have been derived through the orderly procedures of due process and have been declared by

the courts not to be unfairly discriminatory. With these exceptions, foreign students and other aliens are subject to the same
laws as American citizens. Similarly, foreign students and other
aliens are guaranteed the same protection under law and the
same civil rights as American citizens. The right of free speech
and assembly is one of the most important of these civil rights.
Guaranteed by the Constitution is the right of free expression
for all, regardless of citizenship. There are times when, irrespective of—or sometimes even because of—being in a foreign country, the foreign student feels an obligation to speak out on some
subject of personal or national concern. In these circumstances
foreign students enjoy the constitutional right to express their
views freely, to join with others in the expression of those
views, and to participate fully in the propagation and publication of ideas, both popular and otherwise, as long as those expressions are made in an orderly and peaceful matter. They have
the same rights to free speech and are subject to the same limitations of freedom of action as are American citizens. Foreign
students should not be frightened by rumors of prosecution or
deportation resulting from the exercise of their rights of free
speech, for those rights are guaranteed to all.

Certain substantive and procedural protections are also
guaranteed against improper investigation, arrest, or conviction
of any alleged violator of the law. Persons so accused cannot be
forced to confess or to give evidence against themselves; they
may remain silent and refuse to answer any questions regarding
the accusations against them, if they so choose. They are entitled to legal counsel in court, and, if unable to afford one,
they may have one appointed by the court. They are entitled to
be released from jail upon posting a bond and are presumed in-
nocent until found guilty by a court, and the burden of proof
of guilt is on the prosecution. These protections also apply to
the foreign student in the United States.

Alien Status in Times of Crisis

While the fact of being an alien and thus subject to certain specific regulations will, for the most part, be an acceptable
condition of the student's life in a foreign country, in times of

crisis the problem of status may have a more serious and possibly negative impact. The reverberations of domestic crises in the home country, the results of family problems, especially those of a financial nature, or personal emotional or academic problems may disturb the even tenor of student life and, eventually, lead to confrontation with the authorities. It is at such times that the student may add to his or her difficulties by an exaggerated fear of the results of such an encounter.

Unnecessary crises may therefore develop when foreign students fear that they will be deported immediately and automatically if they are convicted, or even accused, of a violation of any law. This is not true; conviction for a single misdemeanor or minor offense, such as petty theft, disturbing the peace, or drunkenness, will have no effect on a student's immigration status. However, conviction for a more serious offense can result in deportation. For example, deportation can occur if a student is convicted of a crime involving moral turpitude for which a sentence of at least one year in confinement is given. Immigration law also provides for the possible deportation of any person who is a narcotic addict or who is convicted of a violation of any law or regulation relating to the illicit possession of, or traffic in, narcotic drugs or marijuana.

Perhaps the most sensitive area, and the one in which foreign students are at a distinct disadvantage, is in relation to academic activities. If, for any reason, foreign students cease to fulfill the requirement that they be full-time students, taking a full course of study as defined by the INS regulations, then they are automatically in jeopardy because they have no legal justification for remaining in this country. Thus, if foreign students violate the rules of their academic institutions and are disciplined by suspension or dismissal from the institution, this involves the additional penalty of loss of student status. In the same way, if they cease to be students through any other reason, such as failure to pay tuition fees, or if they are not maintaining their status according to the specific requirements of the immigration law—for instance, if they are not taking the mandatory full course of study or if they are engaging in unauthorized employment—then they are "out of status" and subject to deportation. In short, as foreign students they cannot be deported for violating university regulations, but they can be deported if they do not maintain proper student status. Sponsored students who violate terms of their sponsoring agencies may lose their financial support and visa sponsorship, thus making them vulnerable to deportation. Crises can also develop when student behavior in this country offends the home government. In such cases passports can be withdrawn or canceled by the home government, thereby making the students subject to deportation. In all these circumstances, the question of maintaining status is of paramount importance to the foreign students during their stay in the United States.

Crises may also occur when foreign students or scholars neglect civil law—for instance, if they do not pay bills or fulfill the terms of a contract or a business arrangement. Contracts may be either written or oral, and both are enforceable by law. Civil suit may be initiated to force payment of legitimate bills or financial obligations.

Laws exist to protect individuals from each other and from arbitrary and capricious actions by government. Although no system is free from faults, the American system does provide important safeguards and guarantees. If the system is to work effectively for them, foreign students must be aware of their rights and insist that these rights be respected by others. At the same time, they must accept their responsibilities under the law and respect the rights of all those with whom they come in contact, whether they be citizens of the United States or other members of the foreign student community.

Legal Responsibilities of Institutions
Enrolling Foreign Students

Institutions authorized to enroll nonimmigrant foreign students must meet a variety of legal responsibilities if they are to retain this important privilege, one that must be sought in the first place by filing a petition with the appropriate district director of the INS (*Code of Federal Regulations,* Title 8, chap. 1, para. 214.3). Smith (1979) has delineated these responsibilities, which are generally of concern to campus foreign student advisers:

1. To operate as a bona fide school and to conduct instruction in recognized courses, to employ qualified professional personnel, and to maintain proper facilities for instruction in these courses and for the supervisory and consultative services for students and trainees.

2. To issue a properly executed Form I-20 "Certificate of Eligibility" to each applicant accepted for admission to the school as a nonimmigrant alien student under the terms of the INA, but to limit acceptance under those terms and issuance of Forms I-20 to those applicants who have been determined by the school to be scholastically, financially, and linguistically qualified for study at the school and who will be full-time students at the school as defined by the regulations.

3. To report immediately to the INS, after receiving notification that a nonimmigrant student has been admitted to the United States for the purpose of attending the school or has been given INS permission to attend the school, whenever (a) the student fails to register personally at the school within sixty days of the time expected to do so, or (b) the student fails to carry a full course of study as defined in the regulations, or (c) the student fails to attend classes to the extent normally required, or (d) the student terminates attendance at the school.

4. To limit any statement that may appear in any of the school's publications or advertisements concerning the approval of the school for attendance by nonimmigrant alien students to the following: "This school is authorized under the federal law to enroll nonimmigrant alien students."

Role of the Foreign Student Adviser

Unfortunately, because of illegal alien problems, aliens in nonimmigrant status suffer by being subjected to increasingly strict controls by governmental authority. It is difficult to argue against such strict governmental controls on the activities of illegal aliens; it is equally difficult to argue for these same kinds of controls or for the excessive monitoring of legal aliens who are engaging in activities permitted by their visa status. The *Adviser's*

Manual of Federal Regulations Affecting Foreign Students and Scholars (National Association for Foreign Student Affairs, 1982a, pp. 4-5) suggests that foreign student advisers keep these distinctions in mind, in order to serve the best interests of the legal nonimmigrants with whom they work. Advisers need to define for themselves and for their students the areas of their responsibilities and authority and to keep within those parameters. Advisers thus have a clear responsibility to advise students of their privileges and responsibilities and of the limitations placed on their activities by United States law and regulations. However, it is not the responsibility of advisers to enforce the laws and regulations or to make reports to agencies of the federal government which exceed the reporting requirements established for each class of nonimmigrant. To perform in this role would be to exceed their authority and responsibility, confuse the administration of the law, and, most important, vitiate the relationship with their students. In this respect it should be noted that disputes sometimes arise between an institution and the INS as to what information should be provided about a foreign student. The discussion of this complex question in the *Faculty Member's Guide to U.S. Immigration Law* (Smith and Baron, 1980, p. 10) provides very useful clarification of this matter.

In many instances foreign student advisers serve as a liaison between the foreign student and the institution. That is, they relate the educational programs in their colleges and universities to foreign student expectations and needs. This peculiar responsibility, which may be seen as part of the legal relationship between the foreign student adviser, as the representative of the institution, and the foreign student enrolled at that institution, lies somewhere between the role of the academic adviser and that of the personal adviser. Today our immigration laws and regulations reflect the control aspects—rather than the developmental, social, and cultural components—of international educational interchange. However, this state of affairs can be changed. With strong leadership from all elements of the academic community (especially from foreign student advisers and others directly involved in international educational interchange) and with clear institutional goals and policies regarding international education, the educational rather than the alien status of the foreign students may be reaffirmed, so that they may obtain the maximum benefit from their academic training in the United States and the larger goals of international educational interchange may thus be realized.

Improving the Educational Experience of Foreign Students and Scholars in the United States

A review of the experience of foreign students and scholars, from the time they first apply for admission to this country to the termination of their stay here, indicates that their major problems derive from the lack of carefully planned long-term policies and from inconsistencies in regulations and in the way they are interpreted and administered by the responsible government officials across the country. The lack of policy in the admission of foreign students to this country was clearly one of the causes of the Iranian student problem, which occurred at a time when the students from that country accounted for 17.9 percent of the entire foreign student population in the United States and the total number (51,310) was three times larger than the next national group (17,560 from Taiwan) (figures from *Open Doors,* 1979-80). Commenting on this fact in a position paper written for his association, John F. Reichard, executive vice president of the National Association for Foreign Student Affairs, noted the accelerated flow of students from Iran over previous years, the disorderly growth of the Iranian student population on campus and our failure to balance that population properly, our inattention to the movement of Iranian students into unprepared colleges and into aggressive proprietary institutions (and the rapid movement out of those institutions by many dissatisfied and confused Iranians), and, finally and most important, the apparent failure of relatively large international educational and cultural interchange programs to produce understanding between the United States and Iran.

In addition to the problem of a lack of long-term policy, foreign students have also suffered from problems in procedures, both in the process of applying for a visa and in complying with the regulations governing their stay in this country. To remedy this situation, the National Association for Foreign Student Affairs, the largest organization in the United States concerned specifically with all aspects of international educational interchange, made a number of recommendations in a position paper delivered to the Select Commission on Immigration and Refugee Policy in the fall of 1980. It proposed five remedies to alleviate the problems associated with visa issuance:

1. The Department of State should develop more precise guidelines for consular officers involved in considering applications for visas.
2. These guidelines should place less emphasis on the requirement that consular officers determine the applicant's intent to return home (since it is difficult to determine or prove intent).
3. Applicants should be assumed to be acting in good faith unless some specific and concrete fact causes consular officers to doubt that they are.
4. Decisions of consular officers should be monitored in order to encourage consistency in the application of the guidelines and of the law and regulations.
5. Decisions of consular officers should be subject to administrative review and, ultimately, to judicial review.

To alleviate problems encountered in the administration of the regulations within the United States by the Immigration and Naturalization Service, the association proposed the following:

1. More precise guidelines should be developed to encourage uniform handling of cases throughout the INS districts.
2. A system of monitoring should be developed by the INS to assure more uniformity in adjudications.
3. The staffing of district INS offices should be increased to provide for more timely adjudication of applications and processing of forms.

4.   The training of line personnel should include materials on cross-cultural communication.
5.   INS line personnel should receive training to enable them to understand the role of the INS in relation to United States policy and international visitors.

Perceptions of the United States by foreign students and scholars and the recollections of their experience while studying in this country are inevitably affected by their treatment as nonimmigrant aliens. The extent to which they see the United States as a nation concerned with the development of educational exchange, rather than one preoccupied with the control of the aliens within its borders, will be reflected in their subsequent reaction to this country. Unfortunately, it is the negative aspects that tend to remain in the memory. The vast majority of foreign students and scholars in the United States are properly engaged in the educational pursuits that brought them to our shores. It would be in everybody's interest, including that of the United States, if the laws governing the status of foreign students and scholars in this country were to stress those purposes of educational, cultural, and international development envisaged by the Fulbright Act of 1946 and reaffirmed in the Mutual Educational and Cultural Exchange Act of 1961.

8

Administration: Coordinating and Integrating Programs and Services

Valerie Woolston

The organization of international interchange activities at United States colleges and universities varies enormously in content and dimension. There are almost as many configurations of "international offices" (the administrative or academic unit or units charged with the responsibility for these activities) as there are campuses. International education interchange activities generally include foreign students, United States students studying abroad, faculty exchanges, and exchange programs. Some international offices also administer joint research projects, international studies programs, and curricular affairs. As the various programs that make up the totality of this international dimension grow and change on campus, it becomes increasingly important that they be integrated into appropriate institutional activities, so that individual initiative can be encouraged while institutional standards are protected. In its broadest context, international education should be equipping

184

as many students and faculty members as possible with knowledge and skills that they will need in our shrinking, interdependent world.

Institutions have designed and continue to develop their own ways of integrating international activity into their total educational program and administrative structure. Particular institutional responses stem from institutional types, sizes, locations, and a number of other variables. For example, the president of a small institution may be able to internationalize curriculum and influence the international elements of programs himself, marshaling the enthusiasm of faculty, students, and administrators; however, at a small institution, it may be difficult to establish student and faculty exchanges and attract foreign students. On the other hand, the president of a large metropolitan school may find it difficult to influence the curriculum and increase participation in international research efforts but may be able to attract foreign students and establish faculty exchanges and exchange programs with a minimum of encouragement.

There has been an extraordinary growth in the international dimension of education on campuses in the United States. The most tangible evidence of this growth is the dramatic increase in the number of foreign students. However, the presence of this burgeoning foreign student population was to some extent obscured by the tremendous enrollment upsurges of United States students and the consequent growth in the size and number of institutions in the 1960s. In the 1970s the foreign student population grew by leaps and bounds, reaching more than 300,000 in 1980; at the same time, the United States student enrollment maintained itself, or slightly declined, and funding for higher education fell on hard times. Thus, in these years the foreign students became highly visible in United States colleges and universities. Today the number of foreign students coming to the United States for academic purposes continues to increase, and current predictions indicate that this trend will continue for the foreseeable future, although perhaps at a slightly reduced rate.

The impact of this growth on institutions is obvious. Not

only have systems had to be developed for serving foreign students within our schools but whole new services and academic fields have developed. For instance, admissions officers have had to become applied comparative educationalists, and foreign student advisers have basically been responsible for developing the new field of cross-cultural counseling. Teachers of English as a second language have developed much new material for the field of cross-cultural communications. A consideration of the appropriate transfer of technology has affected nearly all engineering and scientific fields at the graduate level, and developmental studies are now incorporated into many majors.

In addition to the growth of foreign student populations on campuses, international programs have also become visible campus units. For the sake of this discussion, international programs will include study abroad programs and any formal or informal international affiliation, such as overseas contracts and the outreach of area studies programs, which encourages the exchange of students or faculty. Although normally outside the regular curriculum of an institution, all these activities contribute to the international dimension of the college or university; and study abroad programs, once firmly established, have in fact become part of the curriculum. Obviously, there is no limit to the ways in which international programs can and do develop; and, as knowledge expands and science and education change, there will be more and more opportunities for faculty exchanges and for collaborative research projects involving scholars from different countries. The institutional responses will vary from the spontaneous development of international projects and programs with little or no central coordination to the establishment of one administrative unit that will be the focal point for all the services required for the institution's international outreach.

It is clear that campuses have grown beyond their classrooms. With the number of variables mentioned above, from institutional differences, to geographical considerations, to differing foreign student populations, and exchange programs, it is not surprising that a huge number of institutional patterns have developed. No one organizational style is best. The priorities, needs, and philosophies of the students, faculty members, and institutions must be considered. Institutions must decide what level of commitment can be made to international education and then develop and maintain activities and structures to support that level of commitment.

Required Services and Programs

In 1980 a survey was conducted for the International Studies Association to find out how institutions organized their international programs. Paul Watson, director of the University Center for International Studies at the University of Pittsburgh, surveyed 420 institutions. Upon review of the 215 responses, Watson (1981, p. 5) concluded that "Structures for things international tend to be created more often than not by accidental opportunities or the ideographic behavior of administrators. . . . Organizational patterns are not really present." However, each type of international program demands that certain services be delivered. Irrespective of the form in which the programs may be developed or the pattern in which the required services are delivered, the international activities of the institution are inescapably intertwined. The presence of foreign students and scholars, study abroad programs for United States students, faculty exchanges, and joint international research programs all have their individual goals and purposes but cannot be reasonably considered in isolation from each other. Thus, although such activities may involve the different programs and services described below, and although these may be either centralized or scattered across the campus, they should be recognized as being interrelated, should be designed so far as possible to be mutually supportive, and must be seen as part of the overall organization of institutional interchange activities.

Office of Foreign Student Adviser. As described earlier in this book, the presence of foreign students on the United States educational scene as a group rather than as isolated individuals was already apparent in the early 1900s, but the first manifestation of a new stage in the development of educational interchange came immediately following World War II with the rapid growth in the enrollment of foreign students in United States colleges and universities. The arrival in increasing numbers of students from other countries stimulated the organization of special foreign student services, which are, consequently, further developed than the other elements of international activity on campus, such as the programs for United States students abroad or faculty exchanges. At this time, when the concept of an institution-wide approach to international activities is becoming ever more popular, the point of departure for this development on many campuses has been the office of the foreign student adviser.

Even in the 1950s, the function of foreign student advising was by no means new. The legislation governing foreign students in the United States, with its assignment of certain legal responsibilities to "an authorized official" of any institution to which foreign students were admitted, served to emphasize the need for the appointment of an individual generally identified as the foreign student adviser. Since the 1950s there have been a number of examinations of the developing role and functions of the foreign student adviser—in particular those provided in the guidelines and other publications of the National Association for Foreign Student Affairs. At the same time, individual practitioners were making intensive analyses of their activities. Of particular historical importance is *The Status of Foreign Student Advising in United States Universities and Colleges* (Higbee, 1961), a research study of the scope of services provided to international students and of the people who provided these services. This was followed some years later by two doctoral dissertations on the on-the-job behavior of the foreign student adviser (Benson, 1968; Miller, 1968), which in turn were the basis for a workshop, sponsored in 1971 by the Field Service Program of the National Association for Foreign Student Affairs, in which the activities of the foreign student adviser were ordered into twelve major functions:

Administers foreign student adviser's office.

Consults with and advises university faculty and staff.

Develops plans and programs.

Participates in academic guidance program.

Coordinates financial aid.

Facilitates fulfillment of immigration requirements.

Advises and counsels foreign students.

Coordinates community relations.

Supports foreign student activities.

Maintains liaison with nonuniversity agencies.

Coordinates efforts to resolve emergencies.

Provides personal services.

These major functions are really convenient groupings of an almost infinite variety of tasks both on campus and in the community. Specifically, in addition to the procedures of foreign student admissions (dealt with in Chapter Six), the services that an institution must be prepared to provide, or otherwise make available, for its foreign students and scholars on campus include reception (assistance from United States port of entry to campus), housing, orientation, English language instruction, personal and academic advising, financial aid, health service or adequate health insurance, campus and community life programs, predeparture orientation, and the organization of alumni relations. Each of these services, which are dealt with more extensively in *The Foreign Student Adviser and His Institution in International Student Exchange* (Putman, 1965), has also been the subject of extensive studies published by NAFSA. In the area of campus and community programs in particular, a number of program models have been published by NAFSA as the result of various pilot projects funded with the support of the Agency for International Development and the United States Information Agency and its predecessors.

Although the list of needed foreign student services includes many that are normally provided to United States students, the following elements in student services may require a different approach when foreign students are involved:

Orientation takes on a different aspect if one is unfamiliar with the United States educational system. Imagine a student's trying to deal with "credits," "quality points," and "course selection" if he has come from a highly structured and prescribed educational system. When an international student arrives on a campus from overseas, his first concerns are "Where am I going to live?" and "What am I going to study?" These two questions must be answered with the help of campus staff and faculty because the foreign student has no family or community support systems in place. Initial orientation usually takes place when the new international student is in profound cultural shock; therefore, ongoing orientation is needed to prepare students for their academic and social life in the United States. Small, continuing workshops or group discussions often fulfill this need. It is important to integrate as many American students in this process as possible in order to expose our students to people from other parts of the world, as well as to get the international students to know as many different Americans as possible.

Counseling a foreign student is very different from counseling a United States student. Traditional Western counseling methods often are misunderstood by foreign students or outside their range of experience. Indeed, the converse is also true. A United States counselor may not have the background to comprehend the students' cultural heritage and experience or their educational system and the sociological foundations surrounding that system. For example, the narrow, limited, strictly academic, and literary approach to schooling in many parts of the world produces students with much different attitudes toward education than the attitudes of an American student who has attended broad-based, public schools. Persons from a different educational and cultural background may need to make academic and personal adjustments as they move into the United States system of higher education and thus require guidance and encouragement as they seek to overcome their problems.

In addition to the particular procedures involved in the admission of foreign students—procedures such as determination of financial capability and visa status—a number of continuing *technical and legal problems* must be dealt with. These would include, as necessary, certification processes for sponsors and for foreign exchange and, most important, legal assistance in the form of advising on the various regulations—such as those of the Immigration and Naturalization Service and other government agencies—that affect foreign students and scholars in this country. Often the legal assistance needed is a form of liaison between the institution and both United States and foreign government demands. In order to protect institutional standards and the rights of the students, both sponsored and unsponsored, and faculty, the authorized school official in charge of immigration liaison (or the "Responsible Officer" for participants in exchange visitor programs) must be aware of the implications of new legal demands of the exchanges and assist the participants in protecting themselves as well as helping them meet their legal and institutional responsibilities. Many foreign student advisers agonize and work "flat out" during periods of political crises and financial emergencies overseas. (See Chapter Seven for particular details.)

Foreign student advisers also must become involved in *social and academic programming,* because foreign students, as resource people on campus, can greatly enrich academic programs. An excellent workbook on the international student as a resource, *Learning with Foreign Students* (Mestenhauser, 1976), has been published by the University of Minnesota.

International students need sensitive academic advisers who can assist them in *choosing appropriate courses.* In the past few years, the concern for appropriate curriculum and the appropriate transfer of knowledge has led to more flexibility while still maintaining standards within degree programs. Faculty members who have had an overseas experience themselves, if they are available and interested, are often excellent advisers for international students. More and more graduate departments are demanding that the research an international student does should be relevant to his home country. This demand has actually developed in response to the foreign students' demands for such relevancy.

Workshops to prepare international students to *return home* have been developed. After spending two to four to six years in the United States, the international student is a much changed person. The return home is likely to be as difficult as the initial arrival period in the United States, and the resulting culture shock may be a significant impediment to the effective use of the education received abroad. In some countries returning students may also encounter certain qualifying requirements in their profession, which may involve a period of retraining before they can embark on a career in their homeland. In order to ease the shock and prepare for any adjustment problems, either personal or professional, reentry transition workshops have been developed for the returning foreign student, organized either immediately prior to departure or over a period of months during their last year in the United States. For, in addition to being a stranger to their own culture, the overlay of United States education and culture is often deeper than the students may have felt while they were studying in the United States. (In fact, in Sierra Leone students who have studied overseas are known as "Beentus." They have *been to* another country to study and are therefore different and recognized as such.)

One item of particular importance to the welfare of the institution is the necessary *liaison* between the university, the local population, and the civic authorities—particularly when the foreign student population has an impact on available housing, police and hospital services, and the elementary and secondary schools. In any case, the international student exchange program will affect not only the institution but also the community in which the institution is located. If unsuccessful, its impact will certainly be felt in the surrounding community and will require strenuous remedial efforts on the part of the college or university administration. If the program is successful on campus, then its beneficial effects will also be apparent within the community. The spinoff need not be organized, though formal community groups have been organized to help the community and the international students mingle. While it may be difficult to achieve, in that it requires both time and interest, the development of an effective community liaison can be very beneficial to the institution. The programs and services which, in addition to home hospitality, are provided by interested members of the community can make a significant contribution to the welfare of the foreign students and scholars and also provide valuable support for the work of the foreign student adviser's office. With the realization that the foreign student or scholar is interested in learning more about the United States community and the way it functions, service activities are complemented by a wide variety of extracurricular educational programs arranged by the community organization with the assistance of local civic, professional, and business organizations. The Community Section of the National Association for Foreign Student Affairs offers both training programs and resource materials for community organizations and volunteers interested in providing programs and services for foreign students and scholars.

The earlier studies on the development of institutional interchange activities demonstrated the role of the foreign student adviser as a *referral* person for all the constituents of the university on matters pertaining to foreign students. This particular aspect and the interdependence of the functions of admission, advising, and teaching English as a second language are further emphasized in *A Guide for the Education of Foreign Students* (Benson and Kovach, 1974), in which ten defined stages in foreign student education, from planning to follow-up evaluation, are displayed in relation to the responsibility or the involvement of different elements of the university.

In the current organization of institutional interchange activities, the role of the foreign student adviser, whether as an individual devoting full or part time to this task or as a member of an international office, will depend on the particular administrative structure of the institution. Despite all the differences of operation, and a determined lack of functional standardization, individuals or institutions engaged in the establishment or further development of foreign student services may be guided by the *NAFSA Principles for International Educational Exchange* (National Association for Foreign Student Affairs, 1981). Within this framework each institution may create its own pattern of activity, perhaps by adapting or adopting programs that have proved successful in institutions of similar size and character and also by seeking the services of one of the NAFSA consultants in the field.

Foreign Student Admissions. The most immediate target

for the letters and requests from students in almost every country in the world who are seeking an education outside of their homelands is, of course, the institution's admissions office. While the function of admissions has long been institutionalized in our schools, the admission of foreign students is a more complex process, involving decisions regarding the evaluation of foreign educational credentials, English proficiency, financial capability, and visa status. All must be assessed and meet both institutional and immigration requirements. In most institutions the responsibility for foreign student admissions is retained in the admissions office, although in the optimum situation there will be a close liaison between the admissions office and the international office or the office of the foreign student adviser.

Foreign student admissions are discussed in detail in Chapter Six. Here we note only that, in order to integrate the international activity of the admissions office into the total administrative structure, the unusual data generated by foreign students must be included in the institution's record-keeping procedures and its computer programming. As national attention focuses on the presence of foreign students in United States colleges and universities, the collection and retrieval of vital statistics become increasingly important. The need for data and the extent of the information required are evident in the forms distributed by the Institute of International Education in its annual census of foreign students in the United States. The fact that 94.5 percent of the institutions surveyed in 1980-81 sent in their responses indicates the general recognition of the significance of this data.

Study Abroad. Within the institution the organization of study abroad opportunities has often originated in the foreign language and area studies departments, run mostly on an ad hoc basis through the continuing education unit of the school. Faculty members of academic departments have also offered study abroad programs related to the subjects they teach. The professors of English history, for example, have designed and led programs in England for the study of British history and culture. Today it is recognized that study abroad can enhance the academic experience of students majoring in any field from architecture to zoology.

Recently a number of factors have led to changes in the pattern of administration of study abroad. The expansion of the activity and the proliferation of study abroad programs (over 800 academic year study abroad programs were run by United States colleges in 1981, as reported in *U.S. College-Sponsored Programs Abroad: Academic Year,* published annually by the Institute of International Education), the increasing complexity of the logistic arrangements, the high cost of programs, and the complications involved in awarding transfer credits between institutions have together persuaded many institutions to centralize their study abroad programs in one office under an administrative rather than an academic unit. The University of Maryland is one such institution. Where there is good coordination between the administration and the faculty members, this more centralized management of the study abroad programs leads to much flexibility.

The services that must be provided by the institution to support study abroad programs are in some ways similar to those offered to international students but differ in other ways. They are set forth in detail in Chapter Three. In the context of the organization of the totality of institutional interchange activities, the following must be taken into account:

- Processes need to be developed to prepare the student who is studying abroad to leave the institution and return to it comfortably a semester or a year later. The student abroad needs to feel that his home institution is supporting him.
- Mechanisms need to be set up to provide for preregistration overseas if preregistration is an option for students on the home campus.
- Study abroad counselors need to be able to evaluate credentials, both United States and foreign, in order to determine transfer of credit and validity of programs; there must be an evaluation of programs and approval by the student's academic department prior to going overseas.
- Good advising is needed to enable students to select programs abroad that will enhance and apply to their degree programs.
- Resource libraries must be developed (the bibliography com-

piled by the Section on U.S. Students Studying Abroad is available through NAFSA and lists appropriate references; see National Association for Foreign Student Affairs, 1982b).

- Logistic support services, such as guiding the student to applicable financial aid and making inexpensive travel arrangements, must be provided.
- Orientation programs must be presented to prepare United States students for their overseas experience; debriefing programs, together with courses designed to discuss education as a cross-cultural experience, also should be offered.

While the above advisory and supportive services bear some relationship to those offered to international students, different services and skills are required if an institution decides to operate and administer its own study abroad programs. The institution must differentiate and make a choice between a wide variety of program configurations. These include programs operated by United States colleges in foreign academic institutions; those run directly by United States colleges in foreign countries but not in foreign academic institutions; those provided by private agencies or by foreign institutions, such as the Sorbonne, where programs for foreign students are supplementary to, but not part of, the regular course offerings; and those in which the United States student can meet the academic and language requirements and enroll directly in the foreign university.

With so many programs already in existence, it is difficult to avoid duplication, and a strong rationale must be developed to justify any new program. The institution that decides to administer its own study abroad programs faces an intricate and often complicated task. Negotiations must be made between at least two bureaucracies, two educational systems, two cultures, and two sets of foreign currency exchange. Institutional support for such programs must be very broad based within both the sending and receiving institutions (a great deal of financial wizardry is also involved). Obviously, the services required will involve many offices in both countries. Groups of students traveling abroad have diverse needs, and the institution must make a commitment to meet such needs. Thus, in the organization of institutional interchange activities, the institution that decides to operate its own study abroad programs will require a very strong administrator.

Faculty Exchanges. Some of the services needed for international students and study abroad students overlap to support faculty exchange programs. Information developed for foreign students is often applicable to foreign faculty arriving on campus. Travel information, visa and immigration information, and orientation materials developed for the study abroad student will apply to the faculty member traveling abroad. Much of the administrative support that a faculty member requires when preparing proposals for a teaching or research experience abroad is very different from the other types of support services. Often the faculty member's greatest need is for a typist and for someone to assist in developing a reasonable budget for the overseas project. Appropriate programming to support exchange efforts might be a seminar on fellowships and grant availability, or something as simple as how to apply for senior Fulbright awards. For instance, Fulbright travel awards are designed to support other grant programs, and fully fund travel to and from the overseas destination. A good coordinator of faculty exchanges will find ways to integrate the United States faculty wishing to go overseas with the visiting foreign faculty on campus. The United States Information Agency, through its International Visitors Program, provides monthly lists of visiting foreign faculty members who are available to lecture on campuses. Innovative means of finding ways to exchange foreign and United States faculty are needed. Often a faculty exchange depends on the availability of a sabbatical or grant funding. Faculty job swapping, or a direct one-to-one exchange, is a popular solution. As well as eliminating some of the financial constraints, it intimately involves whole academic departments in the exchange as well as the individual faculty member, since the department must host the visiting faculty member.

In the area of faculty research and exchange, it seems obvious that academic department heads will be involved with the exchanges and will select countries and research projects that will benefit the home teaching and research programs. In fact, the professional interaction between individual educators doing collaborative research in many different parts of the world generally defines the exchange activity in most institutions. This causes a proliferation of efforts within institutions and makes institutional focus difficult. In order to define their interests, and to coordinate international research and exchange efforts, many institutions are centralizing the function in an administrative unit outside of academic departments. Whether the efforts of faculty exchanges are centralized or not, there is almost no substitute for the mutual respect and understanding developed between professors and researchers when they work with colleagues on mutual problems.

Exchange Agreements and Contracts. When a particular research capability meets a developmental need in a foreign country, exchange agreements are often drawn up between academic departments or institutions and foreign towns or countries, as well as foreign academic institutions. An exchange agreement may take the form of a simple arrangement between faculty members in the mathematics department of a United States university and their colleagues in the same department in a foreign university. Or it may be an elaborate agreement or contract between a multiversity in the United States with all institutions of higher learning in a developing country. The University of Maryland has such an agreement with the universities in Sri Lanka. Contracts and exchange agreements may also be made between a university and more than one other party, such as an agency of the United States government and a foreign government; or the arrangements may involve a university and an international organization or a private agency (such as a foundation). In all such cases, there is clearly a need for administrative oversight on the part of the institution itself.

The transnational movement of scholars generated by these individual or institutional faculty exchanges and collaborative agreements is a major factor in the advancement of knowledge and the further development of contemporary education. Through their study, teaching, and research, the international scholars make an impact on campus; through their interaction with colleagues in other institutions, they contribute to the academic life of the host country. Their influence is also felt through their participation in the international symposia, conferences, and workshops that gather together the worldwide educational community in the exploration of new frontiers in their respective fields of study.

Staffing

The organization of institutional international interchange activities presupposes the assignment of necessary staff—not the casual appointment of someone who happens to have free time but personnel with certain skills and knowledge. The evaluation of foreign educational credentials, for example, requires an expertise in addition to that normally required of the institution's admissions officers; and the legal obligations imposed by the Immigration and Naturalization Service on any institution where foreign students are enrolled must be handled by someone with both training and experience. Some sophistication is also required to deal with the various sponsors, such as foreign governments that are directly responsible for their funded students, or the sponsoring agencies that administer on behalf of the donors a variety of international, national, and private scholarship programs for foreign students and scholars. At a major university this may require liaison with fifty to one hundred different sponsors. Thus, although the assignment of the personnel in charge of the institution's interchange activities may range from one or more full-time staff members to a part-time individual responsibility, there is an inescapable need to make provision for training, for the acquisition of basic resource materials, and for the opportunity for professional development through participation in workshops, conferences, and other learning experiences.

There are no hard and fast rules about the amount of staff time that must be devoted to the interchange activities, but there are certainly recommended staffing standards, although these may be affected by the pattern of institutional administration and the extent to which responsibilities are combined in one or more offices or dispersed among a variety of schools, departments, or administrative units. In the specific area of advising United States students on study abroad, for example, one half-time professional and one half-time support staff member are needed to provide effective service in a college of up to 1,500 students with an active interest in opportunities abroad (National Association for Foreign Student Affairs, 1979c, p. 25); in the more intensive and continuing task of foreign student advising, a ratio of one professional plus supportive staff to every 350 foreign students is recommended (National Association for Foreign Student Affairs, 1979b, p. 4). The information obtained by W. R. Butler in his 1980 survey on services to international students (reported later in this chapter) indicates that that goal has not yet been reached, since the ratio that he found was 284 students to one full-time staff member, figuring both professional and clerical staff.

The reason for these discrepancies may be found not only in budget priorities but also in the way that each institution makes use of the options available to combine the particular responsibility for interchange activities with various teaching or administrative functions. However, no international educational interchange activity can be successfully administered without the provision of basic educational and training opportunities that will enable the staff to function effectively.

Emerging Organizational Patterns

As mentioned previously, all types of international programs have emerged on our campuses to meet the needs of international education. As the international dimension of education has become visible and viable in United States higher education, administrators begin to wonder what type of organization makes sense for their own campuses. Hence, in the past few years, there have been several rather extensive surveys of institutions; and many educational associations have recommended methods of surveying campuses prior to setting up international programs (see Kenworthy, 1970). The National Association for Foreign Student Affairs has developed a consultation project funded by a grant from the United States Information Agency, so that experienced international administrators can consult with campus officials on various aspects of their programs, from admissions, to English as a second language, to study abroad, or an all-inclusive international programs consultation. The program has been in existence since 1964, and approximately 1,100 consultations have been made.

As soon as there is a recognized need for an international education activities office on campus, the first question that arises is: Should all international services and functions be centralized in one office, or is decentralization a better tack to follow? Each institution must survey its own mission, goals, and resources, both human and material, to respond to that question. In Paul Watson's survey of 215 institutions in the fall of 1979, three profiles of institutions emerged (Watson, 1981). The first group of institutions had a central office with overall responsibility for international studies and programs (135 institutions identified themselves in this category). Slightly more than half of the offices contained study abroad functions. Fewer than one in five contained foreign student services. Some of the offices reported to vice presidents, some to deans and provosts. Most of the schools with a centralized office reported that there were area studies on their campuses but that very few area studies offices reported to the centralized international office. Central offices were normally funded from regular institutional budgets, not from external funding. In other words, centralized offices were very different from institution to institution.

The second profile was that of institutions with area studies and no centralization of services (137 schools were in this category). In these schools area studies were housed in appropriate academic departments. Usually the study abroad and foreign student services areas were separate. Personnel were generally supported on institutional budgets, while programs were supported by external grants.

The third profile was of institutions with study abroad offices and/or foreign student services only (there were 125 such responses). Over half of the schools in this category reported study abroad program management. In only one fourth of the cases were study abroad and foreign student services under the same administration. Foreign student services frequently reported to student personnel structures rather than to the central international effort.

In October of 1980, William R. Butler, vice-president for student affairs at the University of Miami, surveyed fifteen departments that serviced international students and scholars at primarily large, public institutions. The survey was conducted through an informal group of vice-presidents of major universities, which is headed by Butler. Some interesting findings in this survey are as follows: (1) The mean ratio of international students to full-time staff (professional and clerical) was calculated at 284 to 1. (2) In most cases the number of clerical personnel matched or was slightly below the number of full-time professionals. (3) Salaries constituted an average of 86 percent of the total operational budget for the departments. (4) The number of staff and the ratio of international students to staff were not consistently correlated with the size of enrollment. (5) The majority of departments did not have a computerized record system, but most indicated a critical need for such.

There are obvious advantages and disadvantages to having both centralized and decentralized international support structures on a campus. In addition, some schools can and should support only foreign student services and/or study abroad programs.

Very few institutions have attempted to centralize all the international activities on a campus. Even within those programs, administrators realize that some important international services remain outside the centralized structure. A hypothetical totally centralized office would coordinate services to students and scholars, exchanges, and curricular and academic affairs. The following functions would have to be provided to service the students and scholars: admissions, arrival orientation, advice and counseling, financial advices, immigration liaison, advice to student and community organizations, end-of-stay guidance, reentry transition programming, coordinating student-sponsor relationships, working on special programs, and coordinating academic interaction between students and faculty. In addition, the office must function as a resource office to other campus offices that support foreign students and scholars, the academic divisions of the school, and to off-campus sponsors and community groups. These services, which support the first-line individuals involved with international interchange, can be provided by professional international admissions evaluators, foreign student advisers, English as a second language teachers, study abroad advisers, and community volunteers and liaison personnel. However, the truly organized and centralized office will also need curriculum developers and programmers, who can affect the academic community of the institution. There need to be personnel who will be responsive to legislative and governmental programs and incentives, work with establishing sensible and coordinated faculty exchanges and visits, and set up close ties with institutions overseas.

A centralized international program allows an institution to focus on its international activities. This is of great importance today because of the variety of opportunities available to institutions willing to be responsive to training and development needs around the world and to support collaborative research efforts. As research and development funding shrinks in this country, special attention should be given to any possible collaborative efforts in order to continue basic research. In a large institution, a centralized office must be supported by a large institutional commitment. Staffing and funding must be adequate. If they are, the international unit can be responsive to almost all other units on the campus. If everything is too centralized, members of the campus outside the unit might leave the internationalizing to the international office alone; however, this is a low risk because of the nature of study and scholarship itself, which is now demanding constant interchange with scholars around the world. This very element of international exchange is becoming so widespread that to completely centralize international interchange is quite difficult.

At the extreme opposite end of the scale is the campus that services international programs in a completely decentralized manner. The services for international students and scholars are incorporated in the regular support services for the campus. Foreign admission applications are processed in the regular admissions office. Advising takes place in the counseling center. Study abroad generally falls under various area studies departments. International faculty are cared for in the academic departments to which they report. English as a second language programs, if available, are taught in the English department or in the continuing education department. A professor in agriculture responds to Agency for International Development projects and participants. A professor of government may respond to initiatives from institutions overseas. The alumni office stays in touch with former graduates. The obvious strength of decentralization is that there are pockets of international activity throughout the campus. It demands many very well-trained people who are committed to the concept of internationalism, and adequate time must be given for them to do an adequate job in meeting their international responsibilities. The weakness of decentralization is generally the lack of knowledge of what is really going on on the campus. Unless there is a very open and strong communication network set up to ensure that everyone knows what is occurring, chaos can evolve. In small colleges particularly, decentralization of services often works well to capitalize on limited resources.

Institutions that provide only international student services and/or study abroad programs may also combine these services or keep them separate. It is difficult to evaluate the relative advantages or disadvantages of combining the administration of these two activities. Apart from the constraints imposed by the organization and division of institutional responsibilities, a critical factor might be the relative size of the two programs on campus. If there is any marked disproportion, then combination probably is a disadvantage. However, the particular advantage in offering a centralized international student service is the energy that emerges when United States and international students and faculty mix. This energy is impossible to "cost out," "account for," or "fund." Yet it is the product that should be foremost in educators' and administrators' minds when developing service support programs. The unity of services assists the student because it tends to cause the institution to deal with all of the student's and faculty member's concerns from a holistic point of view. For an international student or faculty member, this is especially important because the lack of support systems can form a void around individuals far removed from their own culture. While most institutions cannot provide full services (and perhaps they should not), it is well for the institutional administrator to recognize the full range of services needed and therefore fulfill that which the institution can best provide.

Decentralized systems of international student services have strength because they force the students to deal with more members of the faculty and staff. However, because of split responsibilities and work overloads, university staff members may not be well trained or have the time to deal with the special concerns of the student who wishes to study abroad. An example of the difficulty with decentralized student services follows.

A student from Mozambique may be receiving a failing grade in physics. (A United States student could receive tutorial help or help in the reading and study skills laboratory. So could the foreign student, but it is highly likely that the cause of the problem is different.) The Mozambique student's problem may stem from a variety of causes, not the least of which is that he is being educated in at least a third language. His tribal language was certainly not his language of instruction in elementary/secondary schooling. He had to learn Portuguese for those years, and now he has had to acquire English to study in the United States. Not only does he need English, but he needs a very sophisticated English to study very complex physics theories. Each language has overlayed a new culture on the student. The cultural implications are probably not clear to the student or to the person to whom he goes for advice. Moreover, the student is a person who has had to learn methods of learning and study appropriate to each of his cultures. Therefore, counselors, advisers, and faculty members who deal with this one student from Mozambique must be attuned to cross-cultural experiences and counseling methodology and to the various educational systems to which the student has been exposed.

Even if a campus has totally decentralized its services, a few individuals will in time develop the necessary expertise for dealing with problems such as those of the student from Mozambique. Consequently, at least the counseling function for foreign individuals will tend to be centralized. Dealing with these kinds of problems requires considerable skill and is time consuming and quite costly. Many schools have students from 25 to 50 to 100 countries. Even if only a few of these students require in-depth counseling, there must be staff members who are capable of dealing with them. Similarly, someone on the staff will have to have an intimate working knowledge of immigration regulations and a personal working relationship with district immigration offices. If these matters are handled by more than one individual in an institution, problems often arise. The regulations affect individuals such as our student from Mozambique in ways that will necessitate a particular kind of counseling for him. For instance, foreign students are required to maintain "full-time" status. The student from Mozambique may not be able to do so if he is advised to drop his physics course. (In fact, with proper advising there are ways to assist him without resulting immigration problems.) The Immigration and Naturalization Service's definition and regulations put more pressure on the student just when he does not need it. Again, it becomes obvious that such a student needs a faculty or staff member who can assist him with both counseling and immigration. To decentralize the services might jeopardize coherent student counseling.

No matter what structural pattern of organization emerges on a campus, it is of utmost importance to realize that many elements are involved in the international education activity— among them, student services, study abroad, international studies programs, and faculty exchanges and research projects. When properly orchestrated, each part of an international program on a campus should support the other programs and should strengthen the total educational program offered by the school.

Structural Patterns to Maximize Commitment

The diversity that exists in our institutions of higher education in the United States will continue to exist. It is our strength. The flexibility allows us to meet others' needs in a way that is not found in any other educational system in the world. It means that there will continue to be as many international organizational patterns as there are institutions willing to commit resources to international interchange. International mobility is here to stay, and the reasons for the increase in it have been well stated. Higher education must participate in this international mobility and contribute to it. Schools must be prepared to welcome students from developing countries as well as from the areas of traditional exchange. Interinstitutional co-operation must develop two-way processes of exchange. Research must face the problems with which man is now faced, and those problems are international in scope.

Institutions must investigate and debate their role in all of this. No longer can we merely let it all "grow like Topsy." The outcome is too important to the international university community. If institutions are unaware of the services and support systems needed to uphold a strong program of international interchange, they must learn about them and be prepared to provide them before they admit foreign students or sign exchange agreements. It is not enough to say "We want foreign students" if no special services are offered to them. It is not enough to say "We want faculty exchanges" if there is no support system for individual faculty members. It is unwise for high-level administrators to allow rifts to exist between academic deans or directors of international programs and deans or directors of international education services. The services should support the academics and research and vice versa. Strong academically oriented study abroad programs cannot exist without faculty and administrative services input, nor can realistic faculty exchanges. International programs on a campus must be integrated into the total university. Strong and central leadership is necessary to any international program. In the interests of the students and the community, the president and the board of any school must be publicly committed to internationalism.

Once a commitment is made, a decision needs to be made about the best way to institutionalize an international program. As campuses grow and change, structural changes may be necessary in already existing international offices. It is of utmost importance to have feedback between the various units involved in the interchange. This is often difficult because often those most interested in international educational exchange on our campuses are in foreign languages, area studies, humanities, and social sciences, while the units that service international development needs are often agriculture, the hard sciences, and professional schools. The international student services office is frequently removed from all these departments. Hence, if a school is to really develop a comprehensive program, formal communication channels must be established.

If there are study abroad programs, there must be ways to analyze the content and make sure the students who participate in them are prepared for their overseas experience. There will be forever a debate over whether the study abroad programs are as academically strong as the academic programs on the home campus. The debate should exist, and the programs should be constantly reevaluated. Structures should be set up to see that this happens.

Foreign students on a campus require very specialized services. It is impossible to deal properly with foreign students at more than a 1 to 350 professional staff to international student ratio. International admissions officers, foreign student advisers, English as a second language teachers, and immigration experts are all necessary personnel.

If overseas contract operations are to be run, an institutional survey is of utmost importance. Almost no institution can claim to have all the competencies and resources necessary to run a broad range of contract operations. Therefore, well-informed faculty members must be used to garner assistance from other institutions. Much institutional collaboration is necessary, and excellent administrative skills are necessary to coordinate such projects. Indeed, continual institutional self-study is necessary if all the resources are to be put to use in internationalizing research or even making limited contractual agreements.

Institutions should be able to look at themselves and say that the international program on their campus assists them in achieving a global education for their students, and helps pre-

pare their students for the world of the future. International issues of all kinds are now a part of our own culture. It is higher
education's job to prepare students to live in their own culture.
Providing a structure for international affairs within institutions
is a necessity.

9

Cross-Cultural Activities: Maximizing the Benefits of Educational Interchange

George C. Christensen
Thomas B. Thielen

Foreign students and scholars can enrich the quality of collegiate activity. With the support of the administration, both the campus and the community can offer needed services and programs for these students and scholars. At the same time, the contributions of students and scholars from other lands can be organized to provide an intercultural component in the educational activities of the institution, both in its formal academic programs and in its outreach to the surrounding community.

The authors wish to acknowledge the assistance of Martin Limbird, director of the Office of International Educational Services and assistant to the vice-president for academic affairs at Iowa State University, for his assistance. His counsel and advice has been crucial to the development of this chapter.

The Iowa State University experience illustrates what can happen when a major university makes a purposeful and consistent effort to take full advantage of the presence of international students and scholars.

Iowa State University is a land-grant university situated in the rural area of Ames. Its foreign student population of 1,486 constitutes 6 percent of the total student enrollment of 24,754 (1980–81 statistics). As described by the university (and as is amply demonstrated in the content of this book), the international student or scholar has, by definition, no single nationality; the term applies rather to all the members of the university who take part in educational activities outside their home countries. The term encompasses the foreign student or scholar on United States campuses and the returned Fulbright lecturer on the faculty, as well as the graduate or undergraduate student from the United States who has taken part in a long- or short-term study or work program in another country. Just as the services and significance of a university community extend far beyond the physical limits of the campus, the interaction of international students and scholars with off-campus citizens can enrich the experience of all these groups.

Iowa State University has attempted to identify the questions that must be faced when an institution seeks to clarify its relationship to the international student and scholar in the context of university goals and priorities. From two faculty studies of institution-wide international education and services integration, it became apparent that one key to serving the international student and scholar was to build an internationalized curriculum, of which those persons were an integral part—a process that has since been facilitated through the coordination of efforts by the vice presidents for academic affairs and student affairs. Under this administrative framework, the international student and scholar can and does effectively serve as a channel for cross-cultural communication. In these times when economic resources are of critical importance, it is also necessary to emphasize that, in addition to their educational potential, international students and scholars, especially those coming from abroad, can also be seen as a significant economic resource.

International Students as Resources

A university's recognition of its international students or scholars as educational and economic resources begins when its faculty and administrators learn to regard these students as an identifiable audience within the college or university community. All too often, the educational potential of inviting a foreign student to be more than a passive recipient of the United States educational system is overlooked. Often overlooked, too, is the underutilized American whose overseas experiences are casually forgotten by the university community. Such neglect constitutes a serious failure on the part of the administration—especially in this period of economic uncertainty, when many United States colleges and universities are criticized by external and often unfriendly forces. For example, some public institutions have been challenged as to why limited spaces in priority disciplines such as engineering are being taken by foreigners whose families do not pay state taxes. Conversely, some institutions have been tempted by "bounty hunters" who promise to provide qualified, well-funded foreign students for exorbitant fees. Whatever the incentive, the presence of foreign students has become a documented fact on most United States campuses.

The second level of awareness of international students as resources occurs when the university examines the extent to which these human resources are being challenged to enrich the academic community by virtue of their breadth of international experience. At this level of awareness, administrators go beyond abstract expressions of support for international education and attempt to quantify the costs and benefits of having the international student or scholar as part of the community. While the costs may be identified within the institutional budget, the financial benefits may be encountered both inside and outside the institution. In the 1970s—following the pioneer work of Richard Farmer (see Farmer and Renforth, 1971), who described foreign students as an intangible export for the state of Indiana —studies were made by the Institute of International Education to estimate their economic contribution to the United States. The figures for 1981–82 show that foreign students pay over

$1.5 billion annually for living expenses only. In seeking to quantify costs and benefits, each institution will determine the costs according to its own fiscal policies and will assess the benefits as either short-term returns or long-term investments.

At the third level of awareness, the institution decides to incorporate the contributions of the international student and scholar into its educational process. Among the fiercely competing forces that vie for budgetary attention, this decision must be emphasized and included as one of the highest priorities. For a responsible university or college to do less would be to abrogate its role as an institution with a world view. Few United States universities can afford to encourage the parochialism that would result from such a decision. This third level of awareness, incorporating the contribution of the international students and scholars, does not occur without appropriate administrative encouragement. Administrative support for the kind of academic atmosphere in which they can function most effectively is not the responsibility of a single dean or vice president. A growing number of administrators believe that the chief academic officer and the chief student affairs officer of an institution can often jointly provide the leadership necessary to help the international members of the campus community make their maximum contribution to the life of the institution. In contrast to the Ibo proverb "A goat owned jointly sleeps outside," it is with shared, balanced commitment that international activities can and do flourish under collaborative leadership.

Role of Faculty in International Activities

At Iowa State University, after we decided to incorporate the contributions of international scholars into the educational system, we specifically sought new faculty and staff members who had international experience. We recommend such a procedure to other institutions. Whenever possible, search committees should specify that one of the skill areas to be examined as a category of excellence will be the candidate's overseas experiences. A thoughtful search committee will also draw the attention of all candidates to the institution's international activities

—for instance, the presence of an international house, international displays, and international campus programs. Inclusion of the publication *The Foreign Student in Your Classroom* (Simerville, 1965) in the packet of materials for new faculty is another way to draw attention to the recognition of desired cross-cultural themes and institutional emphases.

New faculty with or without overseas experiences may well need an introduction to the services available to foreign nationals, who may become the newcomer's advisees or students. To this end a descriptive brochure outlining services to the international student and scholar can be added to the new faculty's reading material. Another helpful aid is the foreign student newsletter, which may describe foreign study and work opportunities for United States students and faculty and therefore help faculty members appreciate the institution's international view of the campus.

Within each academic department, attitudes toward the international student and scholar are developed as a part of departmental priorities. One way to keep attention focused on the international dimension is to encourage faculty discussion of cross-cultural communication resources available on campus. With the encouragement of foreign student advisers and others who work extensively with the international student and scholar, seminar themes can be developed for presentation at faculty meetings, as well as for staff in-service training programs. Among the most well-received themes is one built on the ethnocentrism of all peoples and their inclination to stereotype. When this is presented with good humor and from a broad perspective, discussion can easily flow into the specific concerns of the faculty members. These discussions need not be exclusively on "the problems of foreign students"; rather, they may help the faculty overcome hesitancy to seek overseas contracts and apply for foreign travel grants. In fact, they may serve as a positive statement of the network of human and other resources on which a faculty member can draw to nurture his or her international interests.

Incentives to encourage faculty to undertake international study and research projects must be clearly stated in published materials for the faculty, including the faculty handbook. In such publications administrative policy toward international involvement can be specified as a part of promotion and tenure guidelines. These publications can also include sections on overseas travel, the availability of research grants from internally generated sources, and application procedures. In these same sections, faculty members may be reminded of the support services available to those staff planning work-study-travel abroad for students. At the same time, persons gathering necessary information for students can collect additional information on such matters as income tax and overseas schooling for dependents. Often this information is already available through the office of the foreign student adviser or the study abroad adviser. For most institutions it is preferable that such information be centralized in one location and that involved staff be given sufficient time to become informed about these matters.

Faculty are sometimes unaware of the administration's efforts to draw on alumni support for international activities. In many cases the alumni association sets aside monies for support of overseas projects for faculty. Faculty who are traveling abroad can also be a rich resource for alumni association interests. Personal contacts through the alumni network can be most useful to everyone involved. Through administrative support and encouragement, faculty members can be brought into this network prior to their departure on approved out-of-the-country assignments. A congratulatory letter from a ranking administrative officer can be highly effective. In such a letter, the faculty member can also be reminded of the specific resources available to him or her: contact with nationals who are part of the foreign student community, alumni association information on key alumni or existing alumni groups abroad, and logistic and cultural information from the study abroad adviser.

Faculty members usually respond favorably to requests for help in acquiring cultural materials from other countries for university purpose. Since 1970 an active effort has been made on the Iowa State University campus to develop international collections of educational materials. These collections are loaned to interested groups on the campus and throughout the state to help them better understand foreign cultures. Where certain items (flags, local currency, and publications) are needed to strengthen a collection, the faculty traveler can often purchase them. The faculty member may also use these collections as part of his or her posttravel presentations.

On their return, travelers may be asked to share impressions of other cultures with the university community. One mechanism that has proved successful is the establishment of an ongoing forum for returned faculty travelers in an informal and cross-disciplinary setting. What once began as a "sack lunch" gathering of Peace Corps volunteers on the Iowa State University campus has become a regular and lively forum for the discussion of international events. Volunteers can coordinate scheduling, and publicity can be arranged to establish a tradition of institutional interest in the returned travelers' observations.

Many universities have published lists of faculty with international interests and experience. At Iowa State University and some other institutions, this information is maintained and regularly updated by computer. Where cost or accessibility limits these alternatives, creative methods may be found to utilize the returned faculty traveler's expertise. In the absence of a printed list of faculty with international interests, a short article in a faculty newsletter can often cause interested persons to identify themselves. Department heads are usually the best sources of information about their faculty's international interests. Expression of high administrative interest in international programs through the activities of such groups as Fulbright scholars or the Society for International Development is encouraged. Further, the foreign student adviser should be urged to bring faculty with international experiences into ongoing contact with foreign students or with United States students who have traveled to other countries. Collaborative agreements for long-term faculty and student exchanges have been generated from such contacts.

The recent development of scholarly exchange with the People's Republic of China has been a reminder that foreign-born faculty members can be rich resources in cross-cultural communication. Often such exchanges have been established through personal contacts of scholars born in China. Materials from the U.S.-China Education Clearinghouse on how to assist newly arrived visitors from the People's Republic of China often mention the role a senior faculty member of Chinese extraction can play in easing the transition for the visitor. Because faculty members of Chinese origin are often among the first to travel to the People's Republic of China, they should be drawn into institution-wide discussions about how to expand awareness of and contacts with China after the recent decades of near isolation from scholarly contact with the United States. The current generation of students will doubtless need an understanding of the People's Republic of China, as well as of other less studied regions of the world. Since there are few major United States campuses where Chinese students are not found, the potential already exists on an informal basis for person-to-person learning about the languages and cultures of the Chinese people.

In the final analysis, the key to stimulating active international involvement and interest by faculty lies in the continuous recognition of international activities by the senior administrators of the institution. Such recognition must be built into the formal faculty evaluation process along with the recognition of scholarly publications and excellence in teaching. Administrative invitations to receptions honoring the international scholar, letters of congratulation for international achievement, and even invitations to serve on committees for the purpose of examining institutional policy regarding international programs demonstrate high institutional interest. Such recognition by both the academic and student affairs officer leaves little doubt that the institution views international activities holistically.

Use of Visiting Scholars in International Activities

Perhaps the most often overlooked channel for cross-cultural communication on major research-oriented campuses is the visiting scholar. Within this category is found the postdoctoral fellow, the visiting junior scientist funded by external sources, or the short-term visitor. Although one may argue that such a visitor is usually interested in specific work with one faculty member on a narrow topic, it is easy to direct attention to other areas of interest within the realm of campus international activities. However, because the stay of such persons is irregular and their types of appointments are varied, it is usually difficult to obtain a comprehensive listing of those who are on campus at any given time. From an administrative viewpoint, there is clearly a need to have an adequate accounting of such persons, if for no other reason than to understand institutional liability should they be involved in an accident on university property. The institution must also be certain that academic appointments conform to affirmative action guidelines.

As a potential channel for cross-cultural communication, the visiting scholar should be sought out by the foreign student adviser. The visiting scholar often has current information about the employment opportunities for fellow nationals who are about to graduate from the university. As a member of the academic community of another country, the visitor can also serve as an adviser relative to collaborative research projects. An active effort should be made to make international visitors feel that they are members of the host institution's community and to encourage each of them to identify with the United States institution after they return home, even though they are not alumni. Among the alumni groups recently established in foreign countries through the Iowa State University Alumni Association, former visiting faculty play important roles in receiving visitors from the campus and in assisting prospective students. One distinguished foreign visitor to the Iowa State University campus has chosen to list this institution—in the biographical sketch found on the cover of the ten books he has had published—as the only university with which he has been associated (as a visiting professor for three years). Such acknowledgment serves as an indication of the affinity which may result from close cooperation with international visitors.

Services for International Students:
A Four-Phase Continuum

At Iowa State University a centralized facility for study abroad advisers has been established within the international educational services office. In addition to having a well-equipped reference library, the staff assigned to this service provide individual counseling and group programming throughout the year to help Americans to maximize the benefits of their international educational experiences and to integrate these experiences into their educational programs. In our view, an international office should make every effort to encourage the participation of as many Americans as possible in overseas learning experiences. Services to this group should begin prior to the students' arrival on campus and extend to the postgraduation period. This period of contact will emphasize institutional commitment to expanding cross-cultural communication.

A conceptual model has been developed to express Iowa State University's view of the international student's relationship with the institution. The model is divided into four phases by those who work most directly in services to the international student. The phases are referred to as the "Four I's": Introduction, Interpretation, Involvement, and Internalization. These four terms encompass the continuum from preadmission contact with a prospective student through relationships with that individual as an alumnus.

Introduction Phase. We believe that admissions counselors should emphasize the presence of intercultural learning opportunities at the university to all prospective students. Students will develop more positive attitudes toward continuing study of traditional languages if they are informed that overseas study or work opportunities can be integrated into degree programs. For those prospective students who have interest in or experience with less familiar cultures and languages, the large number of international students on many campuses presents a potential for acquiring informal learning and enrichment when formal classes are not offered. Where an international studies minor or emphasis exists, the knowledgeable admissions counselor can inform students about career opportunities available to them through involvement with international programs and activities.

University administrators are often interested in comparing the distribution of foreign students on one campus with the national distribution. These data are published annually by the Institute of International Education. Where apparent imbalances occur at one institution, positive efforts can be made to encourage applications from target countries which are underrepresented among the institution's foreign student body. Such efforts can be justified educationally as a means of exposing all students to the largest possible breadth of cultural values through contact with persons from a variety of countries. Although ninety-five countries have student representation at Iowa State University, efforts are under way to attract applicants from five additional countries.

With regard to the admission of foreign students, we believe that the university with an international mission will seek to establish institutional goals. The adage that successful completion of an academic program is closely correlated with a careful selection process by the institution as well as by the prospective student is even more true for a foreign participant than it is for a native student, who is more familiar with the educational system. Thus the admissions information that is sent to prospective foreign students should contain, in simple terms, a statement of the academic requirements for admission, the level of English language proficiency that will be needed, and a realistic estimate of the financial requirements. Students should be admitted only after it is determined that they are likely to accomplish their academic goals; the egalitarian principle of encouraging any student to enroll in any program of study does not always benefit the foreign student or the institution.

One reason frequently cited by foreign students for selecting one United States institution over another is the promptness with which attention is paid to their inquiries. Cross-cultural communication begins when the institution provides information to the prospective foreign student. Prearrival information is provided personally to prospective students in other countries by Iowa State University alumni who meet with the potential newcomers during summers in the home countries.

Recognizing that orientation for the new foreign student is often a frantic series of half-understood bursts of information, the helpful foreign student adviser will view orientation services in an ongoing perspective and not try to present all necessary information prior to the beginning of classes. Student travelers who have returned to the campus are often willing to help plan and carry out orientation services for foreign students. They represent an important resource to the institution. These persons recognize the need to emphasize survival skill acquisition in key areas, such as how to find adequate housing if it cannot be arranged in advance, how to complete the registration process, and how to use the library. From the beginning, students are invited to help chart their own instructional path through the institution, ever mindful that the tools acquired will need to be applied in a different geographical, cultural, and economic setting. Completing the circle of orientation, the network of overseas alumni can be described as a support group willing to assist returning graduates in their adaptation to the home country.

The process of registering provides an opportunity for the new foreign student to enter into the life of the institution. Thus, the foreign student adviser should encourage students to explore activities that enable them to share their culture or that complement avocational interests. Intercultural communication barriers often are overcome through participation in hobbies, sports, or other extracurricular events. For example, through helping his residence group win an intramural contest, the foreign student can become known for his abilities, rather than being the "guy who speaks with an accent." One graduate student at Iowa State University used his experience in his country's air force to become a key member and trainer of the skydiving club. New foreign students at Iowa State University are given a complete list of the approximately three hundred campus organizations and are encouraged to seek relationships that might improve their existing skills or competencies.

During the introduction phase, the clash of cultures is addressed on the Iowa State University campus in a way that may be unique to the institution located in a rural setting. For many Americans on campus, Ames is the largest community in which they have ever lived. For the vast majority of foreign students at the university, it is the exact opposite. The confrontation of rural versus urban backgrounds, values, and attitudes represents a significant challenge. To address this situation, programs are scheduled during the arrival period to describe the social and cultural milieu in which the university is located.

There is an active curiosity about the largely urban foreign population among the domestic students. This curiosity can be channeled into needed one-to-one English language tutoring programs by the enterprising foreign student adviser. Undergraduate honoraries, campus service groups, and returned American travelers (alumni of American Field Service, International Farm Youth Exchange, Youth for Understanding, and Rotary scholars) have been involved in regularly scheduled language conversation groups with foreign students through the efforts of the international student services staff. Members of the retired persons' association have also been involved in these one-on-one meetings. The involvement of this group has provided rich rewards for all participants. The foreign student in particular learns about the role older persons play in our society.

Community service provides an interesting means for non-Americans and Americans jointly to help persons who have just arrived in a university community. One such example in Ames is the International Student Furniture Exchange. This agency currently has on loan household furniture and equipment to nearly five hundred foreign students and their families. Over 120 volunteers, approximately one third of them foreign students themselves, provide the labor to make this nonprofit agency operate. This service has existed in Ames for over twenty years, with leadership support from a variety of groups, including the YMCA, the university residence hall system, and private citizens.

Evaluation of the introductory services is an essential factor in maintaining an effective level of activity. Based on two recent evaluations, the needs of the new foreign student are largely being met at Iowa State University. An internal evaluation of the Office of International Educational Services—in which foreign students, as well as faculty and staff, were surveyed—indicated that there were few areas of concern with the programs and services provided in the introduction phase (Fystrom and Peterson, 1980). These findings confirmed the data presented by Lee and colleagues (1981) on the needs of foreign students from developing countries. A number of new efforts should be undertaken, however, in order to introduce prospective United States students to international education opportunities on our campus. For example, the services available through the overseas work-study-travel adviser need to be given greater emphasis during summer orientation programs. The adviser's role in campus career-planning assistance must be enhanced to expose United States students to professional opportunities abroad. Finally, the newly arrived American student who comes from overseas to study on our campus needs to be better utilized as an information source.

Interpretation Phase. The progression from introduction to interpretation is replete with examples of ways in which problems may be solved and opportunities provided for mutually beneficial activities for the community of international students and scholars. The elements of the interpretation phase of services to the international student to facilitate cross-cultural communication are encapsulated by Krutch (1973) in his thoughtful essay "How to See What You Are Looking At." Once the foreign student has the basic tools for survival in a new environment, questions about "why" social institutions and cultural values are as they are can be responded to. To cite Krutch's approach, the questions often asked about a foreign society—such as "What do the people laugh at?" and "How do they celebrate?"—provide opportunities to interpret the host society. For the foreign student, continuing orientation sessions, involving local resource persons, on such subjects as the United States legal system offer opportunities for a lively exchange of ideas. The local group serving the needs of dependents of foreign students, the Friends of Foreign Wives, offers extensive interpretive services in this domain. Professional persons in the community who serve as resource persons often appreciate the opportunity to take part in these interpretive sessions. They learn that unfamiliar cultural and official practices may be the cause of miscommunication.

Unfamiliar practices in the classroom and residence hall are among the many causes of initial culture shock to the foreign student. Culture shock may result from midterm examinations and grade reports. Poor results on examinations during the early months on campus can be traumatic to the foreign student. Often it is little more than a cultural miscue that is causing the student's failure to achieve. Possibly the student merely needs help in acquiring appropriate study skills or in dealing with problems that result from cultural misunderstanding. The miscue, however, may well be the result of the faculty member's unfamiliarity with foreign cultures. For example, one foreign student was chastised for failing to meet his professor the following day after being told "I think it would be a good idea if we got together tomorrow."

Misunderstandings can be minimized through continuous contact between teaching faculty and those who provide support services to the foreign student. For example, student affairs staff members (those involved in admissions or the English as a foreign language program or foreign student advisers) and selected students can join in discussions with faculty groups in order to understand cultural differences when problems occur. At Iowa State University, faculty groups in three colleges have participated in discussions on how to advise and instruct students from other cultures. Seminars for clerical staff who have extensive contact with foreign students can also be organized by these same resource personnel.

Foreign students themselves can be specifically drawn into interpretive roles when institutional policy recognizes their value as interpreters and informants. As the important work by Mestenhauser (1976) on learning from foreign students illustrates, one major institution—the University of Minnesota—has made great strides in this area. Foreign students at Iowa State University are employed to take part in the team teaching of an introductory course on Third World cultures. In addition, foreign students voluntarily meet with faculty who are planning to take leaves of absence in the students' home countries. In explaining to teachers and librarians how to make the best use of educational materials collected from other countries, the foreign student can help to interpret the function an object plays in the everyday life of his or her fellow citizens. Foreign students who are invited to visit American homes or who are asked to give presentations about their country to local groups and to schoolchildren are pleased to have these materials available to help them interpret their homeland to their new American friends.

In much the same way, international students of United States origin can be involved specifically in an interpretive role. Returned travelers should be challenged to present their experiences to a variety of audiences. Such presentations enable administrators and faculty to acknowledge the importance of approved foreign study programs and evaluate the learning that has occurred during the traveler's international experiences. Prospective student travelers also benefit from attendance at these presentations. It is enlightening, too, for foreign students to attend these meetings, at which the challenges of learning in a foreign culture are described by others.

Cross-cultural interpretive opportunities are also present when university officials are asked to describe "the problems of foreign students" or similar topics to undergraduates who are fulfilling a class assignment. The enterprising official will act as a catalyst to bring the inquiring student into contact with a foreign student who can personalize the story. We also receive numerous off-campus requests for foreign students to give interpretive presentations about their culture. In such instances a preliminary meeting between the host and the student is routinely arranged on campus prior to the presentation; in addition, an effort is made to include follow-up hospitality or personal contact beyond the specific presentation. Important and long-lasting friendships can be forged when this interpretive contact is extended into a continuing relationship.

Faculty who teach international studies courses often appreciate the interpretive skills of foreign students. These can be used to complement classroom activities. Student affairs staff can assist these faculty in maintaining contact with foreign students and in stimulating exchange programs and study abroad programs in the geographical area being studied. The importance of the participation of international students and scholars on campus in these classes can be made known through articles on international studies activities in the foreign student newsletter.

One specific area needing development in the interpretive phase is the utilization of the international student in preparing international research proposals. All too often, faculty seem unaware of locally available human resources possessing intimate knowledge of the society and country to be studied.

In summary, within the interpretation phase, the potential for increased cross-cultural communication by the international student and scholar is limited only by the imagination of the administration and the faculty. As they are made aware of their untapped potential as individuals, international students and scholars may be expected to respond by volunteering their efforts in a variety of cross-cultural activities. For example, one university official was fond of telling foreign students they were taking advantage of only 50 percent of their opportunities to learn if they showed curiosity only about the subjects directly related to their field of study. The intent of this statement was to provoke interest in the wider integration of their discipline with the workings of the university and society. There is, however, one practical problem. The interests of widespread curiosity must compete with the opportunities that international students and scholars have to gain tangible rewards for their specialized skills. This suggests that there must be equally tangible rewards if cross-cultural communication is to be extended. It is in these circumstances that the initiation of formal programs to create interest in other cultures is often the responsibility of the chief academic and student affairs officers.

Involvement Phase. The involvement of international students and scholars is made possible in part by external funding. In terms of dollars, local and private sources of funds for this purpose usually exceed available and state funds. For example, Iowa State University alumni annually allocate funds for travel grants and scholarships to support international education. Two foreign alumni recently gave the university telex equipment and supplies in order that international communications might be strengthened. Valuable free consultation has been provided by local industrialists who have hosted visits of overseas students and scholars. Local interest groups usually appreciate the value of improving cross-cultural communication in order to enrich the institution and the community.

Involvement also can be facilitated through the development of various projects. Funding for this kind of activity has been available from the United States Information Agency and the Office of International Training of the United States Agency for International Development, which for many years have supported programs by granting "seed money" to institutions through the offices of the National Association for Foreign Student Affairs (NAFSA). Iowa State University has received several of these grants. One was used to expand the civic involvement of students sponsored by Agency for International Development, as well as other students from the developing world. Another model program, funded by the Cooperative Projects Committee of the National Association for Foreign Student Affairs, resulted in the preparation of a multimedia slide/tape program demonstrating how the foreign student can contribute to cross-cultural communication in a community. The most recent NAFSA-funded project exemplifies the joint involvement of academic and student affairs staff. Building on the already extensive alumni network maintained by the administration of one college at Iowa State University, a foreign student adviser with an interest in research on foreign alumni attitudes joined a faculty member in writing a successful proposal to experiment with a novel data collection process. Although the grant itself was modest, the process of getting the grant demonstrated a key principle in stimulating international student involvement: cosponsorship by the person serving as a catalyst with relevant individuals and groups in order to demonstrate that they are personally involved. Administrators are thus given an excellent opportunity to overcome artificial territorial limits within the university by involving international students and scholars with university projects.

Another grant, a major award from the United States Department of Education, was recently won by a team led by the study abroad adviser and an anthropology professor. This project integrates work in fourteen academic departments relative to the development of educational materials highlighting the international interdependence of Iowa. It is expected that this project will contribute greatly to Iowans' understanding of their roles in an interdependent world. Special materials have been developed for loan to public school curriculum specialists, to local and regional librarians, and to student teachers and extension personnel through the university. The involvement of faculty, staff, students, and community members is likely to be the most significant result of this project.

Programming, which describes much of the involvement phase, represents one of the most critically important but often misunderstood functions of those who assist the international student and scholar. Such assistance is best appreciated when the programming activity is viewed as a vehicle for the international student and scholar to help the community learn more about the world. Several times each year, public attention is drawn to the International Friendship Fairs hosted by area schoolchildren who welcome scores of foreign students to their classrooms, to teach and answer questions about their homeland. To respond to a public interest in music of other countries, campus radio station leaders requested foreign students and their American friends to produce an international potpourri of music from reggae to rhumba. This continues to be of great interest to local radio listeners. In addition, when they learned that a group of legislators had been invited to visit Taiwan, a team of students from that country organized and put on a predeparture information seminar for them.

Export-oriented business leaders across the state have shown interest in the involvement phase. Foreign students from thirty-seven countries have been invited to be guests of forty Iowa firms with overseas trade potential. Prior to the one- to three-day meetings at a firm's headquarters, participating students are briefed by student affairs staff on how to share cultural and social information with the business leaders. Prearrival information is also given to the firm to increase the potential for valuable exchange of information. More than just "plant tours," these contacts give local business leaders a chance to see the foreign student as a source of information about distant lands. When these business leaders are asked to pay the out-of-pocket expenses of the student visitors, they are never reluctant to do so. On purely economic grounds, such exposure to the future leaders of foreign industry, government, and educational circles is offered at bargain rates. As one important business leader put it, "These students are future ambassadors of Iowa when they return." He considered it important that they learn about the role of the decision maker in American private industry. Support for this type of interchange is provided by state leaders, as well as by business people, industrialists, and others who may be described as proponents of the American economic system. In any event, where a preconceived stereotype of the United States industrial leader interferes with the foreign student's understanding of United States society, these international contacts have helped to break down artificial barriers to the most common denominator—people-to-people communication.

Iowa State University and the state of Iowa have been recognized for the integration of local industry and university interests in the area of international contacts. Programs imitating the university's Foreign Student Contact Program have been initiated elsewhere in the Midwest and also are being considered in other parts of the United States. The university appreciates the fact that international students are recognized as being useful to the state's business and industrial leadership. Thanks to these experiences, business leaders have supported international education in their contacts with governmental officials.

Reluctance on the part of some faculty members to involve international students as educational resources can be overcome. For example, a cultural orientation and language program for faculty members planning to undertake field research in rural areas of Central America was developed at Iowa State University. Specialized curricula were prepared for small groups of faculty. Persons who organize orientation activities for students in intensive English courses were asked to design a two-year program. Students from the target countries became "host families" in reverse for the prospective researchers. Community members with years of on-site language experience (but often lacking university-level language-teaching credentials) served as Spanish instructors. This program has been highly successful. It has been a source of satisfaction to administrators who encouraged cross-disciplinary enterprises and to the teachers who drew on their own experiences in Central America. The program also satisfied the need of participants to absorb practical information in a short period of time.

Another example of involvement is at the undergraduate and graduate instructional levels, where interdisciplinary courses dealing with international issues have involved foreign students and scholars as paid contributors. Course coordinators are constantly seeking contributions from qualified students. Thus, involvement of international students as cultural informants in undergraduate and graduate courses has been appreciated by faculty members and by United States students.

In addition to the traditional classroom-oriented efforts toward curricular change, the university has a clear responsibility to encourage the American student to seek educational experiences abroad. In our view, universities must make every effort to help Americans learn about other cultures through travel, study, or work abroad. International students and scholars from other countries should be utilized to a greater degree than at present in preparing Americans to be aware of and sensitive to the mores and values of their nations. There has been a tendency to rely heavily on Americans for such advice, and the availability of contributions from foreign nationals on campus has been overlooked. A secondary result of predeparture counseling by foreign students and scholars is the establishment of international friendships and understandings.

International students can be effectively involved in a variety of curricular and service activities in support of the internationalization of the campus. For example, Iowa State University has a graduate training program for foreign students conducted under the auspices of the World Food Institute. The institute focuses on the provision of adequate and nutritious food supplies for the world's people through appropriate research and education. Teams of graduate-level international students and scholars, along with their major advisers, design multidisciplinary research programs dedicated to the solution of problems involving food production, distribution, and utilization in developing countries.

Another example of involvement is the exchange program

developed through the joint efforts of student affairs staff and foreign language faculty. In this program American students find jobs in Iowa and then trade these jobs for jobs found by German students in Germany. The exchange is organized with the assistance of the German Academic Exchange Service. Plans are under way to establish reciprocal exchanges with additional countries. On the advisory board that oversees this project are several faculty members who themselves have taken part in work or training programs abroad. Involvement in projects of this type offers special rewards to the international scholar, who can act as a catalyst to help a promising United States student become an international student. It is especially gratifying when students taking part in such a program can also earn enough to cover their expenses. The business community has been supportive of this program. Participating employers, especially those with international ties, are quick to see how they benefit an Iowa student by hiring a German student.

A third example of international involvement has been the recognition by personnel directors of multinational companies of the advantages of bilingualism and international experiences in the employment of new staff. Creative leadership is needed in higher education to prepare college graduates to take advantage of this movement in corporate employment practices. Institutions that prepare their students for the world market will not only turn out employable graduates but also will be highly visible to prospective students, both American and foreign. In our opinion, cooperative education at the international level must be given high priority by educators, industrialists, and business leaders.

In an eloquent statement about the importance of the movement away from a segmented view of humanity, Kerr (1980, p. xix) says: "The proper concern of education is the whole world, not just a part of it. Any educational effort that, in its totality, concerns itself with less than what can be known about all countries and all peoples of the world is incomplete." Colleges and universities must find ways to encourage American students who want to combine studies in an academic discipline with a foreign language in order to enhance future career possibilities. The argument is strong for a bilingual approach to the various areas of study present in the American educational system.

One minor but still significant example of international human resource use is involvement with the expanding interest in foreign foods. With the encouragement of the student affairs staff, many nationality clubs at Iowa State University have planned and organized (but rarely cook) special meals for student residence groups. The cosponsorship role of the foreign student office became unnecessary after several years of successful experience. These projects continue as an ongoing part of residence hall programming.

Foreign student advisers also meet with new residence hall staff each year to describe the resources available from their offices. New hall counselors have shown significant interest in the intercultural tools available to enhance cross-cultural learning in the residence setting. As a result of these sessions, many areas of international misunderstanding can be dealt with more satisfactorily. There is continuing emphasis within the Office of Student Affairs to help set the institutional agenda for international learning.

Internalization Phase. In the internalization phase, the international experience in college is built into the student's life development. This period requires a great deal of attention by the thoughtful educator. In their national needs assessment study, Lee and colleagues (1981) found that foreign students from the developing world were particularly concerned about their opportunities for practical work experiences in their field prior to departure from the United States. For a significant number of those polled, this represented the greatest need, as well as the area in which there was the least expectation for a satisfactory solution. Further research in this area is under way at Iowa State University (Limbird, 1981). In addition, an important study on legal and other constraints to practical training was recently funded by the Office of International Training, United States Agency for International Development, through the National Association for Foreign Student Affairs. The study was conducted by the University of Nebraska, with assistance from educators whose institutions make up the Mid-America State Universities Association (MASUA).

Increased emphasis is being placed on the needs of the international student in the final stages of residency at Iowa State University. In our view, international students should receive opportunities for practical experiences along with theoretical training. Institutions that offer such experiences will, we believe, be more likely to attract qualified international students in the future.

Whenever possible, the graduate student planning to work abroad should be encouraged to conduct field studies in the country of interest. Preparation for such work requires extensive planning, particularly when travel and research funds are not immediately available. Nevertheless, field research in other countries, under domestic faculty direction, helps to keep the student's perspective on the kinds of challenges he or she will face after graduation.

The significance of formally bidding farewell should not be overlooked in planning activities—such as receptions, seminars, and workshops—held during the final stages of the international student's or scholar's stay. The formal goodbyes, combined with such help as shipping information and documents, prepare the individual to return to the reality of the native culture and can be vital to the establishment of lasting relationships.

These events and all the hoped-for results will not happen unless there is careful planning. Professional staff in the Office of International Educational Services, in collaboration with faculty advisers and student organizations, are responsible for coordinating these predeparture events at Iowa State University.

American colleges and universities need to make greater efforts to maintain contact with international students and scholars after they terminate their formal relationships with the institution. Meaningful alumni ties need to be promoted and cultivated by the institution's alumni and development offices. These continuing relationships will result in better international understanding.

Techniques for Encouraging
Cross-Cultural Communication

Faculty involvement as a channel for cross-cultural communication beyond the traditional classroom role has been addressed earlier; however, several specific techniques that have been successful in encouraging cross-cultural communication are worth noting. In order to gauge faculty support for the recommendations of the President's Commission on Foreign Language and International Studies (1979), an ad hoc committee of international scholars at Iowa State University was named to advise the vice president for academic affairs. A similar committee was formed to gather information and propose policy with regard to institutional ties with the People's Republic of China. In the latter group's efforts, the visiting scholars from the People's Republic of China were involved as a part of the data-gathering effort. In these and many other cases, faculty have demonstrated willingness to contribute to the institution's international dimension. Such groups help to evaluate faculty commitment to proposed international projects and programs. International scholars also appreciate having their opinions sought relative to broad international policy matters. These persons also can be helpful in suggesting curricular changes to prepare students for the challenges of a global society.

Another way in which international students are recognized and their continued contributions encouraged has been through annual receptions and programs for international club leaders and returned overseas travelers, organized and hosted at the vice presidential level. Such demonstration of interest in these persons has paid rich dividends in expanding international awareness on campus.

Iowa State University's approach to internationalizing the curriculum involves the integration of the active interest of the vice president for academic affairs, the vice president for student affairs, and the faculty. No college or academic department can ignore any longer the university's overall international mission. A university must assume the initiative at the highest administrative levels in facing and solving problems related to its international goals. Transcollegiality must permeate the institution in all its international activities. In order to provide for the minimal needs of all undergraduates, the university has an obligation to create and maintain internationally related academic programs that have the potential of reaching all students. Every student should be encouraged to examine another society in depth. In the final analysis, whatever the techniques used to achieve this goal and to foster cross-cultural communication, the essential elements for success will be authoritative administrative approval and backing, the support of internationally minded faculty, and the participation of international students and scholars and interested members of the community.

Conclusions

In our experience, top-level administrative commitment to international programs and to international students and scholars is absolutely necessary if a university is serious about maintaining a viable international mission. It helps considerably if the vice president for academic affairs and the vice president for student affairs are actively and personally involved with the institution's international commitments. Their enthusiasm and zeal must, in our view, serve as direct encouragement to the "professionals" in international affairs. All too often, these professionals have no one to turn to for support and guidance within their institutions. Their careers suffer, international academic and research programs languish, American international students and scholars lose their initial enthusiasm, and international students and scholars from other countries are essentially ignored by local citizens. Everyone involved has been shortchanged.

Developments throughout the world demand that American universities stress international affairs, encourage research that pertains to world problems, and promote Third World studies as basic and important elements of their educational missions. As educators, we must serve American citizens who need to understand, appraise, and participate in international affairs; citizens who serve in foreign countries as employees of United

States firms, organizations, and governmental agencies; foreign nationals who come to our institutions as students; and foreign nationals who remain at home and seek the educational help and assistance of our universities in developing their resources and in improving the lives of their people.

According to the president of the Carnegie Foundation for the Advancement of Teaching, "We simply must do a better job of alerting students to the larger contours of the world, of helping them to see the broader ramifications of their actions, and of conveying the urgent need to marshal all our resources as we confront the critical choices of the future. Is there hope for man? Of course there is, provided we can extricate ourselves from immediate preoccupations that loom so large, to confront creatively the issues that urgently press upon us" (Boyer, 1977, p. 78).

Can American universities and colleges afford to support international education, international research, international service, and, most of all, international students and scholars in their institutional scale of values? They cannot afford to do otherwise.

10

Economics: Analyzing Costs and Benefits

Hugh M. Jenkins

Item pricing, cost accounting, and the ominous threat of zero based budgeting all demonstrate the current preoccupation with economy—with the thrifty or sparing use of available resources. Our concern today at the national or international level, particularly in the fields of health, welfare, and education, is not so much what we need but what we think we can afford. It is against this background of political parsimony that the institutional administrator must examine and assess the relative costs and benefits of interchange activities and of the enrollment of foreign students.

It is a climate of opinion that cannot be ignored. For as one delves more deeply into the nature of these costs and the significance of these benefits and the way they are calculated, it becomes abundantly clear that the pecuniary equation cannot be viewed in isolation. National policies and national priorities regarding the funding of education, especially at the postsecondary level, will determine how some costs may, or may not, be absorbed. The reaction of state governments to the presence of foreign students will increase or decrease the margin of acceptable expenses in state colleges and universities. Within the institution one must consider the way disbursements are assigned to different cost centers and the importance of the income derived from foreign students in different departments, or even different courses of study. It is the totality of all these policies, procedures, and circumstances that will affect the final reckoning. In the United States, with its assortment of over three thousand public and private colleges and universities, this reckoning will be determined by the unique combination of factors which will directly or indirectly affect the appraisal of costs and benefits in each institution.

The administrator charged with making this assessment will find little guidance for making the examination. As is pointed out in the study *Foreign Students and Institutional Policy* (American Council on Education, 1982, p. 37), any discussion of the economic impact of foreign students on the United States and its higher education institutions is limited by two factors: "First, research on the economic effects of educating foreign students is still in an early stage. Second, the diversity of the U.S. higher education system inhibits the collection of generalized data." Even the existing information reflects differences of opinion or presumption—not only between the host countries that have the largest foreign student populations (and consequently tend to be the most concerned about the relative costs and benefits), but also among researchers and others familiar with the problem in the same country.

Despite this current confusion, the question of costs and benefits requires immediate answers at the institutional level. Today, for the colleges and universities in the United States, these answers are not easy to determine. In addition to the possible impact of national and state considerations and the current condition of the local economy, there is the uncertainty of the effect of projected overall increases in tuition fees and living costs on future foreign student enrollment and the consequent level of income that may be anticipated. For these reasons it is important to explore ways in which various costs can be recovered, as well as the potential for direct gains that may be derived from resources developed in the international educational interchange activity. Also to be taken into account are the possible long-term benefits that may accrue from the international outreach of the institution, such as the development of foreign alumni groups and interinstitutional contracts for joint research and other cooperative exchange activities.

National Considerations

Although at the national level the designation of the costs of foreign students to the host country will depend to a large extent on its overall pattern of educational funding, the identification of the costs, even in those countries where education is nationally subsidized, will in the last analysis still depend on the situation in the different institutions. At the same time, while the assessment of benefits to the host country will depend on the way these are perceived and evaluated in relation to the national economy, the appraisal at this level will also have its repercussions on the way benefits are determined at the institutional level.

The complexities of the problem are clearly presented by Blaug (1981), who examines all the qualifying factors that the institutional budget maker may take into account when attempting to quantify the costs and benefits. Speaking purely from an economic point of view and ignoring other factors, Blaug concludes that in Great Britain the net cost of foreign students does exceed their economic benefits. In coming to this conclusion, he is in sharp contradiction to the findings of a previous study of the same subject (London Conference on Overseas Students, 1979). To do justice to the arguments put forward by Blaug and his colleagues it would be necessary to reproduce in full the report of the research study and the supporting data. Failing this it seems appropriate to record some questions and comments of those who, while more directly involved in the activity of international educational interchange, are of necessity also concerned with the economics of the operation.

Some of the statements challenged by Blaug are of particular interest because they are fairly generally accepted by a number of people in the United States educational community and elsewhere: (1) the statement that money brought into the country by foreign students contributes to the balance of payments (Blaug concludes that this depends on what might be termed the idiosyncrasies of the international money market); (2) the statement that foreign students' expenditures in the host country contribute to the national economy (Blaug suggests that this is a mixed blessing in that extra spending may decrease unemployment but also may increase inflation); (3) the statement that foreign students serve as a stimulus to exports (Blaug contends that exports to any particular market are influenced by a host of factors, among which the impact of foreign students or alumni is questionable). Supporting the different point of view expressed in the earlier British study, a number of leading experts on higher education in Western Europe, attending a seminar in Bellagio, mentioned a number of widely accepted justifications for international student exchange, including the following economic considerations: "Exchanges enhance the balance of payments position of the country in which foreign students pursue their higher education both because they spend money in it while there and because they favor the country in commercial and relationships in which they may be involved professionally on returning home" (Burn, 1978, p. 14).

How can one explain the marked difference between the strongly supported findings of Blaug's study and the firmly held opinions of a number of other experts? One possible explanation is that the various qualifying factors included in the study are so specific to Great Britain that they may not be applicable to other countries, and that even in Great Britain the findings may be affected by different time spans and other circumstances. A second explanation is that external factors, such as the way in which economic facts are perceived and presented, may be sufficiently significant to affect the issue. Thus, in a discussion of costs and benefits in Canada, the Canadian Bureau for International Education (1977, p. 17) concludes that "expenditure of money by the Canadian taxpayer, through grants to institutions, is roughly equal to the amount of money imported into Canada by incoming students," so that Canada breaks even financially.

Here in the United States, although some part of the costs of educating foreign students is derived from United States sources, "the money coming from foreign sources to support foreign students is considerable" (American Council on Education, 1982, p. 38). In 1981-82, for example, over nine months of the academic year, foreign students spent $1,543,815,900 (*Open Doors,* 1980-81, p. 60) for living costs alone. Since as much as 83.1 percent of foreign student support may originate outside the United States, the arithmetic indicates that, including tuition costs, foreign students bring some $2 billion into the United States each year (*Open Doors,* 1980-81, p. 26). By the same calculations, $500 million must come from United States sources, through federal and state taxes and funds donated to private institutions. Both these sums have a significance of their own within the national economy.

The point at issue is the significance of these national considerations for the institutional planner. Let us suppose that the contributory principle of government expenditure is strictly adhered to and that the large sums of money brought into the country by foreign students are, as such, irrelevant. This means that, as far as its education budget is concerned, the government will withhold any funds used for foreign students in order that the difference between costs and benefits may be recovered through increases in foreign student fees—which will almost certainly result in a marked decrease in foreign student enrollments. At the institutional level, where a combination of other factors (including the money brought from outside sources) may mean that there is a favorable balance between foreign student costs and benefits, this reduction in enrollment, especially if it is in one department or course of study, could have some very negative results. Thus, the institutional planner, who will be affected by but may also affect government policy, should be aware of developments and trends in the determination of foreign student costs and benefits at the national level.

State Considerations

Whereas at the national level foreign students tend to be thought of in terms of statistics, there is a much greater awareness of their presence—particularly those enrolled in state colleges and universities—at the state level. At state institutions budgetary policies and the determination of foreign student fees can be directly affected by the climate of opinion among the state residents and their elected representatives. Even though the economic impact may not be direct, private institutions also will feel the repercussions of any unfriendly attitudes that may exist. Thus, the costs and benefits of foreign student education take on a local color and have an added significance at the state level.

On the cost side, the import of the contributory principle of government expenditure can be a powerful issue in state politics. Although there is no set formula for computing the precise or average cost of educating a foreign student, the existing presumption that, in general, tuition fees do not cover the full cost of education can easily lead to some simple arithmetic about the dollar savings that could be made if there were no "subsidies" for foreign students. The specific application of the contributory principle, as far as international educational interchange is concerned, is described clearly by the American Council on Education (1982, p. 42): "Foreign students are neither taxpayers nor the dependents of taxpayers." Although this is an oversimplification that cries out for further examination, it is used to justify the claim that foreign students are therefore a burden on the local taxpayer and that they are taking places that rightly belong to local students. This argument has been used frequently by state legislators in their attempts to make substantial increases in foreign student fees. Confronted by this challenge, institutional administrators not only must have cogent arguments about the costs of foreign students in relation to their own institutions, but also must provide ample evidence of the economic benefits that accrue, both to the institution and the local economy.

Among the benefits the tangible evidence of the spending power of foreign students and their families can have a positive influence on public opinion and the policies of state governments. Perhaps it is for this reason that a number of studies have been made, or are being made, of the pattern of foreign student expenditures. In his report "Foreign Students in Iowa—A Preliminary Estimate of Social and Economic Benefits and Costs," Limbird (1979) provides an interesting example of the additional economic impact of foreign students on the local economy, specifically on Ames, Iowa. Noting that Iowa State University did not deny admission to qualified Iowa residents in favor of foreign students, who are thus an addition to the student population, he points out that the money spent by foreign students in the local community amounted to over $2 million, including $960,000 for off-campus housing (pp. 14-16). In the same vein, the now familiar report "Foreign Students in Indiana: Our Intangible Exports" (Farmer and Renforth, 1971) indicates that foreign students and their families spent an estimated $17,629,400 in the state of Indiana in 1969-70. Clearly, these figures do not tell the whole story; this part of the story, however, can be very meaningful to state residents.

At the same time, foreign students have an added significance at the state level as the visible representation of potential foreign markets. Although Blaug (1981) contends that the role of foreign students in stimulating exports is questionable, the business community seems to believe otherwise. In Iowa, for example, the state university encourages encounters of foreign students with "export-oriented business leaders" (see Chapter Nine). As Limbird reports, "Iowans in general have encouraged international education and commercial exchange as a two-way street. The overall feeling has been, and continues to be, that—seen in a larger perspective—Iowa enjoys an absolute benefit from its overseas contacts" (p. 26).

In his paper "The Economic Impacts of Foreign Students in the United States," Winkler (1981, p. 1) also recognizes that "the economic impacts of foreign students vary depending on the perspective of the viewer." He goes on to be more explicit: "In particular, local economies, state economies, and the national economy all view the economic impacts as being somewhat different both in size and nature." Foreign student spending in the different states in the United States—for nine months and excluding tuition—ranges from $955,350 in Alaska to $258,830,550 in California (*Open Doors,* 1980-81). The illustrations in Indiana and Iowa suggest that this source of income does affect the state considerations and perspectives on costs and benefits. These considerations at the state level may be important factors as one seeks to determine the economics of interchange activities at the institutional level.

Institutional Considerations

Although there have been studies of the costs of higher education in general and the economic impact of the institution on the local economy, only recently has attention been focused on the specific costs of foreign students to colleges and universities in the United States. It is a relatively unexplored field of study, and the closer examination now being made demonstrates the difficulty of collecting generalizable data. Thus, the reckoning of costs and benefits will remain a particular exercise, related to the circumstances that pertain at each institution. Certain goals and procedures, however, apply to any institution in its examination of foreign student costs and benefits. These broad institutional considerations may be described as follows:

- The acknowledged goals of (1) seeking to maintain a viable organization and (2) offering a high-quality education as inexpensively as possible.
- The accepted definition of *average costs,* simply described as the share of the total institutional fixed expenditures and current expenditures that must be assigned to each individual student at the current level of enrollment, and *marginal costs,* the measurement of the incremental cost for each additional student.
- The importance of the changing relationship between average costs and marginal costs in making any predictions about the benefits or adverse effects of increases or reductions in enrollments on the twin goals of viability and quality for the institution or for some unit within the institution.

Even in the application of these general principles, economists point out that there is room for divergence of opinion, both in the classification of fixed or current expenditures and in the significance of marginal and average costs in terms of institutional goals. It must be noted, too, that there is no "flat rate" for the average and marginal costs within the institution, since these will vary in the different fields of study and between undergraduate and graduate education.

The considerations noted above provide a framework within which administrators can examine the facts and figures in their own institution and make decisions that may lead to an increase or decrease in the foreign student enrollment. They must also take into account certain possible consequences of their decision for the institution:

- A planned increase in foreign student enrollments involves the long-term danger of becoming overly dependent on the continuing level of foreign student applications.
- A planned decrease in foreign student enrollments, although it may produce long-term economies for the institution, may be disastrous in its immediate effect on certain units within the institution.
- A major increase in foreign student fees may lead to a decrease in foreign student enrollment, which may be sufficient to increase the average costs for all the students.
- If tuition fees are used as a method of controlling foreign student enrollment, the composition of the foreign student population may be adversely affected.
- Increases in tuition fees and other expenses may discourage prospective sponsors of foreign students, who provide a substantial and assured source of income.
- More domestic students might be attracted if the institution offers an educational program that is timely, relevant, and international, both in content and participation.

Institutional Costs and Benefits

Conscious of the national considerations that may affect the economics of the institution's interchange activities and working within the confines imposed by state perceptions and institutional policy regarding the costs and benefits, administrators must prepare a balance sheet of the items of income and expense that are specifically related to the foreign students at their institutions. Failing any positive direction, the costs may be limited to the need to deal with the legal responsibilities imposed by the regulations governing the attendance of nonimmigrant alien students at the institution, while the benefits may be seen solely as those derived from tuition fees and income from the use of dormitories, food service, and so on. Apart from that, there may be little or no provision for any services over and above those provided for all students. Under a more reasonable and responsible administration, there may be a number of specialized services designed to meet the recognized particular needs of foreign students, while the benefits may accrue from a variety of deliberately developed sources of income.

Whether the commitment be minimal or more comprehensive, the itemized costs and benefits must be dealt with in accordance with the institution's fiscal administration and budgetary procedures, in which methods of assigning certain expense items to different cost centers will directly affect the "price tag" for the foreign student services and other international interchange activities. Thus, the guidelines, such as they are, for determining costs and benefits must be in the checklist of the items and services to be included rather than in any suggested or estimated costs for them. Because of the variations in institutional practices in dealing with specific budget items, and the effect of such variations on the overall cost for any one item, the National Association for Foreign Student Affairs— after fifteen years of campus consultation in foreign student advising—still avoids proposing a sample or recommended budget for the foreign student adviser's office or international office. Instead, it indicates the necessary elements in a quality foreign student program and the optimum staff requirements to meet this standard, leaving it to each institution to determine how these items will be taken care of within its own budget.

At least five factors may be included in the assessment of the economic costs and benefits of the institution's foreign student program: (1) the specific costs related to the foreign student activity; (2) the possibility of recovering all or some of these costs through an across-the-board surcharge or special fee for foreign students; (3) the possibility of obtaining some reimbursement for the costs related to sponsored students or contract programs through the inclusion of an administrative charge and/or discretionary fund in the financial agreement with the sponsor or contractor; (4) the exploration of opportunities to develop new support, specifically for foreign student programs or services, through fund-raising activities; (5) the identification and development of various extended benefits from foreign student and foreign alumni activities which may reduce costs or provide additional income for the institution.

Specific Costs. Specific costs include staffing, office facilities, rent, and professional development.

Recommended staffing requirements for international educational interchange activities are specified in Chapter Eight. While a number of institutions may find it impossible to maintain these standards, they do nevertheless provide a good yardstick by which to measure the extent of the institution's feasible commitment. As another practical alternative, the natural combination of the two educational interchange functions on campus—foreign student advising and study abroad activities for United States students—may well provide the opportunity for economies (either at the professional or the secretarial level—or both) in the staffing of an institutional international office.

Costs for standard office facilities will have to include additional funding for items such as telephone, postage, and publications. Communication with foreign students, especially up to the point of arrival and registration, will require overseas airmail correspondence and the preparation of special pamphlets. Subsequent to arrival on campus, there may be an unusual number of long-distance telephone calls, visits to the district office of the Immigration and Naturalization Service, and similar special needs, all of which will require a more than average allocation of funds.

Rent may have to be paid for a place for meeting with the public and dealing with general inquiries from foreign students and also for a private office where the adviser can consult with the student without interruption.

In the rapidly growing field of international educational

interchange, it is imperative that staff have the opportunity to keep up to date with new developments. Thus, provision must be made for the purchase of publications, for membership in professional associations, for attendance at conferences, and for participation in seminars and similar educational activities.

Compensatory Charges. There are at least two ways in which the costs that are directly attributable to foreign student activities may be properly offset by special fees or surcharges to the foreign students. The extra cost of dealing with foreign student admissions (not including the costs of a recruitment program, which may be considered as an institutional investment and certainly should be seen as an institutional responsibility) may be reflected in the application fee for foreign students, which should be put at a level to take care of these extra charges. The special services provided by the foreign student adviser's office may be offset by a regular surcharge—in addition to tuition fees—which is imposed across the board for all foreign students enrolled at the institution. This is *not* an increased tuition fee (about which there has been some legal question of discrimination). Moreover, the funds derived from such a surcharge should be used exclusively to pay for the services for which they are imposed. The amount of the surcharge must be sufficient to ensure that the income produced is not dissipated by the added cost of collecting and administering the funds so received.

Reimbursement of Administrative Expenses. The acceptance of foreign students who are sponsored by national or international public and private agencies, whether it be the student on an individual scholarship program or a group of students under a contract program, involves a number of special responsibilities—in addition to those required by the immigration regulations—for the foreign student adviser's office. These may include the administration of the scholarship funds, the submission of reports, arrangements for the visit of sponsoring agents, and a number of similar chores. At the same time, there is always an implicit, and sometimes explicit, assumption that the foreign student adviser will strive to ensure that the participant or scholarship student has a successful educational experience.

A reasonable value may be placed on the professional and secretarial services involved, and this amount may be included in the agreement with the sponsor. Because the welfare of the foreign student may also require unexpected expenses in times of crisis, some institutions have requested and received from sponsors discretionary funds that may be drawn on by the foreign student adviser to meet an urgent need.

A great deal of staff time and effort can also be spent in responding to the many demands made on the institution to receive short-term educational or professional visitors. To respond positively to these requests is in the best interests of the institution; thus, even though no fee may be charged for these visitors, the services rendered by the foreign student adviser's office in planning such visits and arranging hospitality may be seen as one of the economic benefits of that office.

Development of New Sources of Support. A number of sources for the support of foreign students and international educational interchange activities—sources that would not be available for other purposes—may be called on without encroaching on the institution's overall fund-raising or development programs. These would include elements in the local community, such as internationally oriented service clubs or church groups, professional persons of foreign origin who are now United States citizens, export-oriented business enterprises, and a group which is receiving increasing attention as a potential source of support—foreign alumni. These groups may provide the funds needed for services and programs and for various other activities of the foreign student adviser's office. There is, of course, a national network of community organizations that offer programs and services for foreign students. These organizations are represented in the Community Section of the National Association for Foreign Student Affairs and constitute a major resource for advice and assistance in ways of developing community support.

Extended Benefits. There are a number of ways in which the presence of foreign students, and the subsequent development of foreign alumni groups, can be used to provide additional sources of income or make possible pecuniary savings in the

institutional budget. Foreign students on campus, for example—
in addition to being utilized for the enhancement of educational
programs, such as country and area studies and courses on
world religions (see Mestenhauser, 1976)—may be used to provide access to nontraditional languages. Serving either as instructors or members of team-teaching groups, they enable the institution to add to its educational program courses that would
otherwise be impossible or extremely expensive. Foreign alumni
groups also can be organized to provide services such as interviewing or advising prospective applicants in their home countries; they can also provide contacts and hospitality in foreign
countries for alumni tours organized by the institution and thus
increase the attraction while decreasing the costs of this activity.

Conclusion

It is apparent that the economics of institutional interchange activities, and particularly of the enrollment of foreign
students, is a very complex subject. Even the experts find it difficult to make unequivocal statements or to agree on any unconditional predictions. The complicated pattern of short- and
long-term advantages and disadvantages, of direct and indirect
costs and benefits, which are sometimes quantifiable but often
may be only presumed, must be viewed in the light of changing
national priorities and institutional policies. The existing confusion at the national level suggests that this question of economics
merits the attention of a multinational task force or international agency. A comprehensive study in an international or
even global context could shed light on the comparative costs
and benefits in international educational interchange, both to
nations and to institutions. When we know who is paying for
what, the extent of the cost involved, and the value of the resulting educational, social, and economic benefits derived, we
shall be in a much better position to make wise decisions about
the future pattern of this activity.

Part Three

Realizing the Potentials of International Educational Interchange

The critical question facing the international educational community today is whether to treat the new dimension in the transnational movement of students and scholars as an extension of the past or to see it as a confrontation with the future. In the immediate future, there must be an examination to ensure that the optimum use be made of existing resources, so that all students receive an education that is appropriate to the current conditions in their home countries. In the more distant future, there may be a reappraisal of the role of colleges and universities in a world where the educational institution is by definition international, its student body by the same standard is multinational, and the concept of the foreign student becomes obsolete.

Looking back over the past thirty-five years, Robert B. Kaplan asks why foreign students have come to the United States in increasing numbers since the end of World War II. Offering significant reasons for this phenomenon, he discusses the potential contribution that United States colleges and universities might make to meet the educational needs of the devel-

251

oping countries. He also discusses the relationship between language, science, and technology and points out how current developments in these three areas have placed the United States in a position where it might share its resources by serving as education broker to the world. To maintain and develop the key role of the United States in international educational interchange, especially in relation to the developing countries, Kaplan recommends changes in funding of programs, in the regulations that govern foreign students and scholars in this country, and in the educational programs that United States colleges and universities offer to the foreign students.

There must be a continuing review to ensure that the best use is made of existing educational resources and that all students receive an education that is appropriate to the current conditions in their home countries. Kenneth J. Cooper analyzes the shortcomings in the education offered by United States institutions to foreign students, especially from the developing countries. He argues that relevance is a factor that relates to all the education provided to all students and that this must be viewed from the perspective of the individual's relationship to the society in which he or she lives. He suggests how education can be made more relevant and, as a model, describes a program at Stanford University that seeks relevance through a multidisciplinary study of development and its impact on the social and cultural environment in the Third World countries.

This last section of the book ends with a chapter by John F. Reichard, who examines the implications of the increasing public attention to the international interchange of students and scholars. He analyzes the resources required to support effective exchanges and suggest how the individual student and scholar, the academic institution, and the world community might achieve stronger common purpose and more effective results through exchange activities.

11

Meeting
the Educational Needs
of Other Nations

Robert B. Kaplan

Since the end of World War II, students from what are known as the less developed or the developing nations have become the largest group in the increasing flow of foreign students to the United States. For this reason, the interaction between their study abroad and the progress of development in their homelands is of vital concern to the United States institutions where foreign students are enrolled. The way in which colleges and universities respond to the needs of these students may well determine the role that the United States will play in international educational interchange, especially as this relates to the process of development in the students' home countries.

Why They Come

The developing nations have sent us their young because they saw the way we lived and they aspired to share in the wonders of the world the United States had created for its people.

In order to improve the standard of living of their people, the nations of the Third World sought greater efficiency in the operation of the structures of government and industry. They recognized the need for people with special training to achieve greater efficiency. They could see that the United States had efficiency —it had a telephone system that worked, a postal system that served the people, a bureaucracy that seemed to respond to the wishes of the people. The men and women who operated these enterprises had been trained by the educational system in the United States. It was a simple leap in logic to assume that men and women from the developing world could be trained in the same way to bring home the benefits of that educational system. And so governments invested what they could to send young people for such training.

In the same way, or perhaps even more dramatically, emerging business and industry looked to the model of the United States. In the middle of the century, American scientists were helping the ravaged nations of Europe to reconstruct; money and industrial know-how were being exported from the United States to develop the raw materials of the poorer nations. Leaders of business and industry realized that it would be more cost-effective to curtail the leasing of skills and to begin to develop localized pools of talent. And business and industry invested what they could to send young people for such training.

The rush toward modernization brought with it, in many countries, a new kind of problem—urbanization. It is an established pattern in development that modernization is first an urban phenomenon. In many developing countries, there has been, and continues to be, a general tendency to assume—almost as an article of faith—that physical movement from a rural to an urban environment assures entry into the modern sector, a better standard of living, and eternal freedom from drudgery and toil. But these new modern sectors could not possibly absorb all who wanted to enter them; furthermore, entry into the modern sector required certain skills not uniformly distributed through any given population. Families which had made the movement to the urban environment saw that their children would have limited opportunities to enter the modern sector unless they acquired at least some of the special skills necessary

for entrance. They assaulted the indigenous education establishment, but in many cases that establishment simply could not
serve all who wished to enter.

In many developing countries, the educational systems
can barely cope with the general literacy problems. Additionally, many of the systems are truncated; that is, they are often
unable to provide education beyond some median level—often
roughly equivalent to a point in the middle of the high school
years (grade 10 or 11) or lower. Even in more highly developed
systems, graduate education has been limited, and the structure
is sharply triangular, rising at a very steep angle from a broad
base to the apex. In many developing nations, the development
model adopted (at least in the early stages of development) has
demanded immediate technological growth; thus, there has been
a tendency to attempt to develop higher education immediately, and subsequently to build down to elementary education.
Such a model appears counterproductive because it does not
permit the student pool to grow with the increasing capacity of
the system; on the contrary, it sharply curtails the student pool
moving into the expanded top segment of the system and therefore frustrates the development of that top level (see Fuenzalida, 1980). The demand for immediate technological intensifi-
cation creates an immediate need for highly trained manpower,
but the rapid development of higher education can neither supply the immediate need for manpower nor establish the base
through which that manpower need may eventually be accommodated. These factors caused many families, like many governments, to look abroad for educational opportunities, and families often sacrificed extensively to make possible the education
of the individual. Unfortunately, the sacrifice, in too many instances, was unwarranted. The disappointment stemmed, in part
at least, from inappropriate choice of an overseas educational
system, or of an overseas educational institution, or of a field of
study within an institution; not all fields of study could be
equally appropriate to a particular system of national development, and individuals were trained for activities far beyond the
capabilities of particular nations or were trained for activities
proscribed within particular cultures (see Kaplan, 1980c).

Other factors also enter into consideration. Many of

those who sought overseas education were in fact looking for an escape from the deadening hands-on labor that their families had been locked into for generations. They sought a kind of training that would involve them in "clean" work and that would keep them from having to soil their hands. At the same time, few developing nations could afford a large cadre of "theoreticians"; rather, they needed skilled craftsmen and supervisors. Their work arenas were field oriented, not laboratory oriented. Two problems developed: on the one hand, students sought a level of theoretical (as opposed to practical) involvement beyond their own capacities; on the other hand, they sought training far beyond the real needs of development in their home countries. When such individuals returned to their homes, they often found themselves overtrained for the kinds of positions available to them; they suffered disaffiliation and often left the developing country to seek more appropriate work in more developed countries. In other circumstances, they accepted underemployment but engaged in it without enthusiasm. In still other instances, even when they willingly accepted underemployment, their superiors resented their more advanced training or they eventually lost their newly learned skills because they had no opportunity to use them. Consequently, even individuals who returned with a sincere desire to serve their societies were forced to seek opportunities elsewhere (see Goulet, 1977b). These circumstances, the apparent rejection in the homeland and the attraction of developed countries, are to some extent behind the process that has come to be called "brain drain." It is undeniable that "brain drain" is conditioned by two sets of forces—those in the training country as well as those in the home country (Glaser, 1978).

Not all those who came to study in the United States did so out of a desire to return to serve their societies; some came for frankly self-serving reasons. Some were enticed by the images presented in American movies—images suggesting that the streets were paved with gold and that there were frontiers still to be conquered. Others came in quest of freedom of one sort or another; some genuinely sought escape from political or religious persecution in the home country, and others came to avoid military conscription in the home country. These are not new motivations; there are distinguished academicians in United States institutions who came to escape military conscription in the 1930s, and some of our most distinguished citizens are off-spring of those who fled the persecutions of Europe in the same decade. There are those who sought, through admission to the educational system, back-door entry to permanent residence—those who never intended to return. Some have achieved their objectives through a variety of means, both legal and illegal. Some have simply disappeared into the great mass of the population; some have married into the society, and some have found sponsors willing to obtain special consideration through Congressional action, to use political influence, to bend the regulations. In brief, there is no question that people came in the category of students with a vast variety of objectives, not all of them inherently related to being a student. But the great majority of those who came as students came to study, and sooner or later they did in fact try to go home.

This flow of international students to the United States is not a static event but a dynamic, ongoing process. For example, the military and economic conflicts that resulted in the formation of Pakistan and subsequently of Bangladesh, the recurrent eruptions of conflict in the Middle East, the coming into existence of a large number of new states in Sub-Saharan Africa —all these events are directly reflected in the flow and distribution of the foreign student population. This movement is also affected by more subtle events, such as the gradual evolution of the Japanese economy, which resulted in the consequent increase of Japanese students. Indeed, it would be fair to say that the flow and distribution of foreign students are conditioned by every change in political and economic events around the world.

In looking for opportunities to study abroad, some of the students from the developing countries were influenced by historical ties and cultural relationships, but there were some obvious reasons why many were attracted by, or drawn to, the United States. After World War II, the United States was the only highly technologically developed nation whose educational system had not been physically disrupted by the war. The

United States saw itself in a paternalistic relationship to the developing world; through agencies like the Agency for International Development (AID), it extended aid to the developing countries and in doing so helped to cement the structures of dependence (Erb and Kallab, 1975). It was in a position to invest heavily in educational endeavors, and not only was its educational system intact, but its industrial system was also intact and hungrily looking for markets to absorb the products resulting from the changeover from wartime to peacetime production. In short, for every perceived need in the newly emerging and developing countries, the United States educational establishment offered a perceived solution. And the fact that the educational sector in the United States is independent of government, fiercely protective of its freedom from government control, and of necessity highly entrepreneurial contributed to the capacity of that sector to compete in a world market in the packaging and delivery of its product.

Circumstances have gradually changed over the thirty-five-year history of the process. At least some academic institutions in the United States have begun to recognize that a paternalistic relationship with other nations is no longer possible. As a consequence, relationships between institutions have begun to develop in such a way that the United States institution and the foreign institution stand as equal partners in promoting genuine intellectual exchanges (Overseas Liaison Committee, 1976, 1977). There has also been a growing recognition that United States technology may not, in and of itself, be appropriate to every other society; indeed, there has even been a dawning interest in the relative acceptability of certain technologies with respect to ecological and cultural values, as distinct from modernization. Regrettably, offsetting these positive developments, the economic situation of some United States institutions has caused the evolution of a significant recruitment effort for foreign students to fill chairs vacated by a declining United States population and to supply tuition dollars no longer available from various segments of the United States student population. Most recently the economic factors in the United States have conspired to put the educational sector in the position of catering specifically to foreign students. This last phase is likely to have both beneficial and detrimental effects on the quality of education. It will probably lead to a greater concern for appropriate training and appropriate technology; at the same time, it has already led to pandering to the needs of other governments at the expense of the quality of education, and it has also led to a confusion between education and training. There is a need for the evolution of standards by the educational sector, and there is evidence that such an evolution has started; in fact, the Western Association of Schools and Colleges has formally incorporated international educational exchanges into its accreditation standards, and NAFSA is continuing to encourage self-evaluation according to principles set forth by the association.

Language, Science, and Technology

Inherent in the process of educating today's students from the developing nations is the problem of the transfer of technology—of the feasibility of transfer and the appropriateness of the technology. It is an unavoidable problem for educator and student, since a great many of the foreign students enrolled in United States colleges and universities are here precisely because of the technological imperatives of national development. The transfer of technology is a complex problem, since it must breach the barriers of both time and space in order to find in the receiving country a reconciliation with old habits and beliefs and an adjustment to a physical environment that is certainly different and possibly hostile. For institutions that seek to serve the special needs of students from developing nations, therefore, the related questions of science, language, and technology and the problems of access to available information are practical concerns of immediate importance. It is for this reason that the whole subject of technology transfer is rapidly becoming a new specialization and is itself the topic of an increasing number of studies, symposia, and scholarly papers.

Education—any kind of education—has been perceived as the mechanism through which individuals and nations can enter the modern sector. The modern sector is firmly established on a foundation of technology, and technology, in turn, is dependent on science. In the final analysis, then, it is science education that has been most widely sought. This notion is certainly supported by the statistical evidence accumulated over the past thirty-five years; some 50 percent of foreign students in United States institutions over the period under consideration have studied and are studying engineering, theoretical science, agricultural science, or health science (see *Open Doors,* 1980-81, p. 17). Now, scientific research, however intuitive, is a rational activity involving observations and analyses, which are subsequently recorded, often published, and frequently stored for referral by the technical community. Such action is considered an integral part of "research," and it is the essential mode by which science advances and through which technology attaches itself to research. Thus, at the center of all science, there must exist collections of knowledge that are continuously receiving new data, refinements of old data, new and revised perceptions, and geometrically growing amounts of associated observations. All this which exists at the core of science has come to be commonly known as "scientific information." It has, over the years, come to be organized in ways roughly consistent with the organization of science itself (de Solla-Price, 1963). In recent years it has come to be managed, more and more, by specialists in the *information sciences,* a whole new branch of knowledge. Precisely because the quantity of information has grown geometrically, such a development has been inevitable. In the twentieth century, and especially in the post–World War II era, both science and its subsidiary information science have burgeoned, have become structurally more complex, and have far outstripped simple communication and management processes. While the idea is not well understood even in some sectors of developed nations, access to scientific information is the key to modernization, and in the end it is this access that those who come to the United States to study are seeking (Crane, 1972).

It is estimated that the volume of scientific information roughly doubles every ten years. How does one gain access to all this information? It first appears in the *primary publications*—the scientific journals that carry original research articles and that have as their audience peer-scientists. These journals have increased in number and size but have tended to serve narrowing audiences of peer-specialists. Since no single scientist can keep up with the volume, even in his own limited field, much of this category of information is digested and made accessible, by the science information specialists previously mentioned, through networks of *secondary* (abstract) and *tertiary* (title and content-page) *publications*. But even these secondary and tertiary aids to the growing literature have proved to be too much to handle, especially for quality retrospective literature searches. So there have developed enormous coded rapid-access storehouses of scientific knowledge. In these ways the collections of knowledge at the center of science have been radically transformed in character, capacity, and detail.

Societies can be evaluated by their capacity to use complex information storage and retrieval systems. In sophisticated and advanced societies, educational institutions are tuned into these systems, and organizations—both public and private—are involved in the generation, flow, and commerce of technically associated ideas and information. It is no accident that the greatest producers of technical information are also the greatest users and are most involved in systems maintenance and systems management. It follows that the highly elegant storage and retrieval programs of the Library of Congress, the National Library of Agriculture, and the National Library of Medicine, for example, complement a need that exists primarily in the United States; and the need, together with the systems designed to serve the need, is essential to the "advanced" status of this country.

Nations that are the most prodigious producers and users of technical information also manage the storage and retrieval systems. A necessary corollary of management is control. Nations in control of the information systems also are in control of the language(s), the code(s), and the software for storage and retrieval. English, as a result, has become the dominant language of science and technology; indeed, it is virtually the *lingua franca* of information science and of science. Consequently, English is the principal language that scientists will have to use in order to gain access to the world information systems and in order to introduce their own research findings into the literature. The International Federation of Documentation (FID), the international society that deals with science information, recommends that material written in other languages be accompanied by abstracts in English, or Russian, or German. In fact, more than 80 percent of the abstracts are in English. Thus, as the increasing world literature becomes part of the system files, it takes on more and more the character of the language and is made to fit the organization of the retrieval system of the country that manages and controls the technical information (Kaplan and Birnbaum, 1980).

Countries that do not currently manage and control technical information are subject to the existing systems and are restricted by their ability to cope with these systems and modify their output in a manner suitable to localized conditions in the countries seeking information. These conditions impose a number of very difficult constraints. In the first place, the countries seeking information must have (or have access to) scientific information specialists who can use these systems and who, at the same time, can filter and adapt the information to situations which may be significantly different from those in the countries that maintain and control the information systems. This transformation from storage in a sophisticated system to use in a localized situation is one of the most trying elements in the transfer of "appropriate technology." This information is not merely a problem of the technical content but also a problem of language, culture bias, and intercultural understanding.

For the nation that seeks modernization and development, access to scientific information is an absolute essential. This implies not only the development of "libraries" (in the sense of "book depositories") but also the development of mechanisms for access to international information networks, including the installation of the appropriate "terminals." Fundamental to this process is the training of the necessary human resources. Certainly there is the need to develop translation capabilities in both directions (from the world languages used in the systems into indigenous—national or official—languages and from indigenous languages into world languages) because scientists must not only be able to get access to information but must also be able to contribute to information systems. Additionally, there is a need to train information managers—scientists who can sift through the enormous bulk of information and select the most pertinent and useful information—and for "appropriate technology" specialists—scientists who can convert available scientific information into usable form for the indigenous environment. It follows, therefore, that the selection and particular training of those who will provide these vital services is a major concern for the developing nations and one that must be shared by the institutions where these students are enrolled.

Because it is one of the major countries involved in information management and control, the language of the United States is the most widely used in information storage and retrieval, and its technology is central in the generation of technical information and in the development of the information systems themselves. Indeed, it is possible to suggest that the United States (together with a small number of other manager-countries) participates in a worldwide information "cartel." To the extent that the United States is at the center of the information necessary to development and modernization, it will remain a magnet for students from the entire world—for students from the developing world because they must have access to information; for students from the other more developed nations because they must be cognizant of the way in which the system works in all settings where it works. In these terms, the continuing flow of students to United States academic institutions remains assured until such time as the United States—for whatever reasons—loses its preeminent position in the world of scientific information.

But, in fact, the situation is somewhat more complicated than has been suggested so far. The problems relating to information management, described above, certainly are central to the larger problem of technology transfer, but there is another equally important issue, that of assimilation. Since every scientific advance is predicated on previous movement, and every invention—while dependent on individual motivation, intuition, and inspiration—also rests on available information and past achievements, today's scientist must have as part of his intellectual baggage *all* the background information that makes contemporary science intelligible. Because a great many of the scientific and technological ideas underlying modernization and development derive from "Western" science, the aspiring scientist from a less developed country must have *free* access to the most up-to-date scientific information and full access to the *entire* historical panoply of international scientific thought. Only then will the contemporary data be comprehensible. Therefore, the foreign student who wishes to study in the United States, even though he may have extensive factual knowledge, must also face the problem of understanding *scientific method* and *basic* science, a problem which may be every bit as significant an impediment as that implicit in a limited ability to deal with English as a language.

So far, the focus of this discussion has been on the scientist and his training, but there is another side to the coin. The science that a student may acquire as the result of training in a developed country may, in a variety of ways, be inappropriate to the environment in which he is going to function (Jequier, n.d.). For example, the importation of computer technology into a country with a long history of a labor-intensive economy may be a disaster in the sense that it may *reduce* employment opportunity, the importation of a chemical technology into a country that has no accompanying technology for dealing with the toxic wastes produced by such an industry may be destructive of the ecology of the area, or the introduction of such a technology as television into a country in which the traditional culture or religion is marked by inhibitions against iconography may be destructive of the indigenous culture (Brown, 1978). In less dramatic terms, one may argue analogically that the training a student from a less developed country may have received in such an academic area as, say, "strength of materials" may be less than useful if the only materials the student learns to handle are those readily available in a developed nation in the temperate zone while the materials the student will actually have to use will be those available in an underdeveloped nation in the tropical zone. Furthermore, there is the danger that the student from a less developed country may be trained to operate in a laboratory environment supported by a sophisticated infrastructure which provides ready access to elegant measuring instrumentation and equally elegant computing resources. On returning to his or her country of origin, that student will most probably have to operate in an environment in which the supporting infrastructure may be nonexistent or certainly much less sophisticated (Eiseman, 1977).

In addition to essential scientific communication, there are also problems inherent in language itself and its impact on the educational progress of a student from a developing nation. Ong (1971) has pointed to the differential evolution of written versus spoken language. While spoken language appears to have evolved perhaps as long as 100,000 years ago, written language appeared no more than 10,000 years ago, and it appeared only among certain groups of human beings. Among those who developed written language, a smaller group developed printing, and that development is of much more recent origin—well under a thousand years. And among those who developed printing, an even smaller group has—very recently, within the lifetime of all those reading this text—developed electronic word processing. In such circumstances, it is now entirely feasible for an individual to sit within the comfort of his own home and to produce and put into wide distribution a whole book, or at least an article. This capability stands in sharp contrast to the significant number of human societies in which the written word in any form is either totally absent or at least rare.

In Ong's terms, the world may be classified into societies that depend primarily on spoken language, societies that depend primarily on written language, and societies in transition from spoken to written dependence (or, perhaps, societies on their way back to dependence on spoken language after having been dependent on written language). In a society that depends largely on spoken language, information can be retrieved only from living memory—that is, the information is not "fixed" but will vary at least with the age, relative fatigue, and relative audience of the information carrier. In a society that depends primarily on written language, the information is "frozen" and therefore can be retrieved in precisely the same form any number of times over very long time duration (Havelock, 1976). Under the latter circumstances, it becomes possible to accumulate not only information but information about information, and information about information about information; that is, it becomes possible to *distance* information—to objectify it.

Among the students coming to the United States to study in its institutions of higher education are students from societies long dependent on the written word, from societies relatively recently becoming dependent on the written word, and even from societies in which the written word is rare or absent (at least in the mother tongue of the student if not in the official language of the country). Thus, the student population is not homogeneous in the ways in which it looks at language, at language learning, at evidence, at truth, at memory, at learning style, and at information itself.

These comments—about information, information science, and information management, about the cumulative character of science, about dependence on oral versus written language, about the appropriateness of training and of technology —all relate to the issues at hand. To the extent that all these matters constitute impediments to the training of foreign students in United States colleges and universities, some decisions have to be made. These issues raise the question of the efficiency of providing training and the appropriateness of the training. Assuming that, irrespective of national or international crises, the flow of students will not diminish, the United States is faced with three choices: it may act to stem the tide; it may act to increase the flow; or it may do nothing, thereby simply allowing the "free market" to operate.

Education Broker to the World?

Because of its fortunate position at the end of World War II as the only major developed nation with an educational system that was essentially intact, the United States was able to serve the needs both of countries trying to rebuild after the war and of countries seeking, *de nouveau,* independence from colonial status and a place among the world powers. As a result, the United States achieved its preeminence in international education, a position it has maintained despite the changes that have taken place in the last thirty-five years. Today, in the light of current educational needs, especially in the developing nations, the continuing abundance and increasing variety of educational resources in the United States suggest that this country has the ability and even a responsibility to serve in some way as the education broker to the world. In addition to being best suited to this task, it is probably the only nation that could carry it out in a reasonably cost-effective manner. To do so, however, will require new approaches and careful planning and organization within the educational institutions that would be primarily responsible for this further development of the role of the United States in international educational interchange. Whatever the advantages that may accrue, the role of education broker will be possible only if the nation's colleges and universities can offer an educational program that has the necessary international dimension.

Why is it both feasible and desirable for the United States to assume such a role? One reason obviously relates to the status of English as a language of wider communication. To a certain extent, the United States stands first among a small number of developed nations which, de facto, exercise a virtual monopoly on information. Until information can be made available equitably in a language-free format, the information monopoly of the English language, of English language–based technology, and therefore of the United States, will remain. It is unlikely that information can be presented in a language-free context in all important areas of science until somewhere in the middle of the next century at the earliest. As already noted, the problem cannot be solved through translation or through the mere elaboration of existing communication network hardware. To the extent that the United States is a major participant in the information monopoly, and to the extent that it needs to disseminate technology to assure world order and to protect and enhance its own economic interests, it will be obliged to become a purveyor of information and of the kind of training that will permit access to the information networks.

In addition to the issue of information per se, there is the issue of technology. The United States educational system is geared to produce training applicable to a very sophisticated, highly developed technology. Insofar as such training is essential for the development of technology and the rapid modernization of newly emerging less developed nations, many will seek this education in the United States. Efforts to provide access to United States education are already well established; the Agency for International Development (AID) has been contracting such educational exchanges for years; the National Science Foundation has been supporting, and continues to support, international training and education efforts; the American Association for the Advancement of Science has long supported such efforts through its Consortium of Affiliates for International Programs as well as through specific project efforts; and the National Academy of Science, individual academic associations, postsecondary institutions (through direct linkages with peer institutions abroad), the United Nations (through programs like TOKTEN), and broadly based organizations (like NAFSA) have all supported various educational exchanges. Although new initiatives are necessary (see Morgan, 1979), the work of these various agencies has already established the United States as a major source in the transfer of technology.

There is also a political side to the issue. The cordial relations between the United States and some developing nations are to a certain extent attributable to the fact that individuals trained in the United States hold key positions in those countries. In addition, close relationships will develop between some foreign students and some of their American classmates. These personal relationships can be most significant in future relationships between the United States and developing countries. Additionally, foreign students, like all students, form close ties with their academic mentors, particularly at the graduate level, and with the institutions of which they are alumni. Unfortunately, few United States institutions have learned to maintain contact with their foreign alumni, and, too often, they do so only to solicit support. As a result, they have failed to develop an important potential for updating and retraining and for ensuring a continuing flow of qualified students to the institution. A screening mechanism, a mechanism for exchange of information, and a mechanism through which interinstitutional cooperation may be promoted are implicit in the maintenance of relationships with foreign alumni. While such mechanisms hardly exist, and only a few academic institutions have begun to think seriously about developing them, such ties between returned foreign students, their former institutions, and their faculty mentors also constitute an important element in future United States relations with developing nations (Overseas Liaison Committee, 1977).

Quite aside from the directly political possibilities, academic institutions, by their very nature and structure, can do things that governments cannot do. Academic institutions can become the instruments for international cooperation, communication, and understanding because they are not constrained in the ways that governments are and thus are not limited by narrow polarized national views. Academic institutions are, in a sense, like multinational corporations. Their concerns transcend national borders, for they are involved in research questions that are transnational, they deal in the universality of human knowledge, and they seek solutions to international problems. Academic institutions thus have the potential to act where governments cannot. These institutions can open channels of communication even when formal diplomatic channels are substantially closed. This condition is more prevalent in the United States, perhaps, than it is in other countries, precisely because there is no national ministry of education to impose national(istic) interests on the academic enterprise. For these reasons, universities are able to substitute education for weapons in international interactions. They are, by definition, permanent refuges for objective study and inquiry—even when such inquiry involves controversy.

One additional major argument can be made: The United States is a nation at such a stage of development that its most viable product is service. Although it sells and will continue to

sell goods of all sorts in the international market, it is also interested in selling services; indeed, when the United States sells
hardware, accompanying softwear and training are often included in the package. Internally, the great majority of workers
in the United States are engaged in service industries. Labor
costs have reached such a level that, in some instances, the
United States cannot compete with more highly labor-intensive
economies. (To some extent, the current debate over the importation of small cars from Japan is symptomatic of this issue.)
Therefore, at this stage in its economic and scientific development, the United States now finds it most cost-effective to pursue scientific discovery and technological invention and to encourage the mass production of technological innovation in
societies with more labor-intensive economies; that is, it is advantageous for the United States to become a producer and
marketer of ideas and services rather than of products. One of
the services it is already prepared to package and market is education; another is the information network which is in part
appended to education and which underlies technology. This is
not to suggest that the United States should simply abandon the
development of its physical resources or the manufacture of
consumer goods or of industrial goods; it might be advantageous,
however, to shift emphasis gradually, over the remainder of the
century, from raw materials and products to services and inno-
vations.

Despite the perceived reasons why the United States
could serve as education broker to the world and the advantages
that would accrue to all parties to this process, a number of
questions need to be examined and conditions met if the United
States and its colleges and universities are to be successful in
this venture. There is, for example, a serious question whether a
highly sophisticated education is appropriate to newly emerging
less developed nations. If not, should United States academic institutions be less inflexible in curricular design and in insisting
on requirements that may not be relevant to the needs of less
developed nations (see Weiler, 1978; Markson, 1976)? The rationale for this inflexibility has grown out of a legitimate concern for educational standards, but the result is that the United

States academic community continues to operate from an essentially paternalistic position; faculties are not yet convinced that the transfer of technology involves first a clear understanding of what technologies are appropriate, of what social and educational systems need to be brought into play to achieve transfer, and of what linguistic and ecological systems may be involved in encouraging the rooting of transferred technology in new environments without forcing the total restructuring of the environments (in other words, of what existing cultural systems can tolerate). Although the awakening sensitivity to these problems is reflected in Chapter Twelve, there is a real danger that the necessary action will be too little and too late.

Many academic institutions do not yet recognize that action in the international arena is desirable and commendable. Consequently, faculty who become involved are not rewarded for their involvement in the conventional ways (with salary, merit recognition, tenure, or promotion) but may in fact be dissuaded from participation in international activities through the indirect operation of negative factors (like being passed over, losing tenure, losing salary, or losing sabbatical time). Academic institutions have been slow to recognize that meaningful international activities need supervision and regulation (in precisely the same way and to precisely the same degree as do other academic activities) if quality is to be maintained. Few academic institutions have consciously and deliberately planned their international involvements, both immediately and in the long-term future. Until very recently professional and regional accrediting associations have taken no interest in international activities. Some academic institutions have admitted international students with considerable cynicism, enticing them without the ability to provide the minimum services necessary to their successful transition into a new educational system and a new culture and language. A reappraisal of the educational programs of United States colleges and universities in the context of international needs and opportunities is certainly a prerequisite if this country and its educational institutions are going to continue to meet the demands of the developing nations.

Finally, there must be a new definition of the meaning of

universality. Scientists in academic institutions have been misled into an assumption that, because the principles of science
are universal, the applications of science must likewise be universal. Those individuals or institutions that have recognized the
existence of some of these problems have been silenced with the
argument that any modification of the existing system constitutes a weakening of academic standards and that any attempt
to meet the needs of less developed countries implies the development of second-class degrees for foreign students. It is not
inherent in any change that standards must be eroded; on the
contrary, standards can be maintained at the highest level *if it
is recognized that the applications of science and of social science are not linked exclusively to familiar Western models.* Perhaps the most cogent argument for the internationalization of
United States education lies in the necessity to deal with other,
non-Western, ecological, cultural, linguistic, social, and economic
systems. The active internationalization of the United States educational sector may require United States academics to develop
new theoretical models that will account for a much larger
chuck of reality—a chunk considerably greater than that present
in conventional Western models.

Conclusion and Recommendations

A number of smaller and less developed nations—nations
whose educational sectors are insufficient to serve the needs of
their indigenous students—welcome foreign students to the extent they are able to do so. Korea and the Philippines have, relatively speaking, substantial numbers of foreign students; the
University of the South Pacific, serving ten tiny independent
states with a total population of only about five and a half million people, accepts "foreign students" from Asia and elsewhere. Egypt's universities have for generations served students
from throughout the Middle East. These less developed states
welcome foreign students *and underwrite the cost of their education* because they believe that the presence of these students
works against provincialism and because they desire to participate in the global network of knowledge, in the free flow of

technical information, and in the value of modernization through technical development.

In the United States, on the other hand, the federal government, while accepting in principle the benefits of international educational interchange, has for the entire period under discussion steadfastly refused to fund at a meaningful level a whole potential range of international educational activities. As a consequence, the matter has devolved on the several states. The reaction of the state governments, depending on the political climate within each state, has varied widely. It has ranged from the provision, in some instances, of special favorable rates for foreign students, to the imposition, in others, of special supplementary fees for foreign students. These phenomena reflect not a concern for international education but a continuing provincialism, a too narrow interpretation of the public charge to serve students from the local community, and a misunderstanding of both the larger educational and the larger economic issues.

Despite all these negative signals, the pull of United States technical education is so great that foreign students have continued to come in increasing numbers. As a result, the United States has benefited in the various ways already enumerated. But the long-term interest of the United States and the long-term interests of the academic sector probably can be best served by much greater attention to international education.

Three kinds of efforts seem desirable: a change in the funding of international educational activities, a change in the regulatory procedures, and a change in the curricula and basic services offered.

In relation to *funding,* it is not too much to suggest that if poorer, less developed nations accept the underwriting of foreign students as part of the responsibility of national government, the United States, as a rich, highly developed nation should do so as well. There are ample reasons for the United States to consider seriously accepting the role of education broker to the world. The cost of doing so would be relatively trivial, and even though the United States taxpayer might have to tolerate some part of the cost, this would probably involve nothing more than the correction of the cash-flow problem. The richer nations could be encouraged to support their students (as Kuwait, Saudi Arabia, and Venezuela, for example, do now) while the other nations, in descending order of GNP, could pay some portion of the educational costs, and the poorest nations could send their students without cost. In the long run, it is highly likely that, overall, foreign students would more than support their own education; in any case, the economic and social benefits would be a worthwhile exchange for any costs incurred by the United States.

The question of *regulatory procedures* is the subject of a more intensive study in Chapter Seven, which discusses the problems that the Immigration and Naturalization Service (INS) can cause for foreign students and scholars. It is sufficient to note here that the Select Commission on Immigration and Refugee Policy (1981) has already recommended diversification of the pertinent visa categories and the involvement of the Department of Education—or (presumably), failing this, some other educational authority within the federal government—in the evaluation of institutions to participate in international educational interchange. It is to be hoped that, as in the past, the educational sector can successfully accredit itself in this as in other areas of activity and that educational institutions will recognize their own responsibilities in the field of international education.

The question of the reaction of United States educational institutions to the enrollment of foreign students and the development of *international curricula* affects the basic question of the kind of education that will be provided in the twenty-first century. The educational sector has the responsibility to provide to all citizens an equal opportunity to achieve a greater awareness of the world. In a time when global interdependence is a reality demonstrated in the daily headlines and is not merely a slogan, too many campuses and faculties remain isolated and provincial. Internationalization of the curriculum is essential to the education of all future generations. Internationalization implies the admission of at least some foreign students; the recruitment of at least some foreign faculty; the development of at least some exchange programs, which would permit United

States students to study abroad and United States faculty to become involved in the solution of worldwide problems; and, finally, the recognition that the curriculum should include some segments that transcend the normal myopic view of the world.

These three kinds of changes will involve more than the educational sector and the government. The private sector, for example, stands to gain much in the way of expanded markets, better basic research, better understanding of market need, and a larger pool of human resources. There is no reason why the private sector should not contribute to the financial support of the whole enterprise; indeed, industry already contributes in significant ways. And philanthropic foundations might be interested in contributing to the enterprise; it is reasonable to assume that they will do so if they are convinced that internationalization is a significant interest of the United States and of the educational sector. Finally, there needs to be a carryover of the notion into basic United States foreign policy, because the exchange of persons eventually depends on a series of country-by-country protocols. As existing protocols are revised and modified over the next quarter-century, the question of reciprocal educational exchanges may be addressed.

At the present moment, the United States contains within its borders one third of the world's formal educational resources. The policies evolved by United States educational institutions—in consort with the federal government in whose charge lie the country's international relationships—will inexorably affect the pace of development for much of the world. The development of this country is inseparable from the development of every other nation; the fate of this country is in very direct ways linked with the fate of the seemingly smallest and most insignificant state. Who would have thought, a year or two ago, that the fate of Afghanistan, of Angola, of the Sudan, could be so linked with that of the United States? Interdependence is made a fact by technology, and technology—while it is certainly at the mercy of philosophy and ideology—is most closely related to economics. The United States educational system is an important "hidden" export; it brings "new" money in precisely the same way that the sale of export goods does; it may turn out to be the most important product the United States has to offer, but its importance depends on the ability of the educational sector to recognize the quality of the commodity of which it has control and simultaneously to recognize the nature and needs of the world market for that commodity.

12

Increasing the International Relevance of U.S. Education

Kenneth J. Cooper

The question of relevance in education has been the subject of increasing debate in recent years. There has been a broadening of vision, as some groups in the United States educational community call for an education that is relevant not only to individual needs for personal advancement but also to citizen responsibilities in a global community. In the field of international educational interchange, the problem of relevance is more complex. Questions are raised about what is taught, how it is presented, and how it will be used. Some educators ask whether courses of study that were created to meet the needs of United States society can be transferred in their entirety to prepare students for careers in another country and a different culture. Some fear that any adaptation of curriculum will prejudice the academic integrity of the discipline. Others deplore the futility of providing overspecialized education, which students cannot readily apply when they return in their home countries. Others simply point out that, for the last more than thirty years, increasing numbers of students from countries all over the world have come to this country for the sole purpose of obtaining the education offered by United States colleges and universities, and nothing needs to change.

Discussion at this level only scratches the surface of a problem that has deep-seated roots and long-lasting implications. As the transnational movement of students and scholars assumes ever greater proportions and as the passage of time now offers a perspective that allows us to evaluate the impact of a generation of educational interchange, there is need for a closer and more penetrating examination of the meaning of relevance in the education of foreign students.

What follows is an approach to relevance in the widest possible context, encompassing the relationship of education to the world we inhabit, the times in which we live, and the future for which we are preparing the students of today. Noting that education is a process of change, we see that the application of relevance is of necessity a changing condition—a condition that, perhaps because of the very nature of education, can never be brought to closure.

The Dimensions of Relevance

Where do our measurements of relevance come from? Relevant for whom, according to whose values? For what purpose? If we do not ask the question directly, at the beginning of our analysis, we are apt to find ourselves engaged in purely procedural questions where we unwittingly discuss "how to?" instead of "what for?" or "for whom?" How do we begin to reconcile the many interests involved: the personal and professional goals of the foreign student; the cultural values and development needs of the student's home country; the particular competence and objectives of the host university and its separate academic disciplines; the value to the host society, to international relations, communication, and mutual understanding, and to the particular organizations that choose to sponsor a student's study or research abroad?

Another dimension almost as difficult as "for whom?" is the dimension of change. Relevance can be and usually is considered (when considered at all) in terms of what has been and is now "in place." It usually is a question of how to expedite procedures that have already been accepted by individuals and institutions as legitimate. United States foreign student counselors of necessity devote far more of their time and energy to administering existing bureaucratic rules and regulations, and helping students adjust to the pressures and demands of United States academic and cultural competition and specialization, than to questioning the possible causes of dissatisfaction and mismatching. And one of the possible causes for the problems people encounter as they try to adjust to particular social structures and institutions is that those very institutions may be in need of change. The social system itself, rather than the individual, may be at fault. To be relevant, then, education itself requires a philosophy that contains a strong dash of experimentation and openness to the future.

Problems experienced at a host university often are caused by an imperfect matching of the goals and assumptions of the various parties involved in international educational interchange. Unfortunately, such problems may not be recognized until after the student has graduated, returned home, and begun to apply what he or she has learned from the international educational experience. New programs at universities around the world are attempting to anticipate these problems before they become the personal problems of international students. That is, these programs attempt to ensure a better match between the educational experience and the ultimate need to put that experience to work, so that the student will have fewer problems and the foreign student counselor will devote less time to making more efficient a system that possibly should be drastically changed and redirected.

But the real problem of relevance is much deeper and the search for it at this level is complicated by the fact that so much of the global interchange of students and scholars at this time is among the highly industrialized capitalist countries and between them and those countries of the Third World that have capital and wish to develop industrially and technologically as fast as possible. Thus at the very moment when there are more foreign students in the United States than ever before, and when new creative strategies are needed to guide the evolution of American higher education into imaginative new channels, the dominant drive behind the quest for United States degrees is to accelerate the now traditional "Western" modernization process in the developing countries themselves.

We need to make a fresh start. When we discuss and analyze "relevance," let us be freed from the shackles of ethnocentrism and let us also be freed from tempocentrism. We should look to the future and "be prescriptive rather than descriptive"; we need to present a challenge, not a history, to deal with current and emerging topics rather than retrospective ones. That very directive is precisely at the heart of any examination of the role of education in society. If we as educators choose to rest on past laurels, we may find greater and greater numbers of graduates being trained to fine-tune what turns out to be a very obsolete machine. How can one "educate for the future"? Might relevance be defined, in part, as an openness to and acceptance of complexity, uncertainty, interdependency, limits, and contradictions? There may be need to experiment with new sets of human values that offer direct challenge to conventional values on which existing power structures rest. To do this we need to think and plan beyond the mere mechanical processing of students and scholars within an existing system, whose inherent contradictions may cause many of the problems we deal with on a daily basis. We need to ask whether United States higher education is relevant to ongoing and anticipated changes in patterns of national and global development.

Specifically, we might wish to examine the prevailing and widespread need—in all cultures and in all academic and professional fields—for an "integrative expert"—a person who has acquired expertise in a professional field and is also able and willing to understand and communicate with other specialists for the purpose of linking their professional knowledge and problem-solving abilities with the realities of their living communities. In the opinion of future-oriented thinkers such as Michael

(1973) and Harman (1975), the integrated experts of tomorrow will necessarily possess emotional and intellectual capabilities that will allow them to be highly flexible—to take in, comprehend, and identify with the extremely complex and often contradictory and conflicting opportunities, demands, and limitations that constitute future development. The effectively educated persons of tomorrow will not only need to have a particular area of expertise; they will also need to see how the focus of their own field links with the larger professional and societal wholes of which it is a part.

If we consider future development in all societies as requiring a healthy supply of integrative expertise, then we might ask how our present educational system measures up to this criterion for relevance. When one talks to educators about the overall purpose of the educational process, or the particular criteria they use to judge the degree of success or failure of educational programs, it soon becomes apparent that, somewhere in the process of administering education, the original, basic questions of "what for?" and "for whom?" are often forgotten. These are the questions that need to be addressed.

When we talk about "relevance," it is safer and surer if we understand, first of all, what "purpose" we are measuring relevance against. Who are the key actors involved, for whom international educational exchange may or may not be relevant? For what purpose or purposes are they involved in the process? If we can understand the objectives of each of the major parties involved, we can talk sensibly about relevance.

Recognizing that the interested major parties concerned with the success or failure of the international educational experience are the student or research scholar, the home country from which the student comes, the host university, the host country, particular sponsoring agencies, and the global community, we need to ask who determines the goals—the individual student or society? Are social institutions responses to the will of the individual collective, or are individual values determined by the images and pathways provided by the social institutions that are already in place—with a life and power of their own? Of course, it is a mix of the two, an undulating dynamic that

swings back and forth in a given society, depending on current
political and economic forces. Each individual, too, acts sometimes in response to impulses based on deep personal values and
sometimes in response to demands from the social order. Certainly, the individual student is caught in this dilemma. Even
the youngest and most unsophisticated student has strongly
held personal values and concerns—some related quite specifically to the desire to satisfy individualistic physical and emotional needs; some related to the welfare of humankind as a
whole. We have all seen young people whose original hopes for
a special kind of self-fulfillment containing a strong element of
social responsibility were gradually eroded by the realistic demands of the very limited and thus competitive avenues open
to them in society. As we continue to carry out our traditional
roles of passing on a culture from one generation to the next,
we in the field of education need to continually ponder to what
degree our educational institutions should be responsive to
fresh new hopes and ideas from students and their perennial
quest for new approaches and for personally and socially meaningful education.

In addition to a consideration of the individual-versus-
the society dynamic, we need to consider the existence of a
global society and the prospect of its survival. Thus, we must
bring into our discussion two other dimensions—the global and
the future. Education began its march through time in various
forums for the principal purpose of passing on accepted survival
techniques from one generation to the next. It was, necessarily,
a localized—that is, a highly ethnocentric—phenomenon. Survival depended on protection of a group's access to necessary
life-supporting resources. Most needs were satisfied by people
organizing in relatively small and, of course, homogeneous
groups, working out sharing and cooperative arrangements. If
one could have viewed the planet earth as a whole several thousand years ago, it would have been apparent that a balance
existed between the demands placed on the earth by its human
populations and the ability of the earth to provide resources to
meet those demands. The people did not "know" anything
about the global picture; nevertheless, it existed—an earth in

balance. As the size of viable human communities became larger and larger and as technologies for gaining access to and utilizing the earth's physical resources became increasingly more effective and more powerful, the old balance ceased to exist. Increasing demands by more people with more and more technological power, combined with a shrinking resource base, have led to countless conflicts through the ages—to the point now that a purely ethnocentric search for satisfaction by each of the earth's separate national and cultural entities quickly leads to confrontation and conflict (North, 1976). Today no one can deny the need for a global consciousness. "Every individual or nation for itself" simply does not work any more—or will not work for very long. In spite of vestiges of colonialism and intranational inequities, the movement through time signals clearly that the constant dynamic from now on is going to bring continuing pressures for a more equitable sharing of a recognizably finite supply of natural resources (Barnet, 1980; Dammann, 1979; Mesarovic and others, 1974; Schumacher, 1973; Tinbergen, 1976). There will be breakthroughs from time to time as new technologies help stretch the yield from this finite resource base. But the costs will be higher, and the pressure to share the increased yield will continue to grow.

All this leads us to repeat that cultural and national centrism is no longer functional. If education fails to incorporate this awareness into its goals, it will fail one of its original purposes—to prepare future generations for survival. This point raises serious questions about the relevance of two dominant characteristics of education in the industrialized, capital-based, market-oriented societies: the stress on individualism and competition. With a series of studies that came out in the early 1970s—*Limits to Growth, Blueprint for Survival, Population Bomb, The 29th Day, Poverty of Power, An Inquiry into the Human Prospect, The World That Could Be, Small Is Beautiful, Mankind at the Turning Point*—it was no longer possible to ignore the clear message that there are physical limits to our environment. Resources are limited, as is the physical environment's capacity to absorb the wastes of "civilized" societies. Ecological awareness is here to stay.

In considering the time dimension, we must realize that education has always had the responsibility of bridging the time barrier. It has had, as mentioned above, the principal task of passing on survival techniques for preserving the status quo from one generation to the next. Assuming that survival in the future will depend on increasing cooperation among cultures and nations, it follows that any education that neglects the issues of long-term survival and future planning will be out of tune and will automatically become less relevant. Tempocentrism is out of style. Education that hugs itself to its own bosom and insists that it has all the answers, that the only urgent need in the world is to "transfer" our technology, is proving to be dysfunctional (Goulet, 1977b). The apparent fact is that we no longer know exactly where we are going. John Dewey, in many of his early writings (1922, 1930, 1936), insisted that a basic ingredient in education relevant to the twentieth century is the freedom to respond to change, to be innovative and open to experience, to let experience guide us.

When we add another dimension, social equity, it then appears that cooperation rather than competition may be the watchword of future development. It is no longer blindly acceptable that some of us shall be rich and some poor, for some to live happy and fulfilled lives and others to starve. The irrationality and inhumaneness of this dualism have become part of the human consciousness and the historical record. Whether or not we devise new social, political, economic, technological, and educational systems that will eradicate this dualism is still an open question. But the *consciousness* is here to stay. Egocentrism and ethnocentrism are out of phase with the times. A different global ethic is required. Dewey had a term for it: "inward corporateness," when people act naturally and unconsciously in a spirit of cooperation and mutual respect for each other's needs and desires (Dewey, 1927, 1930).

In summary, the condition of life on earth now and in the future demands that education be multi- and intercultural and future oriented. Forms of cooperation rather than competition for access to limited resources will lead toward national and cultural survival—group survival. A two-pronged recognition—that we are all on a small and valuable planet and that everyone on the earth has an equal right to survive—should form the basis for analyzing the degree to which education is relevant for the 1980s and beyond.

Relevance and Reality

How do students perceive the purpose of studying at a foreign university? They want the "best" education available, so that they can develop to their fullest potential and so that they can get a good job in the general area of their professional interests. They almost always have a companion desire: to broaden themselves culturally. They want to know more about the world from firsthand experience and to gain added perspectives of their own cultures. When most people decide on a new educational experience, they probably hope it will help them to lead a professional life that is interesting, remunerative, and good for their self-image. And most people would like their work to be helpful rather than harmful to the society at large. They would like to make a positive contribution to "knowledge" and to the welfare of their fellow human beings. Few technologists would actually *choose* to design or build neutron bombs. For the same reason, few would actually prefer to use their marketing skills to increase the sales of a breakfast cereal they knew to be harmful to children's health.

The achievement of this last purpose—utility of one's professional work to the larger public good—is a hard one to measure. What we do need to think about is the degree to which prospective students' perceptions of their purposes are altered through the actual process of study and living outside their countries. How can anyone judge the relevance of their evolving experiences, whether it be to their predeparture visions or to their changing selves *necessarily* adapting and adjusting to new environments? The metamorphosis is usually so idiosyncratic that we can only suggest ways of asking questions that will reveal whether a student's objective is one he or she had before leaving home or one that emerged abroad. But how can anyone say what the emergence resulted from? It could have been due to natural personal development or to changing aspirations and self-image related to the particular milieu characterized by the specific research focus of one's academic department.

All of us who have worked in international education have had our own personal experiences talking with alumni about their educational sojourns. My own interviews with Stanford graduates in countries in Africa, Latin America, Asia, and the Middle East led me to question, seriously, the relevance of their Stanford/United States experiences in relation to their perceived roles once back in their own societies. Most of the alumni seemed to have benefited in terms of personal growth, job remuneration, and self-image. Almost without fail they spoke positively about their overall study abroad experience. They valued the opportunity to make friends from other cultures; they enjoyed their broader sophistication resulting from life outside their own cultures.

But the majority of foreign alumni wished they had had, at Stanford, a better preparation for the broad-based concerns and responsibilities they found themselves challenged with shortly after returning home. The specialized, single-discipline, high-technology, United States market–oriented training was seldom very relevant to the complex cultural nuances and inherently interdisciplinary nature of the problems faced by their own societies. A small but critically important group of alumni expressed dismay that they had not had the opportunity while at Stanford to point their studies and research more toward addressing some of the very particular critical social, political, economic, and technological problems facing their societies. Others were concerned about the even more subtle problem of having the course of development of their societies strongly influenced by the particular technologies, business practices, and cultural values they had inherited from their United States educational experience.

There is the practical versus the theoretical problem. Many students find little opportunity to apply directly the knowledge acquired at a United States college or university. Foreign students often find themselves in positions with significant responsibility shortly after their return home. They are less likely than their American counterparts to be plugged into a middle-level position in a large corporation or academic institution where they are expected to carry out work already under way—one small piece of a larger whole. The foreign graduate often is expected to be able to pull together many disparate pieces, to integrate and oversee and initiate long-term comprehensive plans, whether he be in academia, government, or private business. And he usually finds himself immersed in a rapidly changing political and economic scene.

Apparently, few graduates had opportunities while at Stanford to anticipate how their necessarily narrow, specialized training might eventually be applied to the complicated, interactive types of problems that emerge in living societies. Nor were they sufficiently challenged to ask difficult questions related to long-term survival and improvement in the well-being of their citizens.

How well are the present educational institutions addressing the range of needs discussed above? If some of the needs regarding global survival call for new ways of organizing society, new ways to approach balance with nature, to reduce inequities, to increase fulfillment of an individual's potential—then it is obvious that imaginative and creative approaches will be in demand. If the old systems currently in place are not working too well (we can each make our own list of failings), then what are the mechanisms in the world today that have the potential to meet those demands? Educational institutions and the individuals that form them seem a logical source. Whether they are a likely and willing source is yet to be determined.

Historically, when individual human and social needs developed and when opportunities for evolutionary steps were present, individual innovators asserted themselves and helped create new institutions and mechanisms for adapting to and creating new environments. Education and educational institutions have sometimes played important roles in the evolving drama of human civilization. In numerous instances, however, it was not the scholar who saw the needs and opportunities for change. Social experiments have taken place, usually without the blessing of academia. The reflective, deliberate, reasoned

thinking characteristic of the world of higher education combined with the assertive change-oriented action of religious and
political leaders and popular social movements has, throughout
history, melded into the variety of societies we see today.

However, the new dimensions to relevance mentioned
earlier—dimensions having to do with the limits to our life support system, burgeoning populations, the need for a far more
balanced approach toward gaining access to the limited supply
of resources, and the ability to destroy human civilization as we
know it today—pose survival questions that did not exist before.
Relevance—relevance of education, of international educational
interchange—now takes on new importance. Education no longer has the luxurious option of sitting back and providing merely
"basic" and reflective interpretations of the past and present. If
we are to improve human welfare and build systems for future
human survival, then educational institutions and the scholars
within them surely will have to play a more conscious role than
in the past. The university will have to ask itself to what degree
relevance to human welfare and long-term survival means responding to competitive job market openings and contemporary
sources for research funding. It must ask itself whether, instead,
it now means taking thoughtful and outspoken steps to lead rather than follow and to suggest new and imaginative experimental development strategies that might even lead to life-style
changes; economic systems based more on cooperation than
competition; decentralized and participatory governance;
change toward more human-scale technological growth.

Will higher education respond to the signals? Who will be
the ones to explore new approaches to living—at the individual,
community, national, international levels? Who will be free
enough and brave enough to ask questions that might lead to
suggestions for change? Will it be the academician—or might it
be necessary for innovative individuals to move out of the university and into other kinds of activities?

It is one thing for a university to be *responsive* to the demands of the present marketplace. United States universities
already do a better job of this than most foreign universities.
But if the university is to be *responsible* and *relevant* to the

deeper needs and hopes of society, it may have to develop entirely new mechanisms that in themselves may offer direct opposition and contradictions to the marketplace. If the universities do not develop such mechanisms, the truly creative and active minds will go elsewhere. But there is little "elsewhere" to go. Therefore, unless the universities are able and willing to be open to the need for *new* ways of thinking and researching and acting, the prospects for meaningful survival in the future are dim.

How Can We Make Education More Relevant?

Our overall task will be to make education more flexible and responsive to the changing times. Education should help people learn how to frame questions that will lead to new answers and new directions, to new theories and new actions. It should help build a conceptual approach to life that is critical and analytical and imaginative. United States higher education has excelled in "how to" without asking itself, very seriously, "what for?" It finds it hard to address its considerable talents and power to existing and rapidly developing societal needs. Why is United States higher education so good at improving the efficiency and power of existing value systems, institutional structures, and technologies and so poor at addressing the truly critical global problems? Shall we, as educators, close our eyes and ears to the difficult questions and resort only to the more manageable and therefore more comfortable tuning up of the status quo? Should we leave the overhaul job to someone else? If so, can we find someone else to do the job?

If students continue to come to the United States to study, carry out research, and work solely on the "how to," they may achieve personal wealth and prestige and bolster the corporate structure and its value system. They will not be of help to the home country in its desire to achieve greater self-reliance and independence. And they will not be helpful to the long-range hope for human survival because they will not be asking "what for?" questions. And they will not develop their fullest personal potential because they will not have explored the depths of creative potential for innovative ideas and behavior that are tapped only when people are asked to stretch themselves and have confidence in their questioning of the status quo. People need to be encouraged to explore new alternatives. Change comes about only when workable alternatives are posed.

The mere restyling of the educational vehicle—the tinkering with its engine by installing computerization and robotization (Sandberg, 1979) or by giving it more power and speed in order to hold its own amidst the mad rush of the competitive job and research funding freeway—is not the answer. Nor are the freeways that roar blindly toward the nowhere of growth for growth's sake. The ever finer tuning of the educational vehicle to conform to the perpetuation of accelerated growth and expansion of present social, political, economic systems—so that its separate parts are, themselves, better—can no longer carry us in the direction of holistic, integrated goals such as improvement in the quality of life, greater equality, human-scale technology, self-fulfillment, or, indeed, even the very survival of human society.

When education has devoted itself to ever increasing specialization, it has succeeded, in many ways, in bringing a better life to many people—in enabling individuals and whole nations to share in the benefits of the past thirty years of economic and technological growth. The United States model of growth—of specialization, production, and consumption (and waste) of material goods—was the path to success. It was successful for many Americans, Europeans, Japanese, Russians—and for small new segments of elite in much of the rest of the world. Now, as with the United States automobile models, the United States model of society has been seriously challenged. We are not at all certain that it will hold together long enough to get us all safely to the twenty-first century. It is even becoming questionable whether it will be able to do so with major adjustments and new parts. It may well be that we should all think of a qualitative change comparable to the change from horse to automobile.

Substantial change in our educational vehicle—probably even more substantial than the change from horse to automobile—will be required. For the challenging world of tomorrow will require more than a faster and more efficient robot or computer. We will need to ask not so much how to get there faster but where we are going. Why should we all be going to the same place? What is the relationship between the basic values and techniques of United States society and the impoverishment of so much of the world? Strategies for educational relevance in the twenty-first century will most certainly have to leave wide open the possibility for new and fresh designs for human society. The old paradigms and the old models will not suffice. Nor, most certainly, will the traditional expectations of international educational interchange (Fuenzalida, 1980). It is in the search for relevance in today's education that we may find the way to bridge the gap between current realities and our aspirations for the future.

What are some of the emerging alternative social patterns (Brandt and others, 1980; Lazlo and others, 1977)? Perhaps they will only be found if there is openness and willingness to experiment on the part of both rich and less well-off countries. New patterns for enhancing human welfare will have to come from many different societies. Just as dependence on one single strain of wheat can lead to ecological disasters, there is the possibility of global social catastrophe if one particular mode of development becomes all-pervasive. Goulet (1977a) expresses eloquently the need for Third World societies to look to their own cultural integrity to find the root ingredients in their optimum formulas for development, and to be less vulnerable to the power and style of the center countries. Although there are certainly those who disagree, many are convinced that Third World development will be able to occur *only* if the present development paths in the powerful countries are altered drastically (Daly, 1978; Carnoy and Shearer, 1980; Wilber, 1979; Lappe and Collins, 1977, 1980).

If we are to consider long-term survival of humankind, opportunities for more equitable societies, and fairer distribution among countries of access to vital resources for development, improving the quality of life for individuals in rich and poor countries alike—then it appears that educational programs for the youthful leaders of the future will have to pose challenges for new and creative alternatives to present social systems and development strategies. The United States does not have all the answers. Other societies will have to be more eclectic in their model-building and strategy choices, and the United States itself, and its educational programs, will need to be open and alert to suggestions from outside. We will need the active participation and contribution of non–United States students and scholars in our evolving educational institutions.

One example of this attempt to broaden the curricula of students is Stanford University's experimental Program in Development Studies, administered by a committee made up of twenty faculty from twelve different academic departments: political science, medicine, Spanish/Portuguese, education, industrial engineering, economics, civil engineering, electrical engineering, business, communication, food research, and engineering-economic systems. This committee promotes an interdisciplinary approach to problems and assists students from a variety of schools and departments who wish to study development problems and opportunities in the highly developed and industrialized areas of the world as well as in the less developed, less industrialized, and nonindustrialized sectors. The program enables students to analyze interactions between cultures and the development process—considering variables such as population size, availability of natural resources, and the wide range of human values and behavior that determine how those resources are acquired, controlled, distributed, used, and protected. Important linkages between ecological concerns and development strategies and the role of technology in development are stressed.

The program also is concerned with the future of the development process. Students consider where present trends are likely to lead humankind, discuss alternative futures that appear possible and desirable, and examine decisions that must be made to give humankind a viable future. They also consider the need for expanded personal perspectives in terms of a new global awareness: the need for improvement in the quality of life within and among nations while recognizing the limitations of the earth's physical life support system and realistic constraints within our different cultural systems. A Development

Studies concentration helps prepare students from the humanities, the sciences, and the various professional schools for understanding and participating in world development by utilizing the combined strength of many separate academic disciplines. (For a fuller description of the core seminar, Ethics of Development in a Global Environment (EDGE), see Feller and others, 1981).

The particular example of how the Program in Development Studies evolved at Stanford may be of interest and useful to others faced with similar strengths and weaknesses at their own institutions. After my interviews with the foreign graduates referred to above, I initiated—in cooperation with several foreign students and their wives—a new course in the ethics of international development. Within a few years, the course became listed for credit in five academic departments and had an enrollment of several hundred. Some of the very best, most imaginative, and concerned faculty in the university became involved in the course. They found it stimulating to work with faculty members of departments other than their own on issues and problems that required a multidisciplinary approach. Eventually we found increasing numbers of students who wished to extend their involvement with our holistic approach to development issues beyond the one course and who expressed a desire to major in Development Studies. We make a serious attempt to provide opportunities for the highly specialized Stanford students to be able to work on research related to their own societies. Of course, the more our faculty become involved in research in countries outside the United States, the easier it will be for them to see the advantages of home country research.

We have found some two hundred courses in twenty-two different departments at Stanford that are decidedly relevant to the issues we have been discussing, related to the ethics of present and future development of societies and sectors of societies. These courses encourage serious basic questioning, with few preconceived assumptions. They seek to involve the student in fresh, holistic questioning and thinking, and to look at root causes of problems. Many ask the student to pose new alternative strategies for development and to suggest probable and possible constraints to such strategies. A framework was needed

that could pull the many separate offerings together into a coherent program. The new Program in Development Studies attempts to do this.

In summary, the 1980s do indeed appear to be a time for
reviewing the goals, purposes, and objectives of international
educational interchange and, in fact, of education itself. Others
in this book have looked carefully at the history and the existing structures and procedures involved in foreign study, research, and teaching. I have tried to broaden the perspective by
suggesting that relevance of education needs to be defined and
tested in relation to the real world, to the awesome challenges
of the future.

13

Summary and Agenda
for Future Interchanges

John F. Reichard

This volume brings together a variety of American perspectives on the phenomenal growth of international educational interchange since the middle of this century—a growth concurrent with deepening United States involvement in world affairs. The authors have charted the development of the phenomenon; the processes that foreign and American students and scholars must go through to study in another country; and especially the efforts of United States colleges and universities to respond to, understand, and manage educational interchange. Some attempt also has been made to assess the educational meaning and potential in the accelerating pace of international student and scholar exchanges. The collective lesson set forth is that international educational interchange unexamined is probably not worth conducting. The examinations begun here raise questions which, taken together, point the way to a desirable and broad policy review of international educational interchange in the years immediately ahead.

In an early chapter, M. Archer Brown stresses that the American student's quest for international understanding and competence through study abroad is as important as the quest of the foreign student in America. The need for mutuality, reciprocity, and a reasonable degree of parity in the sending and receiving of exchanges was a theme sounded strongly in the original Smith-Mundt Act (1948) and the subsequent Fulbright-Hays Act (1961), but under these laws funding has generally been appropriated at a two-to-one ratio in favor of students and scholars coming to the United States. Furthermore, for understandable functional reasons, colleges and universities have often administered the two categories of exchanges separately; in the process, however, they have lost opportunities to utilize the benefits of each exchange flow to support the other.

Several of the authors—Ellen Mashiko in Chapter Two, Hugh Jenkins in Chapter Five, and William Patrick in Chapter Six—deal principally with the processes whereby foreign students find out about and get into United States colleges and universities. In view of the increasing interest of foreign students and scholars in United States higher education, the enormously detailed communications requirements that must be met over vast geographical and linguistic distances, and the heterogeneity of United States colleges and universities, the situation seems ready-made for a computer age. Through improved storage and transmission of data, institutions are already better able to inform, assess, and admit students, and Mashiko's suggested model clearinghouse offers a method for further improvement of existing procedures (Chapter Two). However, there will be limits far into the educational future on the extent that United States higher education—even with the strong support of professional organizations in international education and governments here and abroad—can make itself known, understood, and accessible to prospective students. Measures to connect the entire global educational community are mounting because the know-how, if not the budget, is falling into place. As a result, an expanding collaboration among academic institutions, professional associations, and governments on information services and marketing strategies will be increasingly needed to ensure that the most useful exchanges are promoted.

Reports of ethically questionable recruitment of foreign students—largely of Third World students by United States colleges and universities, but occasionally of United States students by some institutions in Europe—have invariably noted the decline or anticipated decline of United States student enrollments. Hugh Jenkins' discussion of recruitment begins to open up the opposite side of the subject: recruitment for appropriate educational and international objectives. While almost every American college and university, from the best to the worst, undertakes some form of recruitment—to broaden and diversify the student population or to seek the best students—various foreign policy and cultural factors, as well as inexperience and a bad press, have made it difficult for most United States colleges and universities thus far to publicize their interest in attracting foreign students. Even if future studies, as suggested by Jenkins in Chapter Ten, should demonstrate that foreign student recruitment is not cost-effective, it is inevitable that American higher education will increasingly consider a major part of the world's student-age population as a prospective admissions pool.

In Chapter Seven Alex Bedrosian outlines the many legal aspects of exchange, highlighting the growing complexity in regulating the vast foreign student population in the United States. The regulation process begins at United States campuses, moves to visa-granting consular offices throughout the world, travels back to port-of-entry Immigration and Naturalization Service officers, and ultimately moves back to campuses. Then periodically the process moves to district immigration offices for a variety of adjudications, sometimes unfortunately even to United States courts. The vast data storage needs and high volume of adjudication activities require capabilities that the INS has not been able to achieve. Foreign student advisers regularly report that as much as 50 percent of administrative time on campuses is related to immigration matters. This heavy cost to colleges and universities in conducting exchanges should be reviewed. When a small number of institutions do not comply with United States government regulations, the INS tends to create more regulations or to change regulation procedures. Frustrated district INS officers have frequently dealt with some

foreign students arbitrarily and insensitively. The employment
of students, which is permitted under circumstances of extenu-
ating need, has often become a contentious matter between
government and campus officers, largely because campus officials rarely have the means to verify a student's need for employment. Ironically, more and more foreign students, especially
students from developing countries, are asking for opportunities
to gain practical experience in their fields while in America.
Inasmuch as an important part of United States business and
industry increasingly operates, or should, in international markets, more attention might be given to permitting foreign students to hold employment in situations where they might
contribute to the competitive participation of American companies in foreign markets.

Much of the emerging policy debate affecting international educational interchange has been triggered by financial
considerations. In Chapter Ten Hugh Jenkins makes a strong
case for expanded study of the economics of exchange: the direct and indirect costs, the short- and long-term benefits of foreign study here and abroad. The course of exchanges will be
troubled and increasingly subject to political ambush until the
costs of exchanges are more fully understood. In Chapter
Four Joan Joshi describes the erosion of financial support over
the past decade for these exchanges, which have vital scholarly
and strategic value to the United States. To halt this decline in
essential exchanges, she suggests increased institutional linkages
and additional reciprocal schemes, such as the International
Student Exchange Program organized at Georgetown University; increased consortia collaboration among private and public colleges and universities to ensure cost sharing in meeting the
most urgent scholarly and development needs; the development
of expanded student loan systems abroad, such as ICETEX
(Colombian Institute for Educational Credit and Technological
Studies Abroad) and similar plans sponsored by Latin American
governments; a new look at the long-suggested world student
loan fund under an international institution such as the World
Bank; a more liberal view of foreign student employment, both
in the United States and abroad; and arrangements that would

enable a greater number of students to complete part of their degree requirements (for instance, research) in home countries.

The complex campus functions and educational emphases in international education include admissions, intensive English, academic and personal counseling in a demanding cross-cultural context, legal guidance and regulation reporting, and introduction to the community beyond the campus. These services, which are described principally by Valerie Woolston (Chapter Eight) and George Christensen and Thomas Thielen (Chapter Nine), did not develop in logical sequence, with uniform structure or equal effectiveness. Consequently, over the years professionals in international educational interchange (chiefly admissions officers, foreign student advisers, teachers of English as a second language, and study abroad advisers), have debated the question of how international services should be organized—whether through mainstreaming and integration into all parts of the university, through a series of special international education service units, or through a major international campus center which has authority over the entire range of institutional academic and service activities. The international center model can have visibility, central mass, efficiency, professional concentration, and the prospect of direction at a relatively high level of administrative authority to recommend it. This model is staunchly advocated by some foreign student office directors, who believe their place on the university totem poll depends on centralizing all or most international education responsibilities in one place. Occasionally such centering includes—in addition to foreign student/scholar services and academic counseling—international studies, foreign language programs, institutional linkages abroad, and so on. Others argue that academic channels and authority in the reporting process are more important in gaining institutional recognition and resources for international exchanges than a central office. Given the diversity of United States higher education, probably neither structure nor the nature of administrative lines alone can assure appropriate status for international education on a campus. What is undoubtedly more important is that those with high authority in the institution attach some central importance to international education and adopt and act on a set of goals and guidelines for their involvement in exchanges. A variety of structures can work well if the plan derives from a sense of mission and a realistic set of institutional policies.

Christensen and Thielen's description of administrative approaches to international education at Iowa State University reflects exceptional institutional commitment to international educational interchange, especially in the utilization of the collective international experience of the university community. They catalogue the chief educational resources: the foreign students themselves, visiting scholars, an internationally aware faculty, the research undertakings of university scholars. While communication and coordination on many college and university campuses among those directly performing specialized services for foreign students and scholars are often inadequate, such personnel are generally forced to have some contact along the course of the exchange program. The degree to which they coexist, cooperate, or even become creative collaborators with respect to the institution's involvement in international exchanges can have much to do with the quality of the educational experience. What is more likely than insufficient contact among foreign student service administrators is the probability of minimal contact between such administrators and those who teach foreign students. Separation between faculty and administrators is not uniquely related to foreign student concerns, but such separation can be especially damaging in the case of foreign students. The close Iowa State University administrative-academic connections illustrate a pattern of collaboration by the two campus sectors in ensuring the success of foreign student programs.

The activities of those who instruct and those who serve foreign students need to be viewed also from the vantage point of institutional heads from time to time. Such review is often difficult to effect in many institutions, except for the wrong reasons—namely, when students get involved in some political fracas or fail to pay their bills. Probably no greater impediment to international educational effectiveness exists than the failure of many university and college leaders to recognize that foreign students and scholars on campus and abroad require added services and academic attention, that special professional skills and experience are requisites for administrators and faculty who seek to meet those needs, and that a body of principles ought to be agreed on for the content, structure, and conduct of the institution's international education programs (see *NAFSA Principles for International Educational Exchange* in Appendix).

Robert Kaplan (Chapter Eleven) has properly recognized that most of the foreign students who come to the United States—or at least their sponsors—want access to science, technology, and management curricula, which they believe will assist their nations to develop. These students now come overwhelmingly from non-Western nations, where language, culture, and the stage of development importantly affect the application of what is learned in the United States. Kenneth Cooper (Chapter Twelve) goes beyond Kaplan in suggesting that the question of the relevance of United States higher education to foreign students is part of a larger question: the relevance of higher education today to all students in a world seriously threatened by social, political, and environmental crises. Can all of the hundreds of thousands of transnational educational choices be connected in some fashion to ensure global survival?

Although the patterns of growth in international educational interchange activities since World War II have been well chronicled in this volume, it has become conventional wisdom in the 1980s to say that United States policy planning for exchanges has been negligible. When policies have been developed by the government or by higher education institutions, they have been regarded as unsystematic and too often inconsistent. The lack of serious policy consideration has been attributed to the comparatively small percentage of students involved in international education, the absence of a central American ministry of education, and the autonomy and diversity of United States higher education. Admittedly, the proportion of students and scholars who have come to the United States has never exceeded 3 percent of the total higher education enrollment in the United States—not nearly as large as in Great Britain, Germany, and France, where the percentage has run as high as 10 percent. Nonetheless, the international student population has not been insignificant in a country where a much greater percentage of citizens proceed to higher education than is true anywhere in the world. The number of foreign student/scholar academic years in the United States in the past two generations has been at least three million, representing more than one million different persons. During this time, perhaps half as many Americans have studied abroad, and generally for shorter periods than the typical foreign student sojourn in the United States.

If there has been an absence of a concerted and coherent American commitment to international exchange policy and practice, it is remarkable that the numbers of foreign students in the United States should have reached one third of a million persons annually, and that very likely two to three times that number would be in United States institutions if they could gain admission and financial support. The vast majority of the five hundred thousand persons abroad who take the Test of English as a Foreign Language (TOEFL) each year ultimately apply to American colleges and universities. As Hugh Jenkins points out in Chapter One, there has been no parallel historically to the flow of students to the United States in recent decades, and every writer in this book emphasizes the growth of foreign student exchange. Although there is a new awareness of this development, the phenomenon has not yet been seen very widely as historic.

How does a nation become the quantitative leader in international education without sustained national or institutional policies? Although the nation officially and the central leadership of most of its institutions of higher education have viewed international education as a lesser priority, or sometimes not viewed it at all, the great number of students coming from (and to a lesser extent going) abroad would not have made their transnational moves in the first instance, and continued to move in growing numbers, without certain encouragement from both government and private sectors and considerable receptivity and responsiveness in at least some quarters of host academic institutions. Jenkins and Kaplan especially have listed the various motives and missions in America's international interchange activities—most of them closely connected with America's extraordinary movement into the world in this century. As much of that world was liberated from colonialism and sought to satisfy through educational advance its rising expectations, larger and larger numbers of students and scholars sought that advancement in the ideas and institutions of an America that seemed the model of national achievement. Mix such circumstances with the growing influence of English as the language of international scholarship and trade and America's traditional freedom of access to education, and there was little need for a great national scheme to attract students.

Even so, the United States government has initiated a scheme or two from time to time to facilitate scholarly exchange, most notably and successfully through the Fulbright Act. The Fulbright legislation has been more influential than it would appear statistically. In thirty-five years three to four thousand graduate students, scholars, and teachers have been exchanged annually. The program has set the standard for United States international education and included a scholarly elite that stimulated departmental and institutional linkages and considerable academic exchange activity independent of the government. The Fulbright offices abroad also have provided an extraordinary network of processing stations for thousands of nongrant students. In addition to the Fulbright Program, there have been the efforts of the Agency for International Development to provide technically trained manpower for development. The Peace Corps has also had an indirect impact on interchange. Peace Corps participants with ingenuity and idealism have made ties that have brought many students to United States campuses.

In addition to actual legislation, the climate for interchanges in America since World War II—a new and optimistic internationalism after 1940, expressed repeatedly from Wendell Wilkie's *One World* to John F. Kennedy's Peace Corps—provided an essential element of support on United States campuses as foreign students arrived in increasing numbers to study in America. University-related citizen groups often took the initiative to establish interchanges, which resulted in an impressive flowering of hundreds of private sector interchange programs and the steady growth of a number of major nongovernmental international education organizations, such as the Institute of International Education, the Council on International Educational Exchange, the African-American Institute, the Experiment in International Living, the Asia Foundation, and Amideast. Among the hopeful catch phrases of this voluntary welcoming and sending of foreign students and scholars were "unofficial ambassadors," "people to people," "open doors," "the world at your door," the "future leaders of the world," and so on.

The dramatic increase in foreign student admissions to the United States in the late 1970s and early 1980s, however, may have been quite unrelated to either official or institutional cordiality. As Kaplan points out in Chapter Eleven, the United States represents to individuals worldwide an exceptional opportunity for personal, academic, and professional achievement. Since two thirds of exchange students now come to the United States with primary support from personal or family resources, many foreign students are undoubtedly bringing with them essentially personal objectives. Those who work with foreign students are aware of this motivation and the frequent conflicts between the stated formal objectives of exchange and unstated private ambition. In any thorough review of America's role in international educational interchange, serious consideration must be given to the appropriate role of government (both federal and state), the private sector (independent colleges and universities, scholarly and professional associations, corporations, foundations, churches, citizen organizations), foreign governments, international organizations, and foreign students and scholars themselves in supporting interchanges. As places of learning and scholarly investigation, do colleges and universities have some obligation to national and world needs? Does state government? Does the Fulbright scholar have a legal obligation to learn about America while lecturing on Greek culture? The various expectations that have supported the present system of international educational interchange are looked at later in this chapter.

While America took few deliberate official steps to encourage exchanges, the American circumstances in the decades following World War II were in many respects ideal for fostering exchanges of students and scholars. Furthermore, there seemed little need to question the topsy-like growth of the phenomenon. Neither the numbers nor the marginal costs of having foreign students were great, especially as United States higher education enrollments soared. American educators generally wanted to help the course of international development and understanding, the nation could obviously spare something for others, and great benefits might result from responding to the desire of students to study in the United States. Given all these positive circumstances, the principal task for United States colleges and universities, as the authors of this volume have recorded, was to establish procedures for facilitating interchanges.

Beginning with the renewed support in the early postwar period from several of America's largest foundations, the process of professional development in international education received enlightened federal support in the early 1960s from what is now the Office of Academic Programs of the United States Information Agency's Bureau for Educational and Cultural Affairs. Grants were provided over a generation to the National Association for Foreign Student Affairs, the Institute of International Education, the American Association of Collegiate Registrars and Admissions Officers, the College Board and other key national networking organizations in the interchange field. Funding for workshops, conferences, consultations, publications, and in-service training provided the means to organize much of the professional know-how and training procedures in the field, facilitating the development of an infrastructure that enabled the United States to cope with its unanticipated role as the world's leading international educational interchange host nation. If this modest support had not been sustained during the enormous growth in the 1970s, the quality of services to foreign students and scholars probably would now be very low. This book suggests that—given additional, often modest, means—those who direct international interchange activities are ready to establish larger and more ambitious administrative support mechanisms and creative educational endeavors:

Administrative

An international educational interchange information clearinghouse (Chapter Two)

A world student loan bank (Chapter Four)

New organization in institutional admissions procedures (Chapter Six)

More sophisticated organization of institutional international educational interchange activities on campus (Chapter Eight)

Educational

Fuller utilization of international intercultural resources on campus and in the community (Chapters Six and Nine)

Multidisciplinary educational programs designed to relate aspects of development to cultural, social, and environmental conditions (Chapter Twelve)

Multinational task forces to examine common problems, such as student fees, legal status, relevance of curricula, and the definition of the costs and benefits of international educational interchange (Chapters One and Ten)

A transition in the campus response to foreign students from a necessary preoccupation with practice and "how-to" specialization to a new emphasis on policy and content in international education interchange has begun. It is being stimulated by the financial crisis in higher education in recent years and a complex set of changes in foreign student affairs. These changes pose several fundamental challenges to the assumptions on which an aggregate policy for interchanges has evolved; they even foster some tension among various constituencies within and outside academia engaged in organizing and conducting interchanges.

The principal assumptions that have collectively supported the growth of diverse American exchange efforts over the past thirty-five years have included elements of pragmatism and self-interest, idealism, and even naiveté. Foreign students and scholars have been viewed as:

- Enriching the context of the United States campus—bringing a cosmopolitan sense and a needed understanding to American students, who must deal increasingly with a number of complex and perplexing international realities, both as professionals and as citizens.
- Contributing intellectual strength and international perspective to the academic life of the college or university, establishing useful academic contacts that enable American faculty and students to go abroad, and building important international networks for scholarly communication and research.
- Becoming friends of the United States and carrying United States values and ideas to their home countries, providing a greater understanding of America to much of the world, and thus strengthening America's position in the struggle against nondemocratic systems.
- Assisting in the development of the poorest nations, thus contributing to political and social stability in the world community, as well as fulfilling traditional humanitarian imperatives to help the less fortunate.
- Representing an asset in the United States economic equation, through monies brought to the United States for tuition and living expenses, and a potential asset in future trade relations conducted by foreign leaders trained in the United States.
- Contributing to the creation of a cadre of persons able to address global needs through the collaborative development of international institutions, systems, and arrangements.
- In sum, increasing the prospects for world peace.

These goals represent a heavy burden for any group of academic sojourners anywhere, at any time. Those with extended experience with international education have tended to be reluctant to claim too much for exchange undertakings and to concentrate generally on immediate academic requirements and expectations, while keeping the faith that their work well done just might contribute to a golden age. To measure the precise causes of war and peace, international economic prosperity and depression, and the political and social success and failure of nations is not easily accomplished and generally requires considerable historical analysis and perspective. While some research and survey activities have tended to document the positive results of exchanges (largely in terms of personal attitudes), United States exchange activities have never been reviewed in any systematic, sustained fashion—and could not be easily reviewed, at least with respect to the broadest national and international goals.

In the late 1970s and early 1980s, a set of troubling realities began to intrude on the idealistic claims made on behalf of foreign student and scholar programs. Many Americans beyond the campus began for the first time to learn about foreign exchange students.

- The foreign student population grew dramatically, almost exponentially. On many campuses there were massive, noticeable concentrations of students for whom English proficiency was an acquired skill. Cultural dissimilarities were apparent and often disturbing. Many students became teaching assistants in universities and often were not understood. Moreover, much of the new population came from OPEC nations, whose new wealth was achieved at a high cost to Americans for their energy needs.
- Substantial segments of the foreign student population seemed, through the magnifying and often distorting power of television, to become politically active in an inappropriate manner. The Iranian crisis sorely tested American tolerance for dissent. Students of other nationalities reported being spied on by countrymen. A media view emerged of ungrateful guests abusing American hospitality and of foreign political squabbles brought to American shores.
- Resources for higher education were seriously eroded as a result of inflation and a slowing of United States economic growth. As institutions examined the costs of all aspects of

higher education and the best uses for declining student financial aid, campus and public financial planners began to wonder what responsibility they had for noncitizens. Some national groups—notably the Nigerians—fell persistently behind in payment of academic fees. Others found themselves unable to meet financial commitments when political events, currency devaluations, family crises, and so on, overtook them. Services to international students, having enjoyed a relatively short tenure on many campuses and rarely connected to institutional power centers, were subject to elimination or devastating reductions.

- The bad practice of a relatively small number of colleges and universities—in unethically recruiting students abroad, selling I-20s, disregarding qualifications of academic preparation and language proficiency in admitting students, or failing to provide adequate campus services or promised educational programs—came to public notice with increasing frequency and threw suspicion on the entire exchange process.

- Americans witnessed a period of adjustment in their nation's world status and roles and were troubled by foreign economic competition, a perceived loss of scientific and defense superiority, inexplicable criticism of America by many who had been educated here, and the failure of others to accept American foreign policy leadership. The foreign student was beginning to be seen by many outside the university as unreliable, even hostile.

Most United States campuses had rarely had to justify the presence of foreign students, but over a relatively short period of time many were called on to do so. The situation was new.

Gradually the brain-drain cloud, which had often filled the exchange sky in the 1960s but had cleared away largely in the 1970s, began to reappear in the 1980s. It cast new shadowing doubt on the course of the exchange programs. The impression grew that large numbers (never substantiated) of foreign students were remaining in the United States on completion of their academic programs, taking jobs away from Americans and, above all, failing to fulfill their missions to carry skills and understanding to other peoples. In addition, possible conflicts in purpose among the proponents of international exchanges began to be revealed. For instance, exchanges had been advanced by some supporters since the outset of the Cold War as an essential element in the worldwide ideological struggle against Communism, especially the totalitarian system of the Soviet Union. Members of the 97th Congress seemed to be influenced by the claim of the International Educational Exchange Liaison Group that the Russians were spending ten times more on exchanges than the United States was.* Influenced by this argument and other concerns with United States competitiveness in the world, Congress proceeded to restore proposed cuts in the Fulbright and related programs, programs designed primarily to reduce tensions among nations, not to provide ideological advantage to the United States. Another instance: Exchanges have regularly been supported through public and private efforts to assist in the economic and social development of Third World nations. At the same time, some exchange proponents regularly cite important trade advantages for the United States when future Third World managers are educated and trained in this country. The economic interests of the United States and developing nations can sometimes be served through educational training and assistance, but the process can also lead to something other than mutual advantage. The potential exists for the United States to provide scientists, technicians, and business administrators with the know-how to compete successfully against the United States in world markets. Moreover, American aid can foster new economic dependencies which tend in time to trouble political relations between the United States and developing countries.

One of the more interesting paradoxes in United States international exchange policy developed in the 97th Congress,

*The IEELG was organized on an ad hoc basis in 1981 by leaders of the principal United States international exchange organizations in order to interpret the importance of exchanges to government and the public. The United States has three, perhaps four, times as many students from abroad as the Soviet Union, where there is no private sector exchange. The important point, of course, is not numbers but the strategic nature of the exchanges.

when several provisions affecting the immigration status of foreign students and faculty were included in an omnibus immigration reform bill, the Simpson-Mazzoli Act, which ultimately failed at passage for reasons unrelated to foreign students. The provisions sought to limit severely the number and nature of foreign scholars who might be employed by United States colleges and universities and to require all foreign students to return home (not simply leave the United States) for two years before being eligible to apply for adjustment to any kind of permanent status in the United States. The Simpson-Mazzoli provisions regarding foreign students and scholars were interesting because (1) they were included in a broad piece of legislation designed to enable the United States to gain control of the massive influx of illegal aliens (which foreign students were not); (2) the provisions were not proposed by or even known to the Department of State, the United States Information Agency, and the Immigration and Naturalization Service (the federal agencies that normally have authority over and certainly the most experience with foreign students); and (3) the legislation produced no current data on numbers of faculty hired or of students adjusting to permanent status but implied a damaging overdependence by American academia and industry on foreign students and scholars in high-technology fields. In the mild furor that followed the introduction of the legislation, the authors of the bill expressed great concern for the plight of developing nations whose best and brightest were being lost to the United States (again, no data were produced on how many students, from what countries, in what fields); at the same time, they decried the unhealthy dependence of the United States on the foreign born to staff its laboratories, classrooms, and industrial operations. The higher education community for the most part, chiefly its great research universities and including much of its international educational component, joined with the nation's high-technology industry in strong opposition to these provisions, making it extremely clear that the nation's universities and industries did depend (as they have for several centuries) on foreign graduates, scholars, and experts because America is not now producing sufficient graduates in engineering and science to meet its highly technical needs; and, even if the numbers were there, America's colleges and universities must attract the most talented in order to maintain international leadership in scholarly and technical endeavors. Ironically, then, educational liberals—who sometimes make extravagant claims that exchange can transform the Third World into a set of viable, productive nations—were demanding that foreign students be allowed to remain here, whereas conservative members of Congress were expressing their concern about the development of poor nations. Such a juxtaposition of traditional attitudes suggests the need for more profound public review of the realities, purposes, and results of exchanges.

Still another paradox. At the same time that some United States postsecondary institutions, public and private, are sending representatives abroad to hunt for paying foreign students to balance educational budgets, some state legislators and the press are calling for a limit to foreign student enrollments because foreign students represent a cost that institutions—especially public institutions—can no longer afford.

One benefit of emerging public controversy in the 1980s over certain aspects of international educational interchange is that it might provide long-overdue recognition that foreign study experiences in the aggregate arise out of a complex of differing—sometimes conflicting—motivations and lead to differing educational and international results. Through more systematic documentation of the exchange phenomenon and closer analysis of its workings, the United States academic community and the American people might gradually develop and implement exchange policy more purposefully and more effectively. Fundamental to this recognition and review should be a new determination by all who play significant roles in the exchange process to seek ways of focusing the academy's and the nation's attention on the objectives of educational exchanges in United States education and world affairs. If international educational interchange continues to be as oversimplified in its interpretation, ignored in its implementation, and unexamined in its results in the next twenty-five years as it has generally been in the post–World War II period, the seemingly irresistible international attraction of United States higher education will assuredly decline, together with a historic opportunity to address some of mankind's major needs.

It has become increasingly evident that educational exchanges suffer from the failure of academic institutions, governments at several levels, and important public sector interests (such as business, industry, and charitable organizations) to identify realistic goals for exchanges, to view the process of exchange as a totality, to monitor its course(s), and to evaluate the results in a systematic fashion. No one expects all colleges and universities to adopt similar purposes and procedures for international educational exchanges, but the failure to establish some sense of institutional and official mission in which students, scholars, and teachers can develop the exchanges successfully assigns the fate of exchanges to institutional chance. To strengthen the effectiveness of exchanges, more systematic attention must be given to data collection and maintenance, research and analysis, and inter- and intrainstitutional consultation. In addition, there must be agreement on standards to guide the institution's exchange activities and on the proper positioning of responsibility for international exchange activity within the college or university.

A prerequisite for comprehensive policy planning is improved data collection (and projection) and the expansion of continuing research activities in the field. The one great success in comprehensive data collection on foreign students has been the Institute of International Education's *Open Doors*, which now provides extensive data on who has come to study in the United States, in which institutions, at what levels, from which countries, in which fields. No comparable data have been systematically developed covering United States students going abroad, but the IIE has made a start that should be encouraged. Who knew, for instance, that 400 United States students were studying medicine in Romania in 1982?

The rapid increase in the foreign student population in recent years led to a rash of projections that, "at current rates of growth," the population would reach one million sometime in the 1990s. Such projections—with no apparent basis other than an exercise in extrapolation—needlessly misled higher education leaders for a period. While foreign student flows are influenced by worldwide political and economic developments that are often unpredictable, it would not be impossible for the international educational community to consult with foreign governments to identify trends, national goals, and incentives for and impediments to exchange flows, as well as to ascertain at least in general terms how United States colleges and universities assess their capabilities in receiving students in the years ahead. It could not hurt institutions to develop an optimum foreign student enrollment goal in their planning.

An enormous current problem in data collection and dissemination has been the absence of reliable data on the status of students and scholars after they complete academic programs in the United States. The United States government, through the Immigration and Naturalization Service, is required to know who enters and leaves the United States in the various educational visa categories. However, all these data have been poorly collected and maintained and have been made available, if at all, only some years after the fact. Even then there has been no detail on the nationality, field of study, and reason— economic, political, or other—for the adjustment of status of those students and scholars who remain in the United States. Who remains and who goes home immediately after taking a degree is not the whole story. As is well known by those in international education administration and teaching, many students remain in the United States for long periods upon receiving their degrees in order to teach, conduct research, and receive practical training in business; they then ultimately go home. Yet without such basic data, the new immigration controls proposed in Congress are based largely on impression and anecdote. Colleges and universities, the major exchange organizations, and the federal government ought to work together to see if they can develop the data which any government needs for wise policy.

Accurate data on student/scholar flows are essential to any kind of systematic planning, but their constant companion should be expanded research and analysis of certain results of exchanges. In the 1950s and 1960s, the Department of State's

Bureau for Educational and Cultural Affairs conducted a series of surveys and analyses on exchange students' views of their academic experiences in the United States and abroad. Such vital research has not been sustained in government or elsewhere. The International Society for Educational, Cultural and Scientific Interchanges (ISECSI), a small, informal grouping of United States and some foreign scholars, has attempted to encourage and publicize such research. In the early 1980s, the Institute of International Education, with initial support from the Ford Foundation, launched an expanded research program focused chiefly on exchange policy. In spite of the hopeful developments, grants for research on exchange have been minimal and infrequent. Furthermore, except for *The World's Students in the United States—A Review and Evaluation of Research on Foreign Students* (Spaulding and Flack, 1976), no systematic effort has been made in recent years to compile and disseminate a catalogue of research undertakings in international education. While it is always difficult to quantify educational results—and the difficulty increases when the whole world is the stage— many critical aspects of the exchange process can be subjected to analysis and evaluation. The sense of what "it all means" is very vivid to many in the field, who find it difficult, nevertheless, to convince anyone else of the value of international education simply on the basis of impression or gut instinct. Unless exchanges are submitted to more critical examination in the next years, and their benefits and limitations assessed frankly, neither governments nor academic institutions will know how much to invest in them.

While the campus is the stage on which foreign students and scholars seek to play out their educational parts, the drama often has many scenario writers and may require a considerable number of production assistants. Foreign universities, foreign governments, the United States government at various levels, scholarly and professional societies, higher education associations, foundations, and industry and citizen groups often play minor or major roles. While the principal international education organizations have devoted major energies to encouraging communication, liaison, and cooperation among these many actors, the rapid growth of exchanges has often overwhelmed their capabilities to bring the various and far-flung constituencies together on matters of exchange policy. Many of the channels of communication that have been opened are weak, providing only perfunctory exchange of information and little policy direction. Within the federal government there have been some successful efforts to coordinate exchange policies among the agencies of the executive branch, but there has been little dialogue between Congress and the executive agencies; and there is no dialogue at all between federal and state government on international exchange, although two thirds of foreign students study in public institutions supported by the states. Between most state colleges and universities and state government, there have been only the barest beginnings of discussion related to foreign students. Several recent developments in Florida, Texas, and Oregon are worth noting.

In Florida, after a bill that would have increased tuition for foreign students at state universities significantly over the regular out-of-state tuition was vetoed by the governor in 1981, leaders of Florida colleges and universities, acting through the Florida Collegiate Consortium for International/Intercultural Education, joined with business and industry and internationally concerned members of the state legislature to draft a broad general resolution in support of international education. The resolution received strong legislative endorsement and has led to regular consultation among campus administrators and various state officials concerned with education. The Texas State Coordinating Board for the Texas College and University System, which has primary authority for public education, began recently to consider increasing tuition for foreign students in that state. A group of chief administrators of international services on Texas state universities responded by organizing the Texas Association of International Education Administrators. In a short time, they were requested by the state to provide various kinds of information to its staff and were in time invited to join a series of task forces appointed by the Coordinating Board to make recommendations concerning state policy on foreign students. In Oregon, where the traditional practice of granting tuition waivers for some graduate foreign students (in order to attract outstanding talent to publicly supported graduate schools) was threatened by budget cutbacks, the Oregon International Council was formed to negotiate with the state a program of tuition waivers in exchange for foreign student contributions to educational activities in Oregon's public schools. Thus, the state would grant a waiver if the foreign student would serve as an educational resource in Oregon classrooms. This simple tradeoff could unlock enormous possibilities for internationalizing the curriculum of American schoolchildren and at the same time increase funding for international education. It could be a historic instance of America's beginning to take international education seriously and recognizing the rich resource that foreign students represent.

The bottom line in any consideration of international education should be, but often in the discussion of it is not, the educational result. Do foreign students gain the education and training to equip them adequately for a variety of professional roles at home? One could argue that—the costs and benefits to the United States aside—three hundred thousand foreign students cannot be wrong. If the United States educational experience had not been largely successful, the swelling numbers of students would not continue to invest their own and their countries' funds. Indeed, at one meeting of international scholars, participants from Africa, Latin America, and the Middle East took United States participants to task for giving United States education for foreign students such a bad report card. "The United States offers the best to our students," they said. "Let's see how to make it even better." Reassuring as such a comment might be, the United States academic community has been slower to look seriously at the educational heart of international educational exchange than at procedural implications. The American Council on Education's valuable 1982 report *Foreign Students and Institutional Policy* was preoccupied with fiscal considerations in exchange, foreign student trends, comparative national policies on exchange, and other fundamental administrative issues. The educational values and impacts in exchanges were scarcely addressed.

Numerous educational aspects of international exchange should be thoroughly reviewed in the decade ahead. These include the implications of heavy concentrations of foreign students in the fields of science, engineering, and business management; the need for greater reciprocity in international exchange flows; the uses of foreign students and scholars and United States students and faculty returning from abroad in internationalizing the American curriculum; comparative studies of the educational effectiveness of educating students chiefly in the United States, as opposed to educating certain students abroad and/or utilizing educational settings both in the United States and the home country; the development of more and stronger institutional consortia and linkages as the organizational mechanisms for international exchange; and the utilization of new technologies in international education (for example, instruction and seminars by satellite); and the expansion of exchanges in other than high-technology disciplines with students from the poorest countries.

While the complexity of international educational exchange activities in the 1980s calls for clearer, more complete national and international perspective and preparation, the principal place for goal setting and policy review in foreign student programs must inevitably be the American institution of higher education. And all levels of the academic community need to be involved. Colleges and universities need to understand the aims of political and professional communities beyond the campus, but the essential international educational tasks fall to those who carry out the fundamental mission of the institution in the classroom, laboratory, and library.

The world's students are more and more frequently turning to American colleges and universities. This situation constitutes an expanding opportunity for the academy, the nation, and the global community to increase knowledge and understanding greatly. Indeed, there is a reasonable chance that Americans and all the peoples of the world might benefit—not only in their efforts to learn but also in their efforts to survive—through the educational exchange of students and scholars. It would be regrettable if this historic opportunity were ignored. Given time, awareness, and attention, the first—and foremost—system of world education could emerge.

Appendix:
NAFSA Principles
for International
Educational Exchange

In early 1980 the National Association for Foreign Student Affairs convened the Task Force on Standards and Responsibilities to address the growing concern that NAFSA and its institutional and individual members had not been active enough in the establishment of useful, recognized standards or principles of effective practice for those involved in the many aspects of international educational interchange. The result of their deliberations was development of a program of self-regulation which will draw on the experience and leadership of the Association and its members, but will also thoroughly involve faculty members, administrators, and others on college campuses who are affiliated with foreign students and scholars.

Embodied within the program of self-regulation is the following set of *NAFSA Principles for International Educational Exchange*. However, the program is much more than a set of standards—it provides for assessment of strengths and weaknesses in interchange in light of the *Principles* and permits institutions to plan their programs and/or improve their services on the basis of knowledge gained through this self-study process.

319

Principles for Institutions

The movement of students and scholars across community, cultural, geographical, and national boundaries has been recognized for centuries as essential to the discovery of truth, new knowledge, and the means of applying what is learned abroad to human enrichment and progress. In the second half of this century, the interchange of students and scholars has grown steadily, become more formalized and an increasing influence upon U.S. higher education and the society as a whole. Indeed, the significance of the interdependence of nations, peoples, and world systems has brought international education into the very mainstream of higher education planning and requirements.

Programs of international educational exchange take many forms and are located in institutions of divergent purposes, sizes, and settings. Regardless of form and content, the value of any program can be realized only when a college or university has made a conscious decision to be involved in international educational exchange and has made a commitment of resources commensurate with the nature and scope of that exchange. Such recognition and commitment require adherence to the following institution-wide principles:

1. The institution should have a clearly stated policy, endorsed by the governing board, setting forth the goals and objectives of the international educational exchange program or programs developed by the institution. This policy should be manifest in the institution's planning and budgeting. Personnel and program resources—administrative and academic—should be sufficient to assure that the program can be operated in ways consistent with the principles presented in this document.

2. The executive staff of the institution should discuss with the faculty and administrative staff the implications of the international educational exchange policy for the academic programs and academic staff.

3. Programs in international educational exchange should be closely related to and consistent with the basic purposes and strengths of the institution.

4. Regardless of program size, the institution should ac-

knowledge its responsibility to demonstrate sensitivity to cultural needs—social, religious, dietary, and housing. These factors must be accounted for in the planning and execution of the program.

5. Special services required by involvement in international educational exchange should be performed by personnel who are trained for their particular responsibilities, and institutional policy should ensure that faculty and administrative staff receive appropriate training for the activities they manage.

6. Administrative staff and faculty should seek to develop and maintain respect and sensitivity toward those from different cultures in the execution of their responsibilities for international educational exchange programs.

7. The institution should periodically evaluate programs, policies, and services, in light of established goals, and regularly review those goals.

Principles for the Admission of Foreign Students

Foreign citizens have usually been educated in school systems that vary from those in the United States. As a result, students from other countries are often unfamiliar with U.S. procedures and terminology. Institutions that admit foreign students must develop a sensitive and flexible admissions policy that reflects an awareness of different academic backgrounds and personal expectations.

To assist institutions in establishing a sound admissions policy and an effective admissions system, criteria for ethical recruitment were developed at a Wingspread colloquium in March 1980. These criteria, known as the "Wingspread Principles," are presented in *Foreign Student Recruitment: Realities and Recommendations,* and are incorporated in the following principles:

1. The admissions goals and policies for foreign students should be related directly to overall institutional goals and policies and include:

• The academic characteristics of students to whom admission is offered.

- The level—graduate or undergraduate—of students sought.
- Geographical areas to be emphasized or discouraged.
- The number of students desired (as a proportion of the student body).
- The extent to which the institution will make financial resources available to foreign students.

2. Admissions materials should be thorough, complete, and clearly written; they should be sensitive to candidates' unfamiliarity with U.S. education and lack of facility in the English language. Care should be taken to include:

- Detailed information about the admissions requirements and procedures.
- Candid, pertinent, and current information so that students unfamiliar with United States higher education may make informed academic judgments.
- Realistic information about full costs of study and living expenses, as well as the availability of financial aid.
- English language requirements and, if admitted initially for an English language training program, the degree of commitment the institution accepts for subsequent education of the student in another of its academic programs.
- Specific information about requirements of academic programs.
- Complete information regarding the conditions of admissions and acceptance, deposits, orientation, and all steps to be followed prior to arrival.

3. Recruitment of foreign students for both academic and English language training programs must be conducted in an ethical, responsible manner.

- The student's educational goals must be ascertained and a responsible judgment made about whether they can be achieved at the accepting institution.
- Admissions decisions should be made using complete files including academic documents, English proficiency reports, and other supporting materials.
- Admissions responsibilities, including issuance of the visa eli-

gibility certificate, should never be delegated to third parties outside the institution.

- Applicants to an English language training program must be given full information about the extent of the institution's commitment to admit such applicants subsequently to another of its academic programs or provide assistance in obtaining admission to another institution.

4. The foreign admissions process should be conducted by personnel who are trained and competent in the interpretation of foreign educational records. These duties may be conducted on a full- or part-time basis as required by the size of the effort.

- At the undergraduate level, foreign student admissions—usually a highly centralized process—should be enhanced by faculty advice.
- In foreign graduate admissions, where deans' offices and faculty committees often play an important role, the advice and recommendations of admissions staff should be carefully considered in the decision process. The important contribution each individual can bring to the admissions decision should be recognized.
- Special reference resources should be acquired and new materials acquired as they become available.
- Admissions personnel should call on the expertise of individuals on the campus, elsewhere, or abroad who can assist in providing sound evaluations.

5. The functions of the admissions office should be coordinated with those units responsible for English language training, academic programs, and student advising services, and there should be regular contact and sharing of information among those responsible for these functions.

6. The institution's foreign student program should be studied periodically in order to formulate any needed adjustments to admissions criteria, procedures, and processes:

- Entering characteristics should be correlated periodically with student retention and other measures of performance.

- Students should be queried periodically about reactions to admissions materials and procedures.
- Other campus offices as well as cooperating agencies should be queried about the effectiveness of the admissions materials and procedures.

Principles for English Programs and Determination of English Proficiency

An extremely important factor in determining whether the presence of foreign students at a college or university will be a mutually beneficial experience for the students and the institution is the students' ability to use the English language. A student who cannot communicate adequately with faculty, staff, or fellow students will encounter significant difficulties in carrying out even limited daily activities. Moreover, serious deficiencies in English will hamper a student in pursuing an academic program at any level. For those students serving as graduate teaching assistants, the ability to speak English effectively in a classroom is especially critical.

For these reasons, an institution must carefully evaluate the English proficiency (overall ability to use the language) of prospective students when they are being considered for admission. In evaluating English proficiency, both level and field of study should be considered, since the most critical question to be answered is how well the student will be able to cope with a specific program at a given institution. Students whose English proficiency seems adequate for a regular academic program often need an English support course or courses in order to function more efficiently in the classroom or to meet an institutional English requirement. Institutions that maintain a policy of admitting foreign students who are qualified academically but who have limited or minimal skills in English must provide half-time or full-time (intensive) programs in English as a second language or refer students to English training programs where they can receive adequate instruction.

In an effort to establish guidelines by which institutions can evaluate their own or other English programs, NAFSA supports the following principles. These standards apply first to the question of determining English language proficiency and then to the training programs themselves. Except where specifically noted, these principles are meant to apply both to academic institutions and to private, proprietary organizations which offer English training programs.

Determining English Proficiency.

1. The procedures and criteria established for determining English proficiency should be clearly defined. While these procedures should be uniform and comprehensive, they must take into consideration differences presented by at least three common situations:

- For students being admitted directly from overseas, English proficiency should be determined on the basis of results from widely accepted tests designed for this purpose.
- For students who have enrolled in intensive English language programs conducted by the institution to which they are applying, additional information should be sought regarding the students' overall use of English, specific strengths and weaknesses, and motivation for continued improvement. In this regard there should be close communication between the admissions office and the English language program.
- For students who have been enrolled in intensive English language programs at other institutions or at private language schools, similar information indicating level of English language proficiency should be sought. Admissions personnel should seek the assistance of any specialists in English as a second language at their institutions for guidance in interpreting such information.

2. Institutions should periodically assess their capacity to successfully determine English proficiency of prospective foreign students in light of the students' performance in subsequent academic programs.

English Support Courses. Students with sufficient command of English to begin regular academic work at a college or university frequently require additional training to prepare them for tasks encountered during their program of studies.

This training is best provided through English support courses taken in conjunction with regular academic courses in the students' fields. These English courses should address the special needs of students whose native language is not English. They typically range from courses which are the equivalent of freshman English to advanced courses in technical English for graduate students.

3. After admission, the institution should employ effective procedures to identify those students who require some specialized training in English in light of the specific course of studies to be pursued. Special care should be taken to provide training in oral English skills for foreign graduate students assigned as teaching assistants.

4. Support courses should be designed and taught by individuals with training in the teaching of English as a second language.

Intensive English Programs. The purpose of an intensive English program is to develop and strengthen the English skills of persons whose native language is not English, usually in preparation for pursuing an academic program at the graduate or undergraduate level. Such individuals generally do not have sufficient command of English to begin regular academic work at a college or university. Some programs administered by colleges and universities enroll only students who have received academic admission to the institution but require short-term training, often in the summer. Most programs at academic institutions maintain year-round schedules and enroll people at varying levels of proficiency who intend to enter degree programs at the same or other institutions. Finally, a large number of programs are administered by private organizations. These latter programs, often housed at academic institutions, enroll students who must continue their academic studies elsewhere. Based on experience from many established programs, it is not unrealistic to expect students who begin at the lowest levels to require a full calendar year to reach levels of proficiency sufficient to begin academic work.

5. Intensive English programs should establish clear goals and objectives for the training they provide. In the most general terms, these goals would be to provide sufficient and appropri-

ate training to enable students to meet test score requirements established by the institutions they plan to attend.

6. In order to achieve these goals, intensive English programs should receive adequate support from their sponsoring institutions. Although no single administrative pattern is required, intensive programs should be sufficiently independent to permit the smooth functioning of all activities and units.

7. The director and core faculty of an intensive English program should have principal commitments to the program. The director should have advanced academic training in the teaching of English as a second language and have teaching and administrative experience, if possible, including overseas experience. Part-time instructors, especially if they are graduate students in a university program, should be taking or have taken graduate work in the teaching of English as a second language.

8. To ensure that students will be adequately prepared for an academic program, the syllabus of an intensive English program should include training in a variety of skills. The most basic are listening (understanding spoken English) and reading (understanding written English). Also of importance for academic work are speaking (in both formal and informal settings) and writing (primarily expository writing needed in most fields of study).

Principles for Foreign Student/Scholar Services

An institution that enrolls foreign students or invites foreign scholars should recognize that individuals from different cultures and educational systems have special needs for advice and assistance. These needs must be met by services that are organized, directed, and funded by the host institution. The scope and level of such services is to some extent dependent on the number of foreign students and scholars. Regardless of their number, however, the presence of foreign students and scholars requires certain basic levels of support which enable them to function successfully in U.S. colleges or universities. The following principles concern the provision of these essential services:

1. The host institution should state clearly its intentions

to provide special services for the foreign students and scholars it brings to its campus. These services should include:

- Advisory and counseling services.
- Mandated and technical services in compliance with U.S. government regulations.
- Coordination and liaison with the community.

2. Regardless of the number of foreign students and scholars, the level of funding, or other circumstances, there must be one unit in the host institution that is responsible for coordinating these services, and there should be clear and widely acknowledged designation of responsibility for these services.

- These duties may require full- or part-time staff, depending upon the size of the clientele. Where possible, it is highly desirable to have a single individual or office designated to provide these advisory services.
- The staff should be knowledgeable about U.S. immigration law and regulations.

3. The institution should provide ample professional services which are fully accessible to foreign students and scholars. The intention of these services is to assure that maximum benefit is derived from the educational experience. The advisory services must seek to remove impediments and to solve problems on behalf of these individuals.

- The advisory staff must work closely with other campus and community resources which can be of assistance before arrival and throughout the individual's stay.
- An orientation program that introduces students to the physical environment, registration procedures, academic policies, housing, counseling and health services, visa requirements and INS regulations, financial matters, and social and intercultural activities should be provided.
- Advisory services should be provided on an ongoing basis with respect to personal counseling, emergency needs, institutional policies, preparation for departure, and reentry to home countries upon completion of stay.
- The advisory staff serve both the institution and the students

and scholars it enrolls; they should, therefore, perform an intermediary role and be a channel of communication between those individuals and outside agencies or institutions.

- The advisory staff should seek to bring an intercultural dimension to the educational programs of the institution and the general life of the community.
- Advisory services should include academic advising—performed either by faculty members or foreign student advisers.

4. The advisory staff should exercise their duties in an ethical and professional manner. They must:

- Adhere to the regulations of the U.S. government, especially those of the Immigration and Naturalization Service.
- Decline awards and unethical requests for service.

Principles for the Provision of Community Services and Programs

The presence of foreign students and scholars on campus and in the community involves cross-cultural relationships and provides opportunities for increased global awareness. Individual contacts and the sharing of a variety of social and professional activities provide the opportunity for mutual appreciation of different cultural patterns and national aspirations.

Although it may serve a wider constituency at the state or national level, the college or university is an integral part of the community in which it exists. Colleges and universities which enroll foreign students and scholars should make, in cooperation with the community, every effort to assist these students in their adjustment to life in an American community. They may also enhance the education of foreign students and scholars by offering a variety of experiences, both on campus and in the community, which will ensure that optimum benefit is derived from the period of study in the United States.

Institutions should be receptive to approaches from the community and should, if necessary, take the initiative in establishing a relationship with the community (a) to explain the needs of foreign students and scholars, (b) to identify the resources represented by foreign students, and (c) to explore and make full use of the willingness and ability of the community to provide services and programs.

Through the office of the foreign student adviser or its equivalent, institutions should provide assistance, advice, and information as requested by the community for the development of programs and services for foreign students and scholars. These efforts should be evaluated periodically.

Community programs and services should adhere to the following principles:

1. Community groups and organizations should seek to provide programs and services that enhance the experience of the foreign students and scholars while increasing the level of international and intercultural awareness in the community.

2. Community programs and services should be developed in cooperation with the university office that provides on-campus service to foreign students and scholars. Each should be competently designed and conducted and, where possible, coordinated with other community efforts.

3. Community programs must embrace a sensitivity to, and appreciation of, the religious, cultural, and national backgrounds of foreign participants and a proper regard for confidential personal information that may be offered by foreign and American participants.

4. Community groups and organizations should provide professional training for volunteers and paid staff to ensure that programs are competently administered and community resources effectively used.

5. Community groups and organizations should periodically evaluate their programs, policies, and services in light of their established goals and the changing needs of foreign students and scholars.

Principles for U.S. Study Abroad

One of the most effective ways to increase U.S. understanding of other languages and cultures and to improve our ability to function effectively in this interdependent world is to provide individuals with opportunities to study abroad. By living and studying in another country, people learn to live with and appreciate different points of view and gain a more global perspective on life's challenges and opportunities.

The institution that endorses the concept of study abroad should provide some form of basic advisory services. Many opportunities exist for American students interested in studying abroad—sponsored programs of their own institution, programs sponsored cooperatively with other institutions, and hundreds of direct opportunities which may or may not have U.S. institutional sponsorship.

These principles apply to the delivery of advisory services as well as to the direct administration of a study abroad program or cosponsorship of a program with other institutions.

1. Within the context of its overall international educational objectives, an institution should have a clearly stated policy about its intentions and goals for facilitating study abroad.

Advisory Services for Study Abroad.

2. Recognizing that programs and advising may be handled by various people on campus, there should be a central point of access to useful information about overseas opportunities. A library of essential study abroad information materials should be maintained.

3. Faculty and staff members who are responsible for advising should be identified and listed in campus reference literature. These individuals should be given opportunities to develop their abilities to provide sound, knowledgeable, and objective advice about study abroad programs. Important components of advising include the following:

- Clarifying objectives for wanting to go abroad.
- Identifying opportunities that are educationally sound and culturally beneficial.
- Determining the quality, value, and appropriateness of a particular study abroad experience.
- Coordinating evaluation of students' educational background with admissions personnel of foreign institutions.
- Understanding the implications of a particular study abroad

experience on graduation requirements, transfer credit, and financial aid.

4. Returning students should be asked to provide evaluations to enable study abroad advisers to determine the usefulness of the program for those students and possible future participants in that program, and to evaluate the usefulness of the advisory services they received before going abroad.

Cosponsoring Study Abroad Programs Administered by Other Institutions. In order to encourage study abroad or broaden the options readily available to its students, a number of institutions have elected to join consortia or cosponsor study abroad programs in which another institution handles program administration. A consortium or cosponsorship arrangement for study abroad should provide opportunities that are consistent with the institution's overall academic objectives, requirements, and standards; the programs should be administered in accordance with the principles for study abroad program administration (see below); and the home campus role in the cosponsorship should be evaluated periodically by faculty, staff, and students to determine if the objectives are being met.

Administration of Study Abroad Programs. Institutions administer study abroad programs in order to establish direct control over the development and provision of a specific kind of overseas learning experience. Many different kinds of institutions operate programs, including U.S. colleges and universities, foreign universities and companies, and proprietary organizations. The types of programs and amounts of structure and support services vary tremendously. Despite the wide range, all should be administered according to the following principles.

5. The purposes and specific educational objectives of the program should be carefully developed and clearly stated in the program bulletin and promotional materials.

6. Accurate, honest, and complete information should be provided to prospective applicants, describing the nature and scope of the program including its opportunities and limitations, how and where instruction will be given, the relationship if any to a foreign institution, grading practices, significant differences between a home campus experience and what can be

expected abroad, information about local attitudes and mores, local living conditions, and the extent of responsibility assumed by the program for housing participants.

7. Applicants should be screened to ensure that participants have the maturity, adequate language proficiency, academic background and achievement, and motivation necessary for success in the type of program and place of study.

8. The program should include an orientation, both predeparture and ongoing, which assists participants in making appropriate personal, social, and academic adjustments. Programs maintaining centers abroad should provide counseling and supervisory services at the foreign center, with special attention to the problems peculiar to the location and nature of the program.

9. The program should encourage extensive and effective use of the unique physical, human, and cultural resources of the host environment, and the academic rigor of the program should be comparable to that at the home campus. There should be clearly defined criteria and policies for judging performance and assigning credit in accordance with prevailing standards and practices at the home institution.

10. Administrative arrangements (such as housing, transportation, and finances) and support services (such as counseling and health services) made both in the U.S. and at the program location abroad should be managed effectively by carefully selected and qualified staff who have both appropriate academic and administrative experience necessary to perform the work.

11. Programs should be evaluated periodically by student participants, program administrators, and a faculty advisory committee to determine the extent to which objectives and purposes are being met. Changes should be made in light of the findings.

References

Altbach, P. G., Kelly, G. P., and Kelly, D. H. *International Bibliography of Comparative Education.* New York: Praeger, 1981.

American Association of Collegiate Registrars and Admissions Officers. *Do-It-Yourself Evaluation of Foreign Student Credentials.* (Rev. ed.) Washington, D.C.: American Association of Collegiate Registrars and Admissions Officers, 1966.

American Association of Collegiate Registrars and Admissions Officers. *A Bibliography of Reference Materials for Evaluating Foreign Student Credentials.* (3rd ed.) Washington, D.C.: American Association of Collegiate Registrars and Admissions Officers, 1982.

American Chemical Society. *Guide to Chemical Education in the United States for Foreign Students.* Washington, D.C.: American Chemical Society, 1981.

American Council on Education. *Foreign Students and Institutional Policy.* Washington, D.C.: American Council on Education, 1982.

Barnet, R. *The Lean Years.* New York: Simon and Shuster, 1980.

Barnet, R. J. "The Search for National Security." *New Yorker,* April 27, 1981, pp. 50–140.

Benson, A. G. "On-the-Job Behavior of College and University Foreign Student Advisers as Perceived by Knowledgeable Faculty Members." Unpublished doctoral dissertation, Department of Administration and Higher Education, College of Education, Michigan State University, 1968.

Benson, A. G., and Kovach, J. W. *A Guide for the Education of Foreign Students.* Washington, D.C.: National Association for Foreign Student Affairs, 1974.

Berendzen, R. "Foreign Students in U.S.—Problem and Opportunity." *U.S. News & World Report,* Oct. 5, 1981, p. 66.

Bernsen, S. "Foreign Students—An Overview." Paper presented at meeting of National Association for Foreign Student Affairs, Washington, D.C., March 1981.

Binyon, M. "Lumumba." *Chronicle of Higher Education,* 1979, *18* (9), 7–8.

Blaug, M. "The Economic Costs and Benefits of Overseas Students." In P. Williams (Ed.), *The Overseas Student Question: Studies for a Policy.* London: Overseas Student Trust, 1981.

Board of Science and Technology for International Development, Commission on International Relations, National Research Council. *The Role of U.S. Engineering Schools in Development Assistance.* Washington, D.C.: National Academy of Sciences, 1976.

Boyer, E. L. "Toward a New Interdependence." In *The Third Century.* New Rochelle, N.Y.: Change Magazine Press, 1977.

Brandt, W., and others. *North-South: A Programme for Survival.* Cambridge, Mass.: M.I.T. Press, 1980.

Brookings Institution. *The International Dimension of Management Education.* Washington, D.C.: Brookings Institution, 1975.

Brown, L. R. *The Twenty-Ninth Day: Accommodating Human Needs and Numbers to the Earth's Resources.* New York: Norton, 1978.

Burn, B. B. (Ed.). *Higher Education Reform: Implications for Foreign Students.* New York: Institute of International Education, 1978.

Burn, B. B. *Expanding the International Dimension of Higher Education.* San Francisco: Jossey-Bass, 1980.

Callen, E., and Scadron, M. "The Physics Interview Project: A Tour of Interviews in Asia." *Science,* 1978, *200,* 1018-1022.

Canadian Bureau for International Education. *A Question of Self-Interest.* Ottawa: Canadian Bureau for International Education, 1977.

Caquelin, H. J. "Education for an Emerging Profession." *Exchange,* 1970, *5* (3), 44-65.

Carnegie Council on Policy Studies in Higher Education. *Three Thousand Futures: The Next Twenty Years for Higher Education.* San Francisco: Jossey-Bass, 1980.

Carnoy, M., and Shearer, D. *Economic Democracy, the Challenge of the 1980's.* White Plains, N.Y.: M. E. Sharpe, 1980.

Center for Applied Linguistics. *Guidelines for Selecting English Language Training Programs.* Arlington, Va.: Center for Applied Linguistics, 1978.

College Entrance Examination Board. *The Foreign Student in the United States Community and Junior Colleges.* New York: College Entrance Examination Board, 1977.

College Entrance Examination Board. *Guidelines for the Recruitment of Foreign Students.* New York: College Entrance Examination Board, 1978.

College Entrance Examination Board. *Financial Planning for Study in the United States.* (Rev. ed.) New York: College Entrance Examination Board, 1980.

College Entrance Examination Board. *Entering Higher Education in the United States.* (Rev. ed.) New York: College Entrance Examination Board, 1981.

College of Wooster. *An International Community.* Wooster, Ohio: College of Wooster, 1980.

Committee on the Foreign Student in American Colleges and Universities. *The College, the University and the Foreign Student.* Washington, D.C.: National Association for Foreign Student Affairs, 1979. (Originally published 1963.)

Comptroller General of the United States. *Report to the Congress: Better Controls Needed to Prevent Foreign Students from Violating the Conditions of Their Entry and Stay While in the United States.* Washington, D.C.: General Accounting Office, 1975.

Council for International Exchange of Scholars. *Annual Report 1980-81.* Washington, D.C.: Council for International Exchange of Scholars, 1982.

Court, D. "Scholarships and University Development in Kenya and Tanzania." *Higher Education,* 1979, *8,* 535-552.

Craig, B. L. "Variations and Themes in International Education." *Educational Record,* Winter 1981, pp. 41-46.

Crane, D. *Invisible Colleges.* Cambridge, Mass.: Harvard University Press, 1972.

Daly, H. *Steady State Economics.* San Francisco: Freeman, 1978.

Dammann, E. *The Future in Our Hands.* Elmsford, N.Y.: Pergamon Press, 1979.

Deutsch, S. E. *International Education and Exchange: A Sociological Analysis.* Cleveland: Press of Case Western Reserve University, 1970.

Dewey, J. *Human Nature and Conduct.* New York: Holt, Rinehart and Winston, 1922.

Dewey, J. *The Public and Its Problems.* New York: Holt, Rinehart and Winston, 1927.

Dewey, J. *Individualism Old and New.* New York: Minton, Balch, 1930.

Dewey, J. *Liberalism and Social Order.* New York: Putnam's, 1936.

Diener, T. "Profile of Foreign Students in United States Community and Junior Colleges." In *The Foreign Student in the United States Community and Junior Colleges.* New York: College Entrance Examination Board, 1977.

Du Bois, C. *Foreign Students and Higher Education in the United States.* Washington, D.C.: American Council on Education, 1956.

Education and World Affairs. *The University Looks Abroad: Approaches to World Affairs at Six American Universities.* New York: Education and World Affairs, 1965.

Eide, I. (Ed.). *Students as Links Between Cultures: A Cross-Cultural Survey Based on UNESCO Studies.* Paris: UNESCO, 1970.

Eiseman, T. "Emerging Scientific Communities: What Role Does Counterpart Training Play?" *International Development Review,* 1977, *19,* 2.

Erb, G. F., and Kallab, V. (Eds.). *Beyond Dependency: The Developing World Speaks Out.* New York: Praeger, 1975.

Farmer, R. N., and Renforth, W. E. "Foreign Students in Indiana: Our Intangible Exports." *Indiana Business Review,* 1971, *46,* 12-16.

Feller, G., and others. *Peace and World Order Studies.* New York: Institute for World Order, 1981.

"Field 'Wide Open' for Translations of Foreign Literature." *Chronicle of Higher Education,* 1980, *20* (4), 1.

Fienup, D. F. "Institutional Roles and Training Issues in International Agricultural Development." *American Journal of Agricultural Economics,* 1974, *56* (5), 1182-1190.

Fienup, D. F., and Riley, H. M. "Training Agricultural Economists to Serve the Needs of a Changing World." Address at conference of the International Association of Agricultural Economists, Banff, Canada, 1979.

Fisher, S. H., and Dey, W. J. *Forged Educational Credentials— A Sorry Tale.* New York: World Education Services, 1979.

Fox, M. J. "Foreign Students in American Colleges." *College Board Review,* Winter 1962, No. 46.

Fraser, S. (Ed.). *Government Policy and International Education.* New York: Wiley, 1965.

Fuenzalida, E. "Relevance and Development Style: An Analysis of the Prospects of Graduate Education for Students from Developing Countries in the Eighties." In H. M. Jenkins (Ed.), *The Relevance of U.S. Education to Students from Developing Countries.* Washington, D.C.: National Association for Foreign Student Affairs, 1980.

Fystrom, L. M., and Peterson, D. M. *Evaluation of International Educational Services, Iowa State University: A Case Study.* Occasional Paper No. 1. Ames: Office of International Educational Services, Iowa State University, 1980.

Glaser, W. A. *The Brain Drain: Emigration and Return.* Oxford: Pergamon Press, 1978.

Goulet, D. *The Cruel Choice.* New York: Atheneum, 1977a.

Goulet, D. *The Uncertain Promise.* Washington, D.C.: Overseas Development Council, 1977b.

Grubb Institute. *Freedom to Study: Requirements of Overseas Students in the U.K.* London: Overseas Student Trust, 1978.

Haas, G. J. "Undergraduate Transfer Credits from Abroad." *NAFSA Newsletter,* 1979, *30* (8), 195-198.

Harari, M. *Global Dimensions in U.S. Education: The University.* New York: Center for War/Peace Studies, 1972.

Harman, W. *An Incomplete Guide to the Future.* Stanford, Calif.: Stanford Alumni Association, 1975.

Havelock, E. *Origins of Western Literacy.* Toronto: Ontario Institute for Studies in Education, 1976.

Henson, H. N. "Evaluating Students' Perceptions of Study Abroad Experiences." *NAFSA Newsletter,* 1979, *30* (6), 145.

Higbee, H. D. *The Status of Foreign Student Advising in United States Universities and Colleges.* East Lansing: Michigan State University, 1961.

Holton, G. *The Scientific Imagination: Case Studies.* Cambridge, England: Cambridge University Press, 1978.

Hubbard, J. R. *Higher Education and the International Student.* Los Angeles: University of Southern California, 1978.

Hull, F. W., IV, Lemke, W. H., and Houang, R. T. *The American Undergraduate, Off-Campus and Overseas: A Study of the Educational Validity of Such Programs.* New York: Council on International Educational Exchange, 1977.

Indiana University. *Educational Opportunities.* Bloomington: Indiana University, 1981.

Institute of International Education. *Costs at U.S. Educational Institutions.* New York: Institute of International Education, published annually.

Institute of International Education. *Evaluating Foreign Students' Credentials.* (reprint from *World Higher Education Communiqué*). New York: Institute of International Education, 1981a.

Institute of International Education. *Survey of U.S. Public Institutional Policies Regarding Foreign Students.* New York: Institute of International Education, 1981b.

Institute of International Education. *U.S. College-Sponsored Programs Abroad: Academic Year.* New York: Institute of International Education, published annually.

Institute of International Education. *Vacation Study Abroad.* New York: Institute of International Education, published annually.

Interassociational Committee on Data Collection (ICDC). "Guide to Data Collection on International Students." Unpublished paper, National Association for Foreign Student Affairs, 1982.

International Education Project. *Education for Global Interdependence.* Washington, D.C.: American Council on Education, 1975.

Jenkins, H. M. (Ed.). *Foreign Student Recruitment: Realities and Recommendations.* New York: College Entrance Examination Board, 1980a.

Jenkins, H. M. (Ed.). *The Relevance of U.S. Education to Students from Developing Countries.* A Report of the Fourth AID/NAFSA Workshop. Washington, D.C.: National Association for Foreign Student Affairs, 1980b.

Jequier, N. *Appropriate Technology: Problems and Promises.* Stanford, Calif.: Volunteers in Asia, n.d.

Kaplan, R. B. "Foreign Students: Should Education Have Limits." Address at the annual conference of the National Association for Foreign Student Affairs, St. Louis, 1980a.

Kaplan, R. B. "A Language Planning Rationale for English for Special Purposes." In J. F. Povey (Ed.), *Language Policy and Language Teaching: Essays in Honor of Clifford H. Prator.* Culver City, Calif.: English Language Services, 1980b.

Kaplan, R. B. "Report to the Select Commission on Immigration and Refugee Policy Concerning Non-Resident Aliens, Specifically Foreign Students." Unpublished document, 1980c.

Kaplan, R. B. "Support Services for Foreign Students." Address at the annual meeting of the Western College Association, Honolulu, 1981.

Kaplan, R. B., and Birnbaum, H. "Language, Information, and Technology Transfer." Address at the 15th American Studies Seminar of the American Studies Association of the Philippines, Laguna, Philippines, 1980.

Kenworthy, L. S. "The International Dimension of Institutions of Higher Education." In *The International Dimension of Education.* Washington, D.C.: Association for Supervision and Curriculum Development, National Education Association, 1970.

Kerr, C. "Global Education Concerns of Higher Education for the 1980s and Beyond." In B. B. Burn, *Expanding the International Dimension of Higher Education.* San Francisco: Jossey-Bass, 1980.

Klitgaard, R. *Harvard International—A Report on Some International Activities at the University.* Cambridge, Mass.: Harvard University, 1979.

Knowles, A. S. (Ed.). *The International Encyclopedia of Higher Education.* San Francisco: Jossey-Bass, 1977.

Krutch, J. W. "How to See What You Are Looking At." In C. Simerville (Ed.), *Ready, Set, Go: A Traveler's Workbook.* Ames: Iowa State University, 1973.

Lamarsh, J. R., and Miller, M. M. "Weapons Proliferation and Foreign Students." *The Bulletin,* 1980, pp. 25-30.

Lappe, F. M., and Collins, J. *Food First: Beyond the Myths of Scarcity.* Boston: Houghton Mifflin, 1977.

Lappe, F. M., and Collins, J. *Aid as Obstacle.* San Francisco: Institute for Food and Development Policy, 1980.

Lazlo, E., and others. *Goals for Mankind.* New York: Dutton, 1977.

Lee, M. Y., and others. *Needs of Foreign Students from Developing Nations at U.S. Colleges and Universities.* Washington, D.C.: National Association for Foreign Student Affairs, 1981.

Limbird, H. M. "Foreign Students in Iowa—A Preliminary Estimate of Social and Economic Benefits and Costs." Unpublished paper, Office of International Educational Services, Iowa State University, 1979.

Limbird, H. M. "Attitudes Toward Planned Work Experience for Foreign Students." Unpublished doctoral dissertation,

Department of Agricultural Education, Iowa State University, 1981.

Lockyear, F. E. "Current Practices in the Recruitment of Foreign Students." In H. M. Jenkins (Ed.), *Foreign Student Recruitment: Realities and Recommendations.* New York: College Entrance Examination Board, 1980.

London Conference on Overseas Students. *Overseas Students: A Subsidy to Britain.* Report of the Working Party on the Costs and Benefits of Overseas Students in the U.K. London: London Conference on Overseas Students, 1979.

Low, D. (Comp.). *Basic Facts on Foreign Study.* New York: Institute of International Education, 1979a.

Low, D. (Comp.). *A Guide to Scholarships, Fellowships and Grants: A Selected Bibliography.* New York: Institute of International Education, 1979b.

Lyman, R. "The Costs and Values of International Education." *NAFSA Newsletter,* 1981, *32* (8); 165, 188–191.

McLaughlin, M. M. *The U.S. and World Development Agenda 1979.* New York: Praeger, 1979.

Markson, C. J. "What Do Foreign Graduate Students Think About Their U.S. Degree Programs?" *Engineering Education,* 1976, *66,* 830–831.

Mesarovic, M., and others. *Mankind at the Turning Point.* New York: Dutton, 1974.

Mestenhauser, J. *Learning with Foreign Students.* Minneapolis: International Student Advisers Office, University of Minnesota, 1976.

Michael, D. N. *On Learning to Plan—and Planning to Learn: The Social Psychology of Changing Toward Future-Responsive Societal Learning.* San Francisco: Jossey-Bass, 1973.

Michigan State University. *International Education at Michigan State University in an Interdependent World.* East Lansing: Michigan State University, 1980.

Miller, R. E. "A Study of Significant Elements in the On-the-Job Behavior of College and University Foreign Student Advisers." Unpublished doctoral dissertation, Department of Counseling, Personnel Services and Educational Psychology, College of Education, Michigan State University, 1968.

Moravscik, M. "Goals and Realities: Can U.S. Universities Offer Appropriate Education to Students from Developing Countries?" In H. M. Jenkins (Ed.), *The Relevance of U.S. Education to Students from Developing Countries.* Washington, D.C.: National Association for Foreign Student Affairs, 1980.

Morgan, R. P. *Science and Technology for Development: The Role of U.S. Universities.* Elmsford, N.Y.: Pergamon Press, 1979.

Myers, R. B. *Curriculum: U.S. Capacities, Developing Countries' Needs.* New York: Institute of International Education, 1979.

National Association for Foreign Student Affairs. *Responsibilities and Standards in Work with Foreign Students.* Guideline Series, No. 1, 1970 ed. Washington, D.C.: National Association for Foreign Student Affairs, 1970.

National Association for Foreign Student Affairs. *Study of Foreign Student Employment and Financial Resources.* Washington, D.C.: National Association for Foreign Student Affairs, 1974.

National Association for Foreign Student Affairs. *English Language Proficiency.* Guideline Series, No. 3. Washington, D.C.: National Association for Foreign Student Affairs, 1977.

National Association for Foreign Student Affairs. *Selection and Admission of Foreign Students.* Guideline Series, No. 2. Washington, D.C.: National Association for Foreign Student Affairs, 1978.

National Association for Foreign Student Affairs. *Foreign Student Admissions, Credentials Bibliography.* Washington, D.C.: National Association for Foreign Student Affairs, 1979a.

National Association for Foreign Student Affairs. *Standards and Responsibilities in International Educational Interchange.* Guideline Series, No. 1, 1979 ed. Washington, D.C.: National Association for Foreign Student Affairs, 1979b.

National Association for Foreign Student Affairs. *Study Abroad: Handbook for Advisers and Administrators.* Guideline Series, No. 10. Washington, D.C.: National Association for Foreign Student Affairs, 1979c.

National Association for Foreign Student Affairs. *Orientation of Foreign Students.* Guideline Series, No. 4. Washington, D.C.: National Association for Foreign Student Affairs, 1980.

National Association for Foreign Student Affairs. *NAFSA Principles for International Educational Exchange.* Washington, D.C.: National Association for Foreign Student Affairs, 1981.

National Association for Foreign Student Affairs. *Adviser's Manual of Federal Regulations Affecting Foreign Students and Scholars.* (Rev. ed.) Washington, D.C.: National Association for Foreign Student Affairs, 1982a.

National Association for Foreign Student Affairs. *Bibliography on Study, Work and Travel Abroad.* Washington, D.C.: Section on U.S. Study Abroad, National Association for Foreign Student Affairs, 1982b.

National Association for Foreign Student Affairs and American Association of Collegiate Registrars and Admissions Officers. *A Guide to the Admission of Foreign Students.* (Rev. ed.) Washington, D.C.: National Association for Foreign Student Affairs, 1979.

National Association for Foreign Student Affairs and U.S. Department of Education. *The Foreign Student in Elementary and Secondary Schools.* Publication No. E-80-14019. Washington, D.C.: U.S. Department of Education, 1980.

National Center for Education Statistics. *Education Directory: Colleges and Universities.* Washington, D.C.: U.S. Government Printing Office, published annually.

National Liaison Committee on Foreign Student Admissions. *Overseas Counselor's Manual.* New York: College Entrance Examination Board, 1976.

National Research Council. *International Mobility of Scientists and Engineers.* Washington, D.C.: National Research Council, 1982.

National Science Foundation. *A Selected List of Fellowship Opportunities and Aids to Advanced Education.* Washington, D.C.: National Science Foundation, 1980.

Nelson, D. *Crucial Issues in Foreign Student Education.* Washington, D.C.: National Association for Foreign Student Affairs, 1975.

North, R. C. *The World That Could Be.* Stanford, Calif.: Stanford Alumni Association, 1976.

O'Leary, J. "Fees Alter Britain's Image." *Times Higher Education Supplement,* Jan. 2, 1981, p. III.

Ong, W. *Rhetoric, Romance and Technology: Studies in the Interaction of Expression and Culture.* Ithaca, N.Y.: Cornell University, 1971.

Open Doors. New York: Institute of International Education, published annually since 1919.

Overseas Liaison Committee. *OLC Papers.* No. 1-10. Washington, D.C.: American Council on Education, 1973-1976.

Overseas Liaison Committee. *An Analysis of the U.S.-Iranian Cooperation in Higher Education.* Washington, D.C.: American Council on Education, 1976.

Overseas Liaison Committee. *Future Nigerian-U.S. Linkages in Higher Education.* Washington, D.C.: American Council on Education, 1977.

President's Commission on Foreign Language and International Studies. *Strength Through Wisdom: A Critique of U.S. Capability.* Washington, D.C.: U.S. Government Printing Office, 1979.

Purdue University. *Report on International Education and Research at Purdue University.* West Lafayette, Ind.: Purdue University, 1979.

Putman, I., Jr. *The Foreign Student Adviser and His Institution in International Student Exchange.* Washington, D.C.: National Association for Foreign Student Affairs, 1965.

Sagan, C. *Broca's Brain.* New York: Random House, 1979.

Sandberg, A. *Computers Dividing Man and Work.* Malmo, Sweden: Arbetslivscentrum, 1979.

Schumacher, E. F. *Small Is Beautiful: Economics as if People Mattered.* New York: Harper & Row, 1973.

Scully, M. G. "Abuses in Foreign-Student Recruiting Tarnish U.S. Colleges' Image Abroad." *Chronicle of Higher Education,* 1980a, *20* (6), 1, 17.

Scully, M. G. "Foreign Student Recruitment—Why? Demographic and Financial Factors, Present and Future." In H. M. Jenkins (Ed.), *Foreign Student Recruitment: Realities and Recommendations.* New York: College Entrance Examination Board, 1980b.

Select Commission on Immigration and Refugee Policy. *Execu-*

tive Summary. Washington, D.C.: U.S. Government Printing Office, 1981.

Simerville, C. *The Foreign Student in Your Classroom.* Corvallis: Oregon State Board of Higher Education, 1965.

Smith, A., de Panafieu, C. W., and Jarousse, J.-P. "Foreign Student Flows and Policies in an International Perspective." In P. Williams (Ed.), *The Overseas Student Question.* London: Heinemann, 1981.

Smith, E. H. "Law Concepts and Legal Rights." In *The Asian Student, Orientation Handbook.* San Francisco: The Asian Student, 1977-78.

Smith, E. H. "Do You Know Your Legal Responsibilities Under New INS Regulations?" *NAFSA Newsletter,* 1979, *30* (5), 124.

Smith, E. H., and Baron, M. *Faculty Member's Guide to U.S. Immigration Law.* Washington, D.C.: National Association for Foreign Student Affairs, 1980.

Snow, C. P. *In Their Wisdom.* New York: Scribner's, 1974.

de Solla-Price, D. *Little Science, Big Science.* New York: Columbia University Press, 1963.

Spaulding, S., and Flack, M. *The World's Students in the United States—A Review and Evaluation of Research on Foreign Students.* New York: Praeger, 1976.

Taylor, H. *The World as Teacher.* New York: Doubleday, 1970.

TOEFL [Test of English as a Foreign Language] *Test and Score Manual.* Princeton, N.J.: TOEFL Program Office, Educational Testing Service, 1981.

Thavikalivat, P., and Gongotena, M. "An Analytical Scheme for Organizing Re-Entry Programs." Paper presented at NAFSA Region IV Conference, Minneapolis, Oct. 1977.

Tinbergen, J. *RIO: Reshaping the International Order.* New York: Dutton, 1976.

Tonkin, H., and Edwards, J. *The World in the Curriculum.* New Rochelle, N.Y.: Change Magazine Press, 1981.

Udell, G. G. (Comp.). *Naturalization Laws.* Washington, D.C.: U.S. Government Printing Office, 1976.

UNESCO. *Statistics of Students Abroad 1969-1973.* Paris: UNESCO, 1976.

UNESCO. *Thinking Ahead: UNESCO and the Challenges of Today and Tomorrow.* Paris: UNESCO, 1977.

UNESCO. *Study Abroad XXII.* Paris: UNESCO, 1978.

UNESCO. *Statistical Year Book 1981.* Paris: UNESCO, 1981.

U.S.-China Education Clearinghouse. *An Introduction to Education in the People's Republic of China and U.S.-China Educational Exchanges.* Washington, D.C.: Committee on Scholarly Communication with the People's Republic of China and National Association for Foreign Student Affairs, 1980.

United States Commission on Civil Rights. *The Tarnished Golden Door.* Washington, D.C.: U.S. Government Printing Office, 1980.

United States International Communication Agency. *The Fulbright Program.* Washington, D.C.: United States International Communication Agency, 1980.

Watson, P. "Report of Survey of Organizations for International Studies and Programs." *National Committee of International Studies and Program Administrators Newsletter,* 1981, *3* (1), 3-5.

Weiler, H. N. "Discovery and Dependence: The Uneasy Relationship Between American Universities and the Third World." Keynote address at the Western Regional Conference of the Comparative and International Educational Society, Los Angeles, 1978.

Wheeler, W. R., King, H. H., and Davidson, A. B. (Eds.), *The Foreign Student in America.* New York: Association Press, 1925.

Wilber, C. K. (Ed.). *Political Economy of Development and Underdevelopment.* (2nd ed.) New York: Random House, 1979.

Williams, P. (Ed.). *The Overseas Student Question: Studies for a Policy.* London: Overseas Students Trust, 1981.

Williams, P. (Ed.). *A Policy for Overseas Students.* London: Overseas Students Trust, 1982.

Winkler, D. R. "The Economic Impacts of Foreign Students in the United States." Unpublished paper, School of Public Administration, University of Southern California, 1981.

World Bank. *World Development Report.* Washington, D.C.: World Bank, 1980.

Index